D1239826

DESIGNING TROUT FLIES

DESIGNING TROUT FLIES

GARY A. BORGER

Drawings by Jason Borger

DESIGNING TROUT FLIES
Copyright © 1991 by Gary A. Borger
First Printing

Published by
TOMORROW RIVER PRESS
P. O. Box 1745
Wausau, WI 54402-1745

All rights reserved, including the right to reproduce this book or any portions thereof in any form or by any means, electronic or mechanical, including photocopying, recording, or by any information storage and retrieval system, without permission in writing from the publisher. All inquires should be addressed to Tomorrow River Press, P. O. Box 1745, Wausau, WI 54402-1745

Library of Congress Catalog Number 90-71770
Borger, Gary Alan   1944-
Designing Trout Flies.
Bibliography.
Includes index.
Key words: 1. Fly Tying. 2. Flies, Artificial 3. Trout Fishing. 4. Insects, Aquatic

ISBN 0-9628392-1-3   (Hardcover)
ISBN 0-9628392-0-5   (Softcover)
ISBN 0-9628392-2-1   (Limited)
ISBN 0-9628392-3-X   (Presentation)

Printed in the U.S.A.

For Nancy
who has supported me with unselfish love and dedication

And for Jason
who has contributed so much more to this project than his artwork

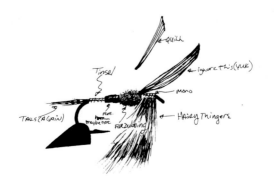

CONTENTS

ACKNOWLEDGEMENTS

I will love thee, O Lord, my strength.
Psalms 18:1

Nancy and I are more than husband and wife. We were best friends first, and we remain best friends in the true meaning. We have been angling companions for 25 years and each has always delighted in the successes of the other. We are business partners, sharing the excitement, the frustrations, the rewards. We are each truly half of the whole we've become. This book is our product. Nancy you deserve more than I'll ever be able to give.

Jason and I have a special relationship, not just as father and son, but as angling companions who think as of one mind. He deserves rich thanks for finding the time from his busy university schedule to produce the stunning artwork that graces the pages of this book. It would be a far less useful book wihout your input, Jas.

My parents, Billy and Shirley, well aware of the fishing mania burning within me, fueled the fire by giving me a much coveted fly tying kit for my eleventh Christmas and encouraging me to follow my heart. Thanks Dad and Mom.

Bob Pelzl has been a close friend for 15 years. We get together each summer for several weeks to teach fly fishing schools at Vermejo Park Ranch in New Mexico and to exchange all the fly tying ideas we've been storing up for the year. It's a grand time of sharing and experimentation. Bob has not only inspired my tying in many, many ways, but he's provided important thoughts on the content of this book. Thanks, and thanks again, old friend!

Mike Dry and I have shared angling experiences for a decade. A decade in which we have also founded and nurtured a video production company. Mike is most insightful and has offered valuable comments on this book's content and organization. My thanks, partner.

John Randolph, Editor and Publisher at "Fly Fisherman Magazine," is a friend of long standing. A friend who took time from his frantically busy schedule to read an early draft of a portion of this book and offer helpful suggestions. I'm grateful, John.

Jim Greenlee and I met over a decade ago during a Citizen Council meeting at the University. Then and there, we began designing a wading shoe, and before long the Ultimate Wading Shoe became a reality. During the process we became good friends. Through his wise council, Jim has also helped bring "Designing Trout Flies" into reality. I'm thankful for such a caring friend.

Diane Andrada took our design ideas and our computer disks and mixed them vigorously with a healthy dose of hard work and her magic Mac to give us this book. What would we have done without you, Diane? You have my most grateful thanks.

Bob Baird helped us through the printing and book assembly maze, turning it into an easily followed, yellow brick road. Thanks, Wiz.

A NOTE TO THE READER

This is a book about the way I design trout flies. It's a book about concepts; a "why-to" book. But it's also a "how-to" book, containing detailed descriptions and tying instructions for patterns that I've developed, or other patterns that I use, because patterns are necessary to illustrate the design concepts I've discussed.

In this sense, "Designing Trout Flies" is very much a personal book. Personal because fly tying, like art, is an expression of individual preference for materials and techniques. Like the artist, the fly tier is always experimenting with new materials and techniques, or modifying existing ones, to achieve a better result. In addition, tiers are always designing—developing and testing new concepts that better fit fly fishing's evolving understanding of the fish and its food organisms. But unlike the artist's work, the fly tier's efforts are critiqued by the fish.

My goal as a fly tier has always been to achieve continual critical acclaim from those fish; to understand why trout take the fly—what features of the natural trigger the fish's feeding response and how specific materials and tying tactics can be used to design artificials that best display these triggering characteristics.

You will note that many of my flies are quite simple. For three reasons: First, my tying time is limited, and easy-to-tie designs mean more flies per hour and therefore more hours on the stream. Second, I keep trying to reduce my flies to their very essence in order to discover what it is that induces the fish to eat them, to remove all unnecessary materials and tying steps, and to do away with complexity for complexity's sake. It is a continual and on-going process. And third, to me, there is great beauty in simplicity. I gain pleasure from carefully crafted flies; from the thoughtful melding of feathers, fur, and steel.

Fly tying is not an art unto itself. It is as old as fly fishing and inseparably linked to it. Inseparably linked because the fisher's success depends in large part upon the tier's skill at representing the fish's food organisms. So whether you tie or buy, there is a real need to understand the design principles behind fly construction. In *this* sense, "Designing Trout Flies" is not a book for just fly tiers. It was written for all fly fishers. Regardless of the patterns you choose to use, and whether you tie or buy, it is my sincere hope that the information in this book will help your flies gain that much sought after, unhesitating acceptance from the shy and spotted trout.

Gary Borger
Wausau, Wisconsin
December 1, 1990

Chapter One

DESIGNING TROUT FLIES

Fly tying has as its basis the intent of deceiving the fish by designing and creating imitations of its food organisms. To produce consistently successful designs, then, the fly tier must understand both the fish and its food organisms. In addition, the tier must have a good working knowledge of the materials used to construct the artificials; information such as color, texture, light transmitting or reflecting quality, and durability. And, the tier must be acquainted with a range of techniques for applying the materials as well as the angling techniques that will be used to fish the fly. For example, if the artificial is to be skated on the surface, then it must consist of materials that represent the natural while simultaneously helping the fly to float, and it must be shaped in such a way so that it not only imitates the natural but will skate as well.

I begin all my designs with the fish. Like other animals, they can see, hear, taste, smell, and touch. There are salmon fishers on the West Coast that take great pains to minimize human odor on their flies, but taste and smell are not of concern in the design of flies. Touch becomes important only if the fish has an opportunity to chew the fly before the angler sets the hook

(see discussion on page 67). Basically, trout and salmon are sight-oriented hunters that occasionally also rely on their hearing. It is these two senses that the fly tier must understand when striving to produce consistently successful designs.

WHAT THE TROUT SEES

The photoreceptive layer, or retina, of the trout's eye contains both rod and cone cells. The rods form only a black and white image; the cones are sensitive to color. The quality of the image produced by the retina depends upon the packing of the rods and cones; the denser the packing, the more detailed the image. In the trout's eye, the cells are packed rather loosely, and the image is of what, we would consider, rather poor quality. In fact, recent scientific experiments indicate that the human eye has about 14 times the resolving power of the trout's eye (see Byrnes, 1990). And thank goodness for that. If its vision were as good as ours, the fish would never take even our most perfectly crafted flies because no real creature has a hook dangling out of its rear and a long chunk of monofilament sticking out of its nose. The trout's eye can detect relative size, overall silhouette (shape), and broad color patterns. But while the retina does not form a highly detailed image, it is extremely sensitive to contrast and motion. Such sensitivity can be crucial in fly fishing: a trout will often take a rather crude-looking dry

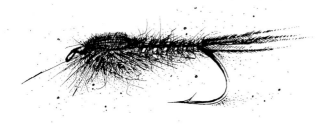

fly if it's presented drag free but reject the same fly if it's dragging. And, such sensitivity can be significant in fly design. A trout may not recognize the exact shape of a mayfly nymph's gills, but it is highly attuned to the movements of these appendages.

The spring creeks near Livingston, Montana, provide an excellent laboratory for observing the ability of feeding fish to visually discriminate between the real and the artificial. At the beginning of the season, before they have been subjected to every deception of the fly fisher, the trout don't spend much time scanning a dry fly. If it's a relatively close match, they take it confidently. By the end of the season, however, they drift backward under both natural and artificial, watching closely for something, anything, that will give the fake away. If they had excellent eyesight, only a glance would be needed to tell the artificial from the real thing. But because the fish's eye forms a poor image, it has a difficult time separating the appearance of real from fake. In this process, the trout become extremely sensitive to drag. Let your artificial move in the slightest unnatural way and it's rejected instantly. Frequently, I've seen these trout reject a natural that fluttered or was blown off course by the wind. For the fish, eating becomes a real craps shoot. Numerous times, I've watched in amazement as a trout snatched a real insect off the surface, shook its head, and dashed off a short distance as if expecting to be hooked. The fish has to eat, but it's eyesight is too poor to separate a good imitation from the natural. For this reason, many of the late-season fish simply stop feeding on dry flies and concentrate on nymphs. The heavy angling pressure of the season has trained them to avoid dry flies.

IMPRESSIONISM IN DESIGN

Because the trout's eye produces such a crude image (relative to our eye), highly realistic flies that satisfy the human desire for perfection in detail are not essential for consistent angling success. For angling purposes, the goal of fly tying, therefore, becomes to create an impression of the food organism, not a carbon copy of it. Fly fisher's have wrangled with this concept for centuries. One of the earliest discussions that clearly put the idea of impressionism into perspective, so to speak, occurs in G. P. R. Pulman's book, "Vade Mecum of Fly Fishing for Trout" published in 1851. He describes the need to suggest size, color, and form which he states together "...constitute the character of the insect...," and goes on further to say that the character "...can be represented without counting the exact number of legs, or microscopically examining the fibers of the wings; on the same principle that, in individual portraiture, what is alone sought to be attained is not minute imitation but individual character and expression."

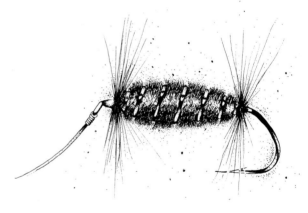

Perhaps the most eloquent and thoughtful arguments for impressionism in flies were put forth by Jack Atherton in his book "The Trout and the Fly." Atherton focused the ideas of many writers; he gave us theory to explain our experiences. Like Pulman, Atherton drew a parallel between fly construction and the goals of portraiture; specifically the work of impressionistic painters such as Renoir and Monet. As the name implies, the impressionists were not interested in a photographic representation of the subject. Rather, they tried to capture the essence of the object: that which made it recognizable. Atherton applied these concepts to fly design. Instead of trying to create patterns that were exact copies of the insect, he sought to represent the essence of the insect; to create an impression of life. And always, it was the impression that the pattern made *on the trout*, not the impression that it made on the angler, that was important to Atherton. He said: "The flies used for so discriminating a fish as the trout should, first of all, have the appearance of life."

Scientific findings have reenforced the thoughts of Atherton and those before him, shoring up the empirical theories resulting from nearly five centuries of careful observations by the best original thinkers in fly fishing. In addition to investigating the visual acuity of trout, scientists have also studied the ability of the fish to respond to various traits of the food item. It is eminently clear from these technical experiments, as well as observations made by fly fishers, that the four characteristics which most strongly represent the essence of life, and therefore trigger the trout's feeding response, are size, shape, color, and behavior. Trout respond to these four traits of the food item whether feeding opportunistically or selectively.

OPPORTUNISTIC FEEDING

Opportunistic feeding periods can occur at any time, day or night, and are marked by a lack of insect hatches and no noticeable, regular feeding activity on the part of the trout. The fish are simply watching for and eating whatever food items come their way. And, while trout respond to size, shape, color, and behavior during opportunistic periods, the fish are not looking for a specific size, a specific color, and a specific shape all coupled with a specific behavior. During selective feeding they are.

When in the opportunistic mode, the trout samples any item in the water column that is suggestive of food: a piece of twig, a pollen cone, a cigarette butt, a strike indicator. But fish are far more likely to grab items that strongly suggest life.

Movement

Movement is the single characteristic that most strongly suggests life, and during opportunistic periods, is the primary trait that triggers the trout's feeding response. A moving pile of junk is often better than a perfectly crafted, but static, imitation. When I was ten, a friend and I were bumming along the stream near home, fitfully attempting to lure some stocked rainbows onto our lines. We began talking with a group of spin fishers who were having lunch along the stream. As a joke, one of them hooked a strip of banana peel on a Mepps spinner and flipped it out into the currents. A 27-inch brown immediately seized the undulating concoction and was summarily wrestled to shore before our coveting eyes and gaping mouths. It wasn't that the trout preferred bananas, it was the undulating movement of that strip that rang the fish's dinner bell. Thus, during opportunistic periods, the fly fisher could do a lot worse than to select a fly which has plenty of movement: fuzzy nymphs, soft hackle flies, the Strip Leech (my favorite), marabou patterns, and the like.

Color

Color can be another important trigger during opportunistic times. Color vision in trout allows the fish to distinguish food items against the background color of the water. Called background space light, this color results from the scattering of light rays by the water molecules. In very clear water, blue light is scattered the most and the water appears blue (this is the same reason the sky appears blue). When free-floating algae (phytoplankton) are present, they absorb red and blue light and the background space light appears greenish yellow. The dissolved organic humus in tea-colored bog water absorbs the blue end of the spectrum, making the background space light appear reddish orange. Underwater flies tied with flashy materials (such as tinsel or Flashabou), iridescent feathers such as peacock herl, or a splash of fluorescent marabou or hair are very successful during opportunistic times because they stand out strongly against any of the background space light colors.

In addition, with increasing depth, water very rapidly absorbs all light. Red light disappears below about three feet; with increasing depth, orange, yellow, green, and blue are absorbed, in that order. In most freshwater systems, all light disappears by a depth of about 30 feet. Usually this is not of much concern to the trout fisher because most of the time the fish are feeding in water less than three feet deep. However, it can be of importance on those occasions when it's necessary to fish deeper water. Standardly dyed red flies become gray and eventually black as they sink below three feet. But again, flashy materials (that reflect any available light), iridescent feathers (that refract any available colors), and fluorescent materials (that absorb available light and then convert and give off the energy as a different color) are all readily visible to the lowest limits of light availability.

Color can also be important for dry flies fished during opportunistic times. Patterns like the Royal Wulff and Adams are such superb fish getters because they are easily seen by the fish and look like something good to eat. Many times, I've had trout rise to my fluorescent orange strike indicator; during opportunistic times, a fluorescent spinner pattern (page 59) can be a very effective fly.

Size

Size can be a determining factor during opportunistic feeding. During such times the old axiom "big fly, big fish" was never truer. The fish are not concentrating on any one food item, they just want something to eat, and because a large item contains so many more calories than a small one, a big fly is often better than a small fly. But be warned, by a big something I mean flies in the four- to six-inch range or longer. One does not catch small trout on them. And too, when you fish big flies, you don't catch large numbers of fish, but boy! when you do catch

one, it will be exciting. If you suspect that big fish are not on the prowl (as during the middle of a bright sunny day), you may prefer to use smaller flies and enjoy the pleasures offered by more average-sized fish.

Behavior

Behavior can also be significant in the non-hatch periods of opportunistic feeding. Skater flies, teased and danced over the surface, can produce explosive rises. Minnow and leech patterns are best fished with an erratic, jigging, twitching, jerking movement that suggests a crippled or weakened prey item. Obviously the design of the fly is important to the type of action trying to be imparted.

What the Trout Hears

During opportunistic times, fish will often use their sense of hearing in conjunction with their vision to find food items. The trout's lateral line mechanism is a very sensitive sonar device that runs along its flank and forward around its mouth and eyes. So sensitive is it that the fish can hear (feel) a nymph swimming or a dry fly drop to the surface. A blind trout placed in a tank with minnows can easily catch and eat them all, solely by the sound of their swimming. Fly designs such as the Marabou Muddler and Strip Leech are so extremely effective because they not only have a great deal of motion in them, but they send out attracting sonic vibrations that the trout can detect with its lateral line mechanism. Sound can also be significant when fishing dry flies during opportunistic periods. Splatting a big hopper imitation down next to an undercut, grassy bank on a breezy afternoon can sometimes produce startling results, and chugging a big mouse fly across the surface after dark can be absolutely smashing.

Dry or Wet?

Trout often move from sheltering lies into the shallows at the edges and tail of a pool, up into the riffles, along the banks of deep runs, or near the shoreline of lakes to feed opportunistically. For the most part, the fish will be concentrating on underwater items for the simple reason that there's usually far more of them. So, many times, during opportunistic periods, I'll use an imitation of a subaquatic invertebrate that I know is prevalent in the stream or lake I'm fishing. It's a good strategy because it suggests to the fish a commonly eaten prey item.

Once, while fishing the high country of New Zealand with my friend Mike Allen, I located a very large brown trout lying in a foot of water and only two feet from shore. A feeding movement by the fish indicated it was taking nymphs, but I wanted to see that big brown come up for a dry fly. A half dozen perfect floats later I was sure the trout wasn't interested in anything on the surface. I replaced the Royal Wulff with a Hair Leg Nymph, to suggest a locally prevalent mayfly, and on the first drift, the fish darted forward and grabbed the sunken imitation.

But by the same token, trout holding in feeding lies during opportunistic periods may be watching the surface and will respond very well to the dry fly. This is especially true when there is a continual dribble of various insect species floating by. If I'm fishing and see a mixed bag of insect flotsam, I'll often tie on an easily seen, buggy fly like the Royal Wulff or the Adams.

And often the fishing is just great. In meadow streams the fish are often very surface conscious because terrestrial insects such as hoppers, beetles, and ants are always being blown into the water, and imitations such as the Bow Legged Hopper, Foam Beetle, or Para Ant are excellent during opportunistic periods.

Thus, during opportunistic periods, it's dealer's choice. Pick a fly you like. Fish wet or dry. Go with a fly for leviathan or chase the average fish. Angle in the daytime or haunt the dark hours. Be serious or make a light time of it. You'll usually find fish to fit your mood.

Selective feeding

Selectivity is a different story. Selective feeding occurs when there is a great abundance of one food item in or on the water. An insect hatch most often produces selective feeding, although a great abundance of non-insect organisms such as scuds or snails can occasionally cause the fish to become selective. During such periods, the fish feed heavily on the prevalent food organism and ignore all others.

Understanding Selectivity

At first, selectivity seems like a trick of mother nature. Why should the trout be locked in to eating tiny insects and pass up a juicy minnow or perhaps an occasional, larger insect? After all, survival for any wild animal requires that it maximize food intake while minimizing energy expenditure. Upon careful examination, however, it's clear that selectivity allows the fish to do just that. Instead of sampling everything that comes along (and wasting energy examining non-food items), the trout sticks with a prevalent, known food source; in a short time with very little energy expended, the fish can fill its gut.

Selectivity can cause the fly fisher great pains, however, because the fish become so tightly fixated on a single food item. Not just a particular type of insect, not just a particular species of a particular type of insect, but a particular stage of the life cycle of a particular species of a particular type of insect. For example, it's common for trout to lock in on the emerging mayfly dun, or egg laying damselflies, or diving caddises, and so on. Selective feeding periods are therefore the time when the correct fly design is essential. But if the match is correct, it is also the time when the angler has the greatest opportunity to take fish.

Since the 1800's, when the dry fly came into vogue, there have been fly fishers who have suggested that trout are more selective to dry flies than to nymphs, implying for the floating fly mystical properties that simply do not exist. When a trout is selective, it is selective, period. I've seen trout on spring creeks in Pennsylvania, Montana, Colorado, Idaho, Wisconsin, and other places feeding exclusively on nymphs just under the film. They would accept only the correct fly presented in only the correct manner. Nothing else would do. It's not that trout are more selective to dry flies, it's just that we as fly fishers have not always clearly understood, nor represented in our dry flies, what the trout sees when it is looking up at insects floating on the surface. In recent years, however, much of the dry fly puzzle has been unravelled, and we now better understand how to dress floating flies to fool highly selective, surface-feeding fish (see Gary LaFontaine's book "The Dry Fly").

Nor is selectivity a matter of choice for the trout. The fish doesn't think "Well today I'm going to eat only size 18 *Baetis* emergers, that ought to drive the anglers crazy." The animal mind doesn't work that way. Rather, as the fish feeds on the very abundant food organism, it becomes entrained on the prey's characteristics. Selectivity, therefore, is not a conscious decision for the trout; it is a trained response. Such training in animals can be very precise. For example, researchers once taught chickens to work as quality control inspectors in a vitamin manufacturing facility, selecting out imperfectly coated pills. But the birds worked too well,

removing every pill except the absolutely perfect ones. They were unable to make independent judgements on the degree of imperfection. The pills were either perfect or not perfect. It's the same for the selectively feeding trout. The fish cannot consciously overrule its training. Once locked onto size 18 *Baetis* emergers, the fish is unable to select anything else.

Thus the fly fisher should not think of the trout as a sly, crafty opponent, but rather as a creature that is a victim of its own genetic programming. To truly understand selectivity, then, we must understand the characteristics of the food organism that entrain the fish's feeding response.

Triggering the Fish's Selective Feeding Response

Selectivity is basically a shallow water phenomenon, and so the fish can clearly see the four major characteristics of the food organism: size, shape, color and behavior. During selective feeding, one of these characteristic (the primary trigger) usually trips the fish's initial, investigative response. Some angling authors have suggested that one of the traits (size, for example) is *always* the most important and have even ranked the four characteristics in order of importance. In reality, any one of the four characteristics may serve as the primary trigger; it is usually that characteristic which is most obvious or unique in the food organism.

But while one trait serves as the primary trigger, the other three (the secondary triggers) must also be present if the fly is to be *consistently* successful. For example, some caddises will run over the water after hatching or during egg laying. Trout crash after them recklessly. In this circumstance, the behavior of the insect is the primary triggering characteristic. But while such fish will readily investigate any dragging fly, most will refuse it unless it is also the correct size, shape and color. Then again, when mayfly spinners fall heavily, the trout become fixed on the shape of the spent flies and steadfastly reject any other shape. Obviously, shape becomes the primary trigger in this instance. But again, if the fly is of incorrect size or color, or if it is dragging rather than floating dead drift, the fish will usually refuse it. During hatches of bright green midges, the fish become quite sensitive to the strong chroma of these insects and scrutinize any item of similar color. However, once the fish gets close, it also wants to see an object of correct size and shape doing what midges are supposed to be doing. If not, the fish rejects the artificial. Size can also be the primary trigger. When the Lilliputian Trico mayflies are on the water, the trout want something of definite diminutive form, but they also expect to see the other three characteristics.

It is this primary trigger, secondary trigger sequence that often causes the trout to reject the fly at the last possible moment. Some authors have suggested that the trout's eye sight is so bad that it effects the fish's aim—in other words, the trout tries but simply misses the fly. Well, just take a few moments to watch a trout feed on naturals and you'll realize that they don't miss. No, a "false rise" is a last-second rejection by the trout. The animal's eye achieves maximum resolution when very close to the imitation, so as the fish draws near, it is able to carefully examine all the traits of the fly. If one or several characteristics of the pattern are incorrect, the trout refuses it. Such false rises should be a tip off that one (or more) of the secondary triggering characteristics is incorrect.

The trout's ability to discern both primary and secondary triggers may be effected by water type. In swift, choppy currents, the fish has little time to examine the fly and cannot see details very well; on flat, slow currents, the trout can examine the imitation carefully and leisurely. For this reason, bushy dries that would fail horridly on the spring creeks can be a raging success on the Madison. So, I design my flies for the most difficult angling situation that I expect to encounter: big, spooky, wild trout in smooth-flowing, crystal-clear waters. Flies that will take trout under these conditions will take trout anywhere. That is why I may also spend an hour or two trying to fool a particularly difficult fish rather than giving up and going on to an easier one. It's the difficult ones that teach us the most if we pay close attention and can refrain from becoming frustrated.

In addition to the primary and secondary triggers, there are other characteristics of the organism that should be considered. What stage of the life cycle is being imitated? How does it look from the fish's level? What presentation tactic will be necessary to ape the behavior of the natural?

When all the questions about primary and secondary triggers and other traits are answered, it's time to consider the materials and tying techniques to best suggest the food organism while still satisfying the needs imposed by the presentation method.

In the chapters on specific food organisms, I've discussed the attributes that trigger the fish's feeding response and how I've used this information to develop my approach to fly design. I've also listed most used sizes and colors of the various designs; use this information as a starting point, then refine existing designs or develop your own as you become familiar with the food organisms on the waters you fish.

MATERIALS AND TOOLS

MATERIALS

Great emphasis is often placed on materials, and with good reason: A fly is only as good as the materials that go into it. On the other hand, *too much* emphasis is sometimes placed on materials; the suggestion is made that it's the material not the fly that catches the fish. So when is a particular material vital to fly design and when is it not? It's vital only if it has unique characteristics not found in any other material. For example, no other material has the particular characteristics of sparkle yarn, but the dark gray shoulder feather of coot can easily be replaced by any other dark gray shoulder feather such as jackdaw or crow.

When selecting materials for new designs or for modifying existing ones, I look at color, texture, quality, ease of application, availability, ability to take dyes, action in the water, floating or sinking properties, ability to trap air bubbles, durability, ease of blending, bugginess, any unique properties, and of course, cost.

Color

Color can be an elusive characteristic. In 1965 I read an article that described a Hendrickson mayfly *(Ephemerella subvaria)* as being the color of "urine-stained fur of a vixen red fox." This posed two immediate problems for me: (1) Where would I find a vixen fox? and (2) How would I know if in fact the fur had been urine stained? (or was the fly tier to do the urine staining?) At that time I was taking a soils course

in which we used a standardized color chart to describe various soil types. "If only there was a standard insect color chart," I thought to myself. There wasn't.

I began to keep track of insect colors, using a variety of color chips as standards. It was a slow process because I wanted a generic chart that covered a wide range of colors. In addition, while I knew that fish had color vision and that color was important in fly design, what I didn't know and couldn't find was just how important color was or how sensitive feeding fish were to various colors. So in addition to recording insect colors, I also began fishing a variety of differently colored flies during hatches. Two major facts emerged: (1) Selectively feeding fish are sensitive to color but do not discriminate between very fine shades of color in the food organisms, probably because (2) there's a range of shades of color in any one species of food organism and because the trout is physically unable to distinguish between very fine shades.

The BCS

From the data I collected for over 20 years, I developed the Borger Color System or BCS. It is not meant to contain every shade of every color that the human eye sees (several million). It is not meant to contain every shade of color of every food organism of the fish (many thousands). What it does contain are colors to which feeding fish are sensitive.

Thus when matching colors of a natural to the BCS chips, you need only select the closest matching chip. But for those who want more accurate data (as might be required for scientific study) colors can be recorded as falling between any two chips. Well over 800 shades can be derived from the BCS in this manner. When recording the color as lying between chips, I list both chip numbers separated by a slash: BCS 60/63. Hundreds more can be derived by recording the color of one chip as shaded by another. For example, smokey gray washed with yellow might be recorded as BCS 108w49. In addition to the actual shade of the color the fly tier should consider such traits as fluorescence, pearlescence, translucency, and patterning such as stripes, bars, and mottles. If the natural is a subaquatic, record its color when wet; if the organism floats on the surface, record its color when dry. This information, as well as data on sizes (determined by the inch, millimeter, or hook scales printed in the BCS) can then be recorded on a replaceable data pad at the rear of the BCS.

The BCS is also handy for keeping track of colors and sizes of successful artificials. Normally the most successful pattern is colored the same as the natural. However, in my studies I've noted that (1) sometimes, one color in the organism is a more important trigger than the other colors, and (2) occasionally a fly that is more strongly colored or even differently colored than the natural will trigger more takes than a fly the same color as the natural.

As an example of the first variable, the adult female of the Great Travelling Sedge (*Banksiola crotchi*) of western lakes has an olive-brown abdomen (BCS 35) through which the bright green eggs (BCS 19) can be seen. The overall effect is that of a dark olive green (BCS 33). However, the best color for the underside of the artificial has proved to be the bright green color of the egg mass. This color can be seen by the fish as the caddis adult runs across the surface to spread its eggs. In this instance, the color of the egg mass is a significant triggering feature of the natural, and over-emphasizing the amount of it in the pattern increases the artificial's effectiveness.

Likewise, scuds of the Bighorn river in Montana are a light gray (BCS 110) to a medium gray (BCS 114). The females, however, carry an easily seen, orange egg mass (BCS 77) in their bodies, and the most successful patterns are not shades of gray, but shades of reds and oranges.

As an example of the second variable, the spinner of the Light Hendrickson (*Ephemerella invaria/rotunda*) has a light rusty brown body (BCS 63). The best color for the spinner pattern is a fluorescent orange (BCS f77). As it turns out, the orange portion of the brown color makes the fly more easily seen in the late evening light when these spinners normally fall (page 59).

I also use the BCS to keep track of the color of my fly tying materials. This makes selection of materials much faster and definitely much easier. For example, I've cataloged all the soft hackles on a number of different types of birds. When dressing a fly that requires a light gray feather (BCS 110), I can look in my catalog and know that scaled quail, jackdaw, and Gambles quail all have appropriately colored feathers (see Chapter 14).

I also keep track of amounts and colors of furs I use when blending. This allows me to easily repeat blends that I find effective. Since materials often darken a shade or two when wet, I keep track of both wet and dry colors. This allows me to select materials for sunken flies without always having to test for the wetted color. In this book, I've used both word descriptions and BCS designations for the colors I've specified. All colors are designated *as they look when dry*. The change in the shade of a color for subsurface flies (due to wetting) has been taken into account.

The BCS fulfills a need for accurate color description that can be communicated between tiers and anglers without error. In this regard, the BCS serves as an easy-to-use color standard for descriptions of the naturals, tying materials, and most successful artificials. It makes my fly designing and fishing easier, and that makes it more fun!

Texture

The texture of the material can be vital to the success of the fly. For example, the texture of nymph patterns is often rather rough. This is produced by using a mixture of coarse and fine filaments, such as furs with the guard hairs left in. On the other hand, dry fly bodies are usually smoother than nymph bodies. For dry flies, the guard hairs are removed before the fur dubbing is applied. Other materials such as wire, tinsel, herl, monofilament, and so on will produce different textures in the fly, and thus achieve different design goals.

Quality

Quality is a nebulous kind of term, implying something positive or negative that may be hard to describe in words. However, in the case of fly tying, there are some very definite aspects to quality. A genetic hackle has very long feathers with short, rather stiff barbs. This is considered high quality for dry flies because the stiff barbs help the fly ride on the surface film and the long feather makes winding the hackle very easy. On the other hand, it is poor quality for wet flies which are supposed to sink the moment they touch the water. In other words, quality reflects the purpose of the material in the fly and how well that purpose is accomplished.

Ease of Application

Ease of application is always a consideration when selecting tying materials. However, this feature may have to take a back seat to other properties of the material if those other properties make the material highly desirable to the fish. Coarse sparkle yarns are not particularly easy to dub, but, boy, do they make great bodies for many fly designs.

Other Characteristics

Then there's availability, ability to take dyes, action in the water, floating or sinking properties, ability to trap air bubbles, durability, ease of blending, bugginess, and special characteristics

that would include the iridescence found in peacock herl; the unique light scattering properties of Crystal Hair, Flashabou, and Krystal Flash; the floating qualities of deer hair; the softness of marabou, and so on.

When designing flies, all the characteristics of the material should be carefully considered in light of what you know about the size, shape, color, and behavior of the natural *and* the presentation method you expect to employ. I've discussed these various properties of materials, as they apply to imitating specific organisms, in the chapters on fly designs.

Threads

To my way of thinking, one of the most important advances in fly tying in modern times is flat (untwisted) nylon, tying thread. This thread has several distinct advantages over twisted silk thread. One, nylon is stronger; which means that the tier will break it less and can pull harder to bind materials to the hook more tightly. Second, it stretches. That slight elasticity also helps the thread to bind materials more tightly to the hook shank. Third, the untwisted nature allows the thread to lie flat and not build up as fast as twisted threads. This in turn allows the tier to use more turns of thread to produce a more durable fly. All threads specified in this book are flat-filament nylon.

There are a whole spectrum of sizes and colors of threads to choose from, but there are only a dozen colors that I use frequently. These are:

Color	BCS Number
white	107
light gray	105
dark gray	119
black	118
brown	102
rusty brown	65
bright olive green	20

Color	BCS Number
dark olive-green	33
primrose	39
yellow	45
orange	77
fluorescent scarlet	81

I keep each color in sizes 3/0, 6/0, and 8/0 and keep them loaded on midge-sized bobbins ready for use. The different sizes are needed for different hooks and for different tying tactics; 3/0 is best for hooks size 10 and larger where materials must be bound very tightly (spun deer hair, for example); 6/0 is a general purpose thread for hook sizes 8-18; 8/0 is best for hooks size 16 and smaller.

TOOLS

Fly tiers love gadgets, and I'm no more immune to this impulse than the next person; I have an ample stock of all manner of tying tools. But over the years, I've come to rely on only a small assemblage of tools for most of my tying. My primary tools, used for the tying of all flies, are the vise, scissors, bobbin, and bodkin.

Vise

The chief function of the vise, the function for which I demand absolute perfection, is holding the hook. If the vise can't hold the hook securely and in such a position that tying is unencumbered, then all the gold plating and extra features in the world cannot make it useful. I like a vise that has an adjustable head angle. For large hooks I normally set the head angle slanted up at 30 to 45 degrees from the horizontal. For hooks smaller than a 16, I like a steeper head angle—as much as 60 degrees from the horizontal. The steeper head angle gives more clearance behind the hook, allowing for easier handling of materials that are tied in at the rear.

I prefer to have the hook at about mid-chest height when tying. This position allows me to look slightly down at the top of the fly but still be able to see the near side without difficulty. (In this same regard, I use a pneumatically adjustable typist's chair so I can sit at precisely the right height relative to the bench top.)

Scissors

Scissors are a very important equipment item for me; I use them actively during all steps of the tying process: to clip thread, cut away excess materials, trim parts of the finished fly, and prepare materials. For this reason, I want scissors of the best quality that I can find. There are three requirements that I have for my primary scissors. First, they must be sharp! And stay sharp. Second, I want flat points, not curved points; flat-pointed scissors are always "right-side-up" no matter how they're laid down on the bench. Curved-point scissors always seem to get put down wrong. If the curve is up when I reach for them, I'll need the curve down, and visa versa. I don't need the hassle of always turning the scissors over. Straight points are just faster and easier to handle. Third, the handles should be relatively long and the blades relatively short; 3 1/2-inch long handles with 1-inch blades work out very well. The long handles keep my fingers away from the fly so I can see what I'm doing. In addition, the long handles permit better control over the opening and closing of the scissor points. The short points allow the scissors to be easily manipulated when trying to get into a rather tight spot.

Bobbin

The bobbin is a tool that allows easy handling of the thread. It's certainly true that flies can be tied without a bobbin. In fact, for the first seven years that I tied flies, I didn't use a bobbin. However, once I discovered this tool, I found that it allowed me to handle the thread better and faster than I could without it. I have always liked the light-weight, wire-arm bobbins in the midge size. It's very easy to change the thread with such bobbins, thread tension is easily set by bending the wire legs, and their light weight makes them ideal for tying small flies. In addition, the midge bobbin is easier to hold in the hand and easier to perform certain thread manipulations with than is a standard-sized bobbin. I have a host of these smaller bobbins, each rigged with a different thread color and/or thread size (see page 13).

There is one problem with the wire-arm bobbins, however: they have no distinctive left or right. Thus, one time when you pick up the bobbin, the thread unwinds clockwise. Next time you pick it up it may unwind counterclockwise. In 1987 I found a solution to this frustration. The solution was so elegant, so simple that I marvelled at my own ignorance. The solution was not mine, and I remember it was 1987 because that's when Darrell Martin's book "Fly Tying Methods" was published. To lessen wax build-up at the base of the bobbin tube, Darrell bends the metal legs of the frame so that the edge of the thread spool (rather than the center of the thread spool) is in line with the tube *(Figure 2-1)*. This way the thread comes off the

spool and goes straight up through the tube. Such a shape also bestows a top and bottom, left and right to the bobbin frame; the thread can only be mounted in one way. The frustration of keeping track of which way the thread unwinds is gone; for me, a very major frustration has disappeared. Now, I always know which way the bobbin spool is turning and can easily unwind the thread or wind it back on by turning the spool with my middle finger (see page 20). Thanks Darrell!

Bodkin

A bodkin is a needle with a handle. It's used to apply head cement, pick out materials accidentally tied under, and roughen the fly body. I like one that has a long, easily held handle and a fine tip. The fine tip is essential for applying head cement to tiny flies.

SECONDARY TOOLS

Secondary tools are essential for dressing many, but not all patterns. For me, these tools include hackle pliers, a pair of medium-weight scissors, several sizes of paper clamps, and dubbing brushes. Hackle pliers come in a variety of sizes and shapes. No one size or shape will do everything that needs done, so I use two types. One is the electrical-circuit-tester clamp, available from fly shops or electronics stores *(Figure 2-2)*. These are very light weight and hold the material quite firmly, so they are excellent for tying small flies and for holding a twisted dubbing loop. They come in a variety of sizes; I find the 2 1/2-inch length to be best. The spring-type hackle pliers *(Figure 2-3)* also work well. I use ones in the 2 1/2- to 3-inch length.

Secondary scissors are used to perform tasks that would be hazardous to the health of the primary pair: snipping lead and copper wires, trimming heavy hide, and cutting hard materials such as monofilament. A good-quality pair of embroidery scissors works very well.

Figure 2-1. *Bobbin modified as per Darrell Martin.*

Spring-back paper clamps (Figure 9-12, page 114) are very handy for holding and spreading materials to be placed in a dubbing loop. They are also useful for holding materials for trimming. I use an assortment of sizes.

A dubbing brush *(Figure 2-4)* makes fuzzy nymph bodies easy to create. I use two sizes: a small-diameter brush to roughen heavy materials and a larger diameter brush to roughen more delicate materials. No this is not a printing error. The larger brush has longer, and therefore softer, bristles than the smaller-diameter brush.

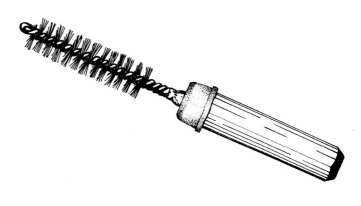

Figure 2-4. *A dubbing brush.*

Figure 2-2. *Electronic circuit tester used as a hackle pliers.*

ANCILLARY TOOLS

These tools are not directly involved in the tying process but are used in preparatory work: a hair stacker, a blender, bobbin threader, hemostats, sharp razor blade or number 11 scalpel blade, and a clip board. The use of these tools is described in the chapters on tying. In addition, I consider a good lamp and uniformly colored tying surface to be essential. There are many lamps available; just be sure the one you get has enough adjustments so it will stay well out of the way while you're tying. I cover the top of my tying bench in the immediate vicinity of the vise with either a blue blotter or a piece of light-green mat board. These colors are easy on the eyes and provide a uniform background against which to view the fly while tying.

Figure 2-3. *Spring-type hackle pliers.*

GENERAL TYING PROCEDURES

Staying Organized

It may seem like heresy to suggest that the tying bench be kept clean and organized, but that's exactly what I'm going to suggest. This recommendation doesn't come from some inherent compulsion for neatness; it's just that neatness increases efficiency. Tying is supposed to be fun, not frustrating, and by having a place for everything and keeping everything in its place, I don't have to spend valuable tying time searching through a hodge-podge of materials and tools for the item(s) needed. Here are some thoughts on staying organized.

1. Keep out only those tools and materials that are necessary for the pattern being tied.

2. When you finish with one pattern, put away all materials and tools not needed to tie the next pattern and take out the additional materials and tools that are needed. This ends the frustration of bench buildup.

3. Tie all the different sizes of one pattern at one sitting. This will save a great deal of shuffling of materials and tools.

4. Keep the tools and materials organized on the bench. Place tools to one side of the vise and materials to the other. *Try to keep the tools arranged with the most used items closest to the vise and the least used furthest from the vise.* Some tiers prefer to use a tool rack to help stay organized. I find it faster not using a rack.

5. Keeping the bench top organized means keeping the storage areas organized. It's no more fun searching frustratedly through the storage areas than it is searching through items on the bench top. I find resealable plastic bags to be a great help in this regard. Materials such as feathers, skins, blended dubbing, and yarns can be sealed in them and clearly labelled.

Using the Vise

Clamp the hook in the vise so that the shank is level; this positioning is the most comfortable for tying. The most secure way to clamp the hook is to position it so that the jaws of the vise are holding the lower part of the bend and the point is exposed *(Figure 3-1)*. The wire in the lower part of the bend is uniform in diameter, and thus the jaws grip the entire area uniformly. Held this way, the hook won't slip during the tying operation. It requires very little effort (and maybe a drop or two of blood) to learn to tie with the hook point exposed.

Figure 3-1. *The best way to grip the hook in the vise.*

To avoid an occasional jab, some tiers hide the point in the jaws of the vise. However, because the wire in the point is tapered (otherwise how could it be a point?), the jaws will only grip the hook at one spot: at the back of the point where the wire is largest in diameter. Thus insecurely held, the hook has a strong tendency to slip during the tying operation. The tier then has a strong tendency to tighten the vise further, putting more pressure on that one spot on the hook. Often such intense pressure is sufficient to fracture the metal of the hook. If the point doesn't break immediately, it often breaks later during the sudden stresses of striking and playing the fish.

Bobbin Handling

A bobbin is a very useful tool, allowing thread manipulation techniques not possible without one. When tying with nylon thread, adjust the tension of the bobbin so that the thread stretches before it begins to unwind from the spool. This will allow you to put maximum pressure on the materials during the tying operation while still allowing the thread to unwind as you wrap.

To get the most maneuverability from your bobbin, hold it by the base of the arms. I grip the bobbin between my index finger and thumb and then hold my middle finger against the bobbin spool *(Figure 3-2)*. When wrapping, I can allow the thread to flow out or clamp my finger against the spool and prevent it from turning. Held this way, it's not only easier to wrap the thread and control its flow, but only the tube gets near the fly. This is doubly important when dressing very small flies where large objects like fingers do nothing but get in the way.

Attaching The Thread

Every fly should start with a solid, thread foundation laid onto the hook before any other materials are attached. When materials are subsequently added, they will be trapped be-

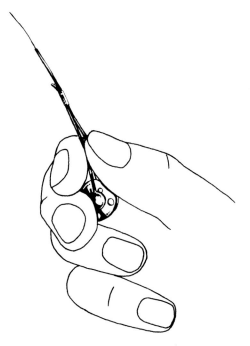

Figure 3-2. *Holding the bobbin.*

tween layers of thread and not against the bare metal of the hook. Materials tied against the bare metal will often spin around the shank, producing a loose, easily dissembled fly.

I use the standard method for attaching the thread to the hook, which is to wrap the thread back over itself. Hold the bobbin in your dominant hand and the tag end of the thread in your materials hand (for a right-handed tier, the materials hand is the left). Starting near the center of the shank, wrap the thread forward in an open spiral right up to the eye of the hook *(Figure 3-3)* and then wrap the thread back over the open spirals, keeping each turn tight against the last one *(Figure 3-4)*. Wrap so that the bobbin is moving away from you as it goes over the top of the shank and is coming toward you as it moves under the shank.

When possible, keep the distance between the tip of the bobbin and the hook shank at about 1 1/2 to 2 inches. If the bobbin gets further away from the shank, the circular pathway that your hand must describe gets cumbersomely large. There are three basic positions where the wraps end:

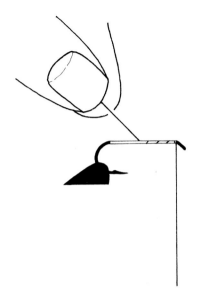

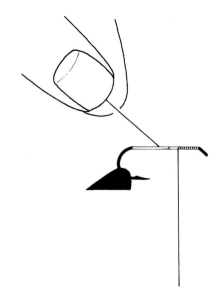

Figure 3-3. *Wrap the thread forward in open spirals.*

Figure 3-4. *Then wrap back over it to lock the thread on the hook*

1. The low-water position, named after the low-water style of salmon fly dressing. This is a position directly above the very end of the hook point *(Figure 3-5).*

2. The standard position. This is the point where the rear curve of the hook begins; nominally it lies almost directly above the barb *(Figure 3-6).*

3. The extended position. This is a point 1/4 to 1/3 of the way around the bend of the hook from the standard position *(Figure 3-7).*

When the thread foundation has been wrapped on, stretch the waste end of the thread taut and cut it as close to the hook shank as possible. The elasticity of the thread will cause the cut end to snap back under the wraps, giving a very tidy appearance to the foundation.

The Pinch

In fly tying, materials are attached to the hook by wrapping over them with the thread. However, as the thread is wrapped around the shank, it crowds against the materials and often

Figure 3-5. *The low water position.*   **Figure 3-6.** *The standard position.*   **Figure 3-7.** *The extended position.*

pushes them out of the way or forces them around the shank into a different position than the one intended. This major problem can be overcome by using the pinch technique.

For example, to tie materials on the top of the shank, hold them between thumb and forefinger of the materials hand and position them on the hook. Maintaining a firm grip on the materials, wrap the thread up between the tips of your thumb and forefinger. Pinch the thread tightly to maintain the tension and loop the thread over the top of the material and down the far side of the hook. Pull the thread straight down, drawing the pinched loop from between your still tightly pinched thumb and forefinger. The loop will settle directly onto the top of the material and hold it firmly *(Figure 3-8)*. Repeat the process two or three times to securely lock the material in place, then wrap in a normal fashion.

By this same manner, materials can be "pinched" onto either side of, or the bottom of, the hook without the necessity of rotating the head of the vise. A true time saver and frustration eliminator.

After locking the materials in place with the pinch technique, you will need to add more wraps of thread to secure the material on the hook. To keep the material from spinning around the hook as you wrap, slide your thumb and index finger along the sides of the hook shank so that they continually pinch the material and prevent it from twisting around the shank. Keep your pinched thumb and forefinger as close to the wrapping thread as possible *(Figure 3-9)*. This tactic can be employed whether the tying thread is to be wrapped forward or rearward.

Dubbing

To "dub" means to twist fibrous materials around the tying thread. Normally, soft underfur (called dubbing fur) of various animals, soft feather fibers (such as marabou), or fine denier synthetic filaments are used for dubbing. These can be spun tightly onto the thread with a minimum of effort.

In the normal dubbing process, a small amount of the dubbing material is held between the thumb and forefinger of the bobbin hand (the right hand, for a right-handed person). The material is brought in contact with the thread and then spun tightly around the thread by twisting it between the thumb and forefinger *(Figure 3-10)*. There are two inherent pitfalls in the process.

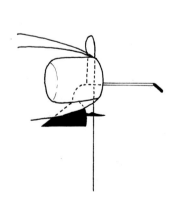

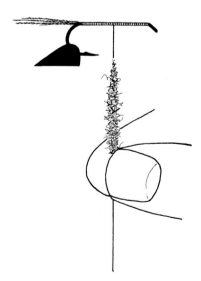

Figure 3-8. *Pinching the thread loop.*

Figure 3-9. *Holding the material to prevent it from spinning around the hook shank.*

Figure 3-10. *Twisting dubbing onto the thread.*

First, most people interpret "a small amount" to mean significantly more than is intended. Small means really small. In still hunting for deer, the hunter is told to move as slowly as possible, and then told that's still twice too fast. When dubbing, take what you feel is a small amount of material; it will still be twice too much. Use only a few filaments of the dubbing material. If you need thicker dubbing, get it by applying several thin layers, one over another. The final product will adhere to the thread much better and form a better body than one thick layer.

The second pitfall occurs in the interpretation of the word "twist." Be careful that you twist the material in only one direction. Twisting counterclockwise and then following that with a clockwise twist doesn't produce particularly tight dubbing. I always twist the dubbing counterclockwise. It's not important which way you twist the material, just do it in one direction and do it consistently.

While prewaxed thread has dramatically eased the process of dubbing, many fly tiers still have difficulty twisting fur or other fibers onto the thread. This difficulty arises because the skin of the fingers is too dry to allow a firm grasp on the fibers; they slide instead of twisting. To overcome this problem, many tiers wet their fingers with saliva before dubbing. While this method is successful, there is a better, longer-lasting solution to the problem: apply one of the tacky dubbing waxes *to the fingers*. But be careful, if you use too much, it comes off on the dubbing and discolors it. Just touch your forefinger to the wax and vigorously rub the pads of your forefinger and thumb together to work the wax into your skin. Then twist away.

The Dubbing Loop

Another method of applying dubbing is to twist it between two strands of thread. The easiest, most versatile variation of this method is through the use of a dubbing loop. The loop is formed during the tying operation rather than as a separate piece of material that must then be tied onto the fly. Typically, to form a dubbing

loop, the tier pulls the bobbin away from the hook about eight inches and places the tip of the index finger of the materials hand at the midpoint of the thread. The thread is then taken up around the finger tip and back to the hook shank where it's wrapped several turns, forming a loop.

However, this simple loop style is not suitable for some dubbing techniques because at the top of the loop the thread is separated by a distance equal to the thickness of the hook *(Figure 3-11)*. When the loop is subsequently closed, this space prevents the threads at the top of the loop from touching. Thus, materials such as hair legs that are placed loosely in the top of the loop tend to fall out after the loop is closed.

Figure 3-11. *The standard dubbing loop has an unwanted space at the top.*

To make a loop that will close tightly at the top, begin in the normal way: pull the thread out, go around your finger and then over the shank, ending with the bobbin hanging down behind the hook. (In addition to using your index finger, practice making the loop around the end of your middle finger; this leaves the index finger and thumb available for handling other materials.) Wrap the thread under the hook on the forward side of the loop, then take the bobbin up over the loop and drop it on the rear side of the loop *(Figure 3-12)*. Pull the bobbin forward under the loop *(Figure 3-13)* and wrap two times around the shank just in front of the loop *(Figure 3-14)*. In this fashion, the tying thread wraps around the loop and pulls the two

Figure 3-12. *Take the bobbin over the top of the loop.* **Figure 3-13.** *Wrap under the loop.* **Figure 3-14.** *Secure the thread by wrapping around the hook shank.*

sides tightly together. This is the method I use for all dubbing loops.

Pretrimming

Many tiers secure materials to the hook and then clip away the excess. But when possible, I prefer to cut away the excess before tying in the material. For example, If I'm tying in several strands of peacock herl, I'll align them into a clump and then trim it so that the ends of the herl are even. This trimmed end is then tied in.

Tying Off

When tying off materials that have been wrapped around the hook (a piece of chenille for example), many tiers switch hands: they hold the material in the bobbin hand and wrap the bobbin over the hook with the materials hand. For example, a right handed tier would hold the materials in the right hand and wrap with the left hand. This is not only a clumsy way to handle the materials and thread, but it does not allow the tier to maintain uniform tension on the thread while tying. Far better to keep the bobbin in the bobbin hand and the materials in the materials hand.

So, this is the procedure I use when tying off. On the last turn of material, I grasp the bobbin and push it toward the rear of the hook. At the same time, I push the material toward the front of the hook so that the thread and material

cross each other right at the shank. Once crossed, the thread can be wrapped and the material released *(Figure 3-15)*. When learned, this method is far faster, less clumsy, and provides more thread tension than switching hands,

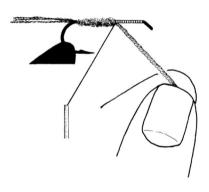

Figure 3-15. *The "crossover" technique for securing materials with the thread.*

With this method, material can be tied off under the hook, on top of the hook, or on either side of the hook. Normally I try to balance the positions where I tie off materials so that some are tied off under and some are tied off on top of the shank. This is especially important when several materials are tied off at one point along the hook shank. For example, if I'm tying a nymph with a wing case, I'll tie off the body material under the head of the fly and the wing case on top of the head.

Cutting Off Materials Under the Hook

This is a problem because the thread is also hanging down under the hook. To avoid cutting the thread, push it out to the far side of the hook with the index finger of your materials hand. Then, use the middle finger and thumb of the materials hand to hold the material while you cut it off *(Figure 3-16)*.

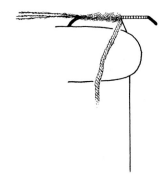

Figure 3-16. *Push the thread out of the way with your index finger.*

The Head

Most of the time, flies are dressed with a thread head. The head is usually made the same length as the eye of the fly *(Figure 3-17)*. With only a bit of practice, the head space is easily determined by "eyeballing" it; measuring the length of the head with a ruler is totally unnecessary. It this book I often refer to a distance I call "head space." It is the length of the head as defined here.

Figure 3-17. *The head is the same length as the eye.*

The Finishing Knot

I don't use a whip finish. The truth of the matter is, I learned to tie flies by myself from the Family Circle's "Guide to Trout Flies and How to Tie Them," and there was no mention of a whip finish. The instructions simply said to place a

couple of half hitches on the head and then lacquer it. Half hitches didn't hold very well, so I began using two double hitches. They worked just great. I've since learned the whip finish, but really don't use it because the double hitch has decided advantages for me.

First, I can tie it much faster than a whip finish. Second, I can direct its placement so that no material gets trapped under the thread as the knot is drawn tight. Third, I can use it on any size fly and with any size thread.

To tie the knot, begin as making a dubbing loop. Go around your finger and then twice around the head of the fly *(Figure 3-18)*. If there

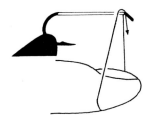

Figure 3-18. *Start the knot as if making a dubbing loop.*

are hackle barbs or other materials close to the head that could get mistakenly wrapped under by these two turns, make them with the very end of the bobbin *(Figure 3-19)*. Take the loop around the eye of the fly, keeping the bottom

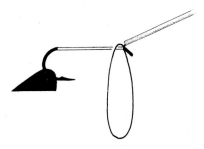

Figure 3-19. *Use the very end of the bobbin to wrap if necessary.*

thread of the loop under the eye and the top loop over the eye *(Figure 3-20)*. As you do so, rotate your finger in the loop so that you can

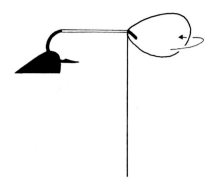

Figure 3-20. *Take the loop around the eye of the fly.*

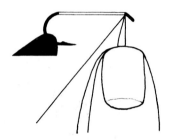

Figure 3-21. *Pinch the loop as you draw it tight.*

pinch the loop between your thumb and forefinger. Your hand will now be on the far side of the hook *(Figure 3-21)*. Pull on the bobbin to draw the knot tight. As it tightens, allow the loop of the knot to draw through your pinch so that the loop gradually gets smaller. By this method you can guide the loop of the knot to exactly the right spot on the head and avoid trapping any materials in the knot.

I've learned to tie this knot using my index finger, middle finger, or ring finger of my materials hand. This allows me to hold materials out of the way with the other fingers, if necessary.

Cutting the Thread

After the finishing knot is tied, the thread is cut away. If the scissors are used to "snip" the thread, parts such as hackle, which aren't supposed to be cut away, sometimes get snipped off

along with the thread. To prevent this, use the scissors to "slice" the thread rather than snip it. Hold the thread under tension with the materials hand. Open the scissor points just a bit (as if to snip) and push them against the thread so that it slides back into the "V" made by the points.

Lacquering The Head

I don't lacquer the head of the fly as soon as I'm done dressing it. Rather, I toss all my flies into a tray and lacquer them when I'm done with the tying session. This is an amazing time saver. In addition, I hold the fly in my fingers and can turn it any way I need in order to get the cement where I want. If I get cement in the eye, I can clean it out readily: I thread a piece of peacock herl (or a pheasant tail barb for tiny hooks) into the eye and then pull it all the way through to whisk it clean.

Tying Tips

To me, a good fly design must not only fool the toughest trout, but must be durable and easy (fast) to tie, because like most tiers, I must juggle my tying time with other commitments and responsibilities—and often my time at the vise comes out on the short end. For this reason, I have adapted my tying techniques for speed whenever possible. Specific speed tying techniques that are used in the construction of a particular fly design are shown in the chapter which discusses that design. I have emphasized them by setting them apart in a window like this:

> *Speed Tying Tip:* A few minutes spent carefully studying the diagrams and descriptions in this book before attempting to tie any fly will greatly increase your speed in learning new methods.

Then, there are specific techniques that may not be speed tying tips but which are used on only a few designs. The first time such a tying tactic is presented, it is discussed in detail. When it's used on another design discussed later, the page number of the original discussion is given as a reference.

MAYFLY
NYMPHS & EMERGERS

NYMPHS

Mayflies occupy a wide variety of habitats in both lakes and streams, from muddy-bottomed pools to boulder-strewn rapids, from coastal waters to mountain freshets. Because they occupy such diverse habitats, the nymphs vary considerably in body details, but there are only four basic shapes. Some species are strongly flattened and have long, powerful legs to cling tightly to rocks in fast currents; the gills of these clinging nymphs are plate-shaped and prominent and contribute to the overall flattened design of the insect *(Figure 4-1)*. They are normally poor swimmers. Crawling nymphs occupy currents of medium flow and are somewhat flattened in cross section and have legs developed for walking. Their gills are plate-shaped or filamentous and smaller than those of the clinging nymphs; however, they beat steadily and so are easily seen *(Figure 4-2)*. Many species of crawling nymphs are good swimmers. Nymphs of the minnow-like mayflies are cylindrical in form; their gills are similar in size, shape and movement to the crawling nymphs *(Figure 4-3)*; they are powerful swimmers. The burrowing mayfly nymphs have a cylindrical body and short, stout, digging legs. Their gills are very large and feather-like and beat in a fluid, undulating synchronization *(Figure 4-4)*. They swim very well, using a most sinuous up and down movement of the abdomen.

Yet, though they are as diverse in form as in habitat, mayfly nymphs do share a number of

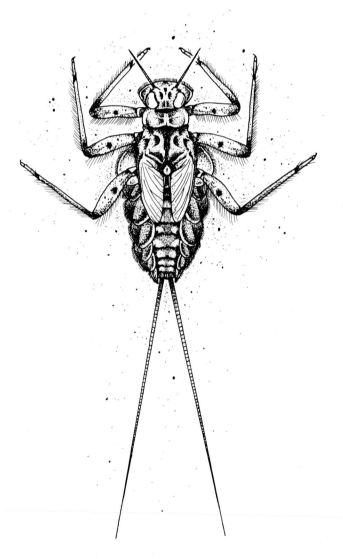

Figure 4-1. *Typical clinging mayfly nymph.*

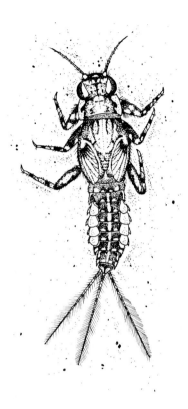

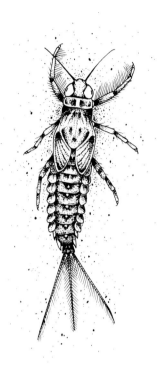

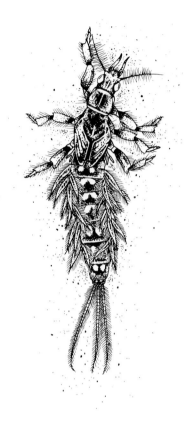

Figure 4-2. Typical crawling mayfly nymph.

Figure 4-3. Typical minnow-like mayfly nymph.

Figure 4-4. Typical burrowing mayfly nymph.

common characteristics that should be incorporated into the imitations. All have well-defined tails, head, thoracic and abdominal regions, gills, wing pads, and legs. The trout's vision is good enough to allow it to distinguish major body parts and note proportions, but the fish does not count legs and tails nor distinguish the shape of the gills. So while the fly tier need not craft a perfect imitation of the nymph, with three tails, six legs, and so on, the artificial should reflect attention to proportionality and overall relational appearance of the various parts of the living insect.

Because of their great ranges in sizes and body shapes, I use three basic patterns to imitate mayfly nymphs. The greatest number of nymphs range between 1/4 to 1/2 inch in length (stan-

dard hook sizes 10 to 16) and are of the clinging, crawling, or minnow-like forms. For these I use the Hair Leg Nymph. For nymphs smaller than size 16 I employ the Feather Leg Nymph. For the very large nymphs of the burrowing mayflies, the Strip Nymph has proven to be a superb imitation. Each of these patterns is based on observations of the underwater appearance of the naturals and is designed to simulate those characteristics that most strongly induce the fish to strike.

Hair Leg Nymph

The legs of all mayfly nymphs are a readily seen characteristic, yet some tiers have suggested that it's not important to imitate the legs because they're folded against the body during swimming.

Many nymphs, however, don't move about by swimming. When these insects are caught in the currents, they drift along with their legs extended, hoping to grab onto something. In addition, the swimming varieties don't swim continuously; they often pause with their legs outspread. Thus it is that trout often do see the legs of the insect. Having fished identical nymph patterns with and without legs, I am convinced that fish will take the legged pattern more readily. Perhaps the presence of legs and/or any movement they may show gives a better impression of life and is therefore a better trigger of the fish's predatory instinct. I've tried many materials to represent the legs of aquatic insects, and for mayfly nymphs size 16 and larger, have found guard hairs to give the best results.

Guard hairs are very desirable because they are stiffer than soft hackle and thus maintain a better silhouette in the fly. In addition they are larger in diameter than cock hackle and so show up more readily. The mottled coloration of the guard hairs of cottontail rabbit, squirrel, hare's mask, and others, nicely mimics the often mottled coloration of many mayfly legs.

I first conceived of using guard hairs for legs in 1971 when I read George Grant's book "The Art of Weaving Hair Hackles." His descriptions of woven hair hackle and its effectiveness were very intriguing, and his arguments were clear and well founded. But the weaving tactic is not practical for hairs shorter than about two inches. Thus, guard hairs were unsuitable for the weaving technique. And it was these hairs that I wanted to use for legs on nymphs. So I experimented with several techniques to make hair hackle from guard hairs, finally settling on a modification of the dubbing loop method shown by F. W. Lawrie in his book "All Fur Flies and How to Dress Them." After dubbing fur is twisted on one side of the loop, the guard hairs are inserted in the loop at right angles to the thread, and the loop is closed and twisted tight. The effect is just right: a three-dimensional hair hackle with dubbing. The dubbing fur helps to anchor the guard hairs in the loop and at the

same time serves as the material for the thorax of the fly. The guard hairs stick out at right angles to the hook shank when the twisted loop is wound on—legs and thorax in one operation. I fished my first Hair Leg Nymph design in the spring of 1972 and was most excited by the results. This tying tactic has remained a favorite of mine since then.

I have tried numerous materials for the tail of this pattern, but with the exception of occasional, experimental forays, I have settled on the barbs of a pheasant tail feather. (For a discussion of feather anatomy and terminology, see page 167.) These barbs are long enough and heavy enough for use on even the largest mayfly nymph patterns. Many mayfly nymphs have rather hairy tails; the bulk of the pheasant tail barbs nicely suggests this feature. Not only that, but the barbules of the feather are large and easily seen, further mimicking the hairs on mayfly nymph tails. In addition, the natural, rusty-brown color of the barbs is a close match for the tails of many naturals. If necessary, pheasant tail feathers are easily tinted shades of yellow, olive, or dark brown.

Fly tiers have used many materials in the construction of mayfly nymph bodies, and I have been just as guilty as the next, trying everything from horse tail hair to molded epoxy and beyond. But always for the Hair Leg Nymph I have returned to furs: synthetic or natural, dubbed or in yarn form, they remain the very best material to simulate the evident, translucent exoskeleton of the naturals.

G. E. M. Skues, who fished the Hampshire chalkstreams of England in the early years of this century, and who is considered to be the father of modern nymph fishing, noted many materials in his writings, but preferred fur or wool. He wrote in "Nymph Fishing for Chalk Stream Trout" that fur or wool was …"so extraordinarily translucent as to let the color of the underlying tying silk be seen through it…." Edward Ringwood Hewitt, the father of North American nymph fishing, adopted Skues' tying styles and material preferences, modifying them to imitate the specific insects of this continent. Big Jim Leisenring, of Allentown, Pennsylvania, who so successfully imported the soft hackle concept of Stewart, used fur bodies on his deadly flies because it was one material which could "...imitate the texture, translucence, and flash of the natural fly as nearly as possible."

Perhaps the most eloquent and thoughtful arguments for fur-bodied flies were put forth by Jack Atherton in his book "The Fly and the Fish." To give the impression of life, Atherton chose fur for the fly's body: "In body materials I am a firm believer in the effectiveness and life-like qualities of fur of some sort...."

Working from an empirical point of view, on the opposite side of the continent from Atherton, Polly Rosborough also came to the conclusion that fur-bodied flies catch more fish: "To be consistently successful a nymph must appear alive to the fish from any angle. When a fuzzy-bodied nymph is saturated and reaches the vision of the fish every filament on the body, tail, legs, even the wingcases, vibrate...."

I work with a wide variety of natural and synthetic dubbing furs, selecting them for their colors, length, and degree of fineness. Seal fur is especially prized for nymph patterns because of its natural translucency, but seal fur is hard to obtain. A most suitable, synthetic, substitute for seal is sparkle yarn, containing Dupont Antron filaments; I blend it with other synthetic and natural furs to produce a very noticeable translucency in the body of the artificial. Normally, I try to blend coarser materials, such as some sparkle yarns or guard hairs, with very fine-fibered furs. The finer filaments act to bind the coarser ones into the dubbing so they can be more easily spun onto the thread.

Not only does blended dubbing give a most life-like effect for creating the body of the nymph, but it also, simultaneously, serves to represent the moving gills of the natural. No, trout do not recognize gills, *per se*, but the almost non-stop beating of these structures is a powerful indication to the fish that the nymph is a living thing worthy of being eaten. The movement of the fur fibers in the imitation cannot possibly ape the precise dance of insect gills, but it can trigger the fish's predatory nature in the same way. This is another reason that I use fine-filament furs when blending materials for the body. These very thin fibers vacillate with the slightest current.

For the wing case of the Hair Leg Nymph, I use peacock herl, period. Herl makes a great body material for many patterns, and Skues, Leisenring, Atherton, and Rosborough have all written glowingly of its trout-attracting qualities. I've always had a fascination with herl because the first trout I ever caught on a fly was on a herl-bodied Slate Wing Coachman. But to use this iridescent material for wing pads?—the idea had never dawned on me. Then, in Joe Brooks' book "Trout Fishing," I saw a color photograph of some stonefly nymphs tied by Dave Whitlock. They had peacock herl wing cases, and the photograph showed off all the sparkle and iridescence of the herl. That photo made me realize the dramatic potential of peacock herl for imitating the inflated, glistening wing pads of the mature nymph. In addition to its unique light scattering properties, herl is also very effective because the barbules are large enough to be seen easily and delicate enough to move in the currents; they add an extra measure of life. Herl has been so effective that I've never strayed to any other material.

I normally weight my nymphs by wrapping the thoracic region with lead wire before applying the body materials. The lead is not meant to sink the fly to the bottom, rather it helps the fly penetrate the surface film. Without it, the dubbed body holds so much air that the nymph will float. Such a small amount of lead does not noticeably effect the cast.

To fish nymphs on the bottom, I prefer to add split shot (or Twist-Ons, or Shape-A-Wate) to the leader. This is better than adding large amounts of weight to the fly for two reasons. First, a great deal of weight on the hook alters the proportions of the fly—making the dressing too bulky. Second, the tier never knows for sure how much weight should be added. When fishing, the angler can use the exact amount of shot needed to keep the fly on the bottom.

The Hair Leg Nymph has become such an integral part of my fly fishing that I feel naked without it. It has been an extremely effective pattern in waters world wide: it has performed flawlessly on big rivers like Canada's Bow and Montana's Bighorn and Madison; the first fish I caught on my first trip to New Zealand was a 25-inch brown—on a Hair Leg Nymph; the wild little browns of England's West Country went wild for it; and the finicky, urbane trout of the gentle spring creeks of our East and West sip it in readily. It's a design that has decidedly proven its worth.

Hair Leg Nymph: Dressing

Hook: Sizes 6-16, standard shank length (2X long shank may be substituted in larger sizes; see hook discussion in Chapter 14.)

Thread: 6/0, color to match body

Tails: Pheasant tail barbs; may be tinted to match color of natural; same length as body

Abdomen and Gills: Blended fur and sparkle yarn dubbing or yarn, color to match natural; brushed out with dubbing brush

Rib: None or tinsel or wire

Thorax: Same material as abdomen but spun on dubbing loop, weighted with lead wire.

Covert: Peacock herl; 8-10 pieces for sizes 6-8; 6-8 pieces for sizes 10-12; 4-6 pieces for sizes 14-16

Legs: Mottled guard hairs from various furs twisted into dubbing loop

Hair Leg Nymph: Most Used Sizes/Body Colors/Hair for Legs/ Naturals Matched (all regions)

Sizes 6-16/Body red brown (BCS 66); may be ribbed with copper wire/ Legs of cottontail rabbit or fox squirrel guard hairs/Matches nymphs of *Ephemerella, Rithrogena, Isonychia, Leptophlebia, Paraleptophlebia*

Sizes 8-16/Body blend of 50% hare's mask, 25% fur from back of fox squirrel, 25% tan sparkle yarn (BCS 61); ribbed with gold tinsel or wire/Legs of cotton tail rabbit or fox squirrel guard hairs/ Matches nymphs of *Stenonema, Heptagenia*

Sizes 8-16/Body dark olive brown (BCS 34); may be ribbed with dark green wire/Legs of rabbit or squirrel guard hairs dyed dark olive/Matches nymphs of *Callibaetis, Epeorus, Siphlonurus*

Sizes 6-16/Body dark brown (BCS 98); may be ribbed with black wire/ Legs of rabbit or squirrel guard hairs dyed black/Matches nymphs of *Ephemerella*, and dark phase of many other genera

Sizes 10-14/Body smokey gray (BCS 108); ribbed with silver tinsel or wire/Legs of cottontail rabbit dyed gray, gray mink, or gray squirrel guard hairs/Matches nymphs of *Siphlonurus, Ameletus*, and others.

Hair Leg Nymph: Tying Instructions

1. Secure the hook in the vise and wrap the thread to the standard position *(Figure 4-5)*. To tie a slightly longer pattern or hide the hook bend a bit, wrap back to the extended position.

Figure 4-5. *Hook with thread foundation in place*

2. Using the pinch technique, attach four to six pheasant tail barbs to the top of the hook shank at the standard position (or, if you choose, at the extended position). These will form the tail of the fly; it should be about the same length as the body. To further secure the barbs, wrap the thread forward, keeping tension on it and placing each wrap immediately ahead of the previous one; end the wraps at about the low-water position *(Figure 4-6)*.

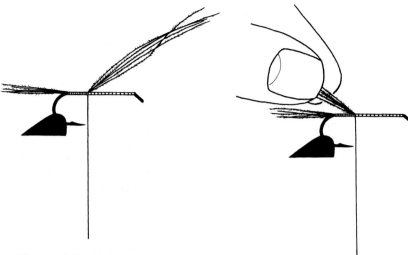

Figure 4-6. *Tailing material secured with thread wraps.*

Figure 4-7. *Breaking off the waste end of the tailing material.*

crawling or swimming species; with a little practice it's easy to estimate the necessary amount.

Figure 4-8. *Lead wire secured with thread.*

3. Remove the waste portion of the barbs.

> *Speed Tying Tip:* To save the time needed to pick up, operate, and put down the scissors, don't cut the barbs, break them off instead. Grasp them firmly and snap them sharply rearward. Keep your fingers close to the hook so that the barbs are bent acutely back over the thread wrapping; they will break easily (*Figure 4-7*). If they pull out instead of breaking, you need to apply more tension to the thread as you wrap.

4. Wrap lead wire under the thoracic region. The lead wire should have about the same diameter as the hook shank. It's not necessary to tie in the lead; just hold it like a piece of tying thread, and beginning at the midpoint of the shank, wrap forward, keeping each turn tight against the previous turn. End the wraps about two head spaces behind the eye. Remove the excess lead wire.

> *Speed Tying Tip:* Again, to save time, don't use the scissors to cut away the excess lead wire. Rather, crimp it against the hook shank with your thumbnail; it will break easily. In addition, you can use your thumbnail to press the broken ends tightly against the hook shank.

5. Wrap the thread over the lead wire, in a rib-like fashion, forward to the head and then back to the rear of the lead. Repeat this two or three times to lock the lead securely in place. Also build up a tapered section of thread wraps at each end of the lead to provide a smooth transition. End with the thread at the rear of the lead (*Figure 4-8*).

6. Pull out about five inches of thread and spin dubbing tightly onto it; start the dubbing about 1 to 1 1/2 inch from the hook and work away from the hook. Build up a wick of dubbing with a taper at each end (*Figure 4-9*). The amount of dubbing used will depend upon hook size and required body size. For the clinging nymphs, the body should be thicker than for the

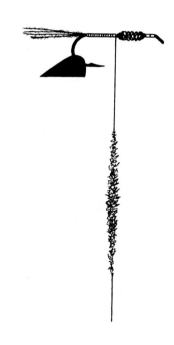

Figure 4-9. *The prepared dubbing wick.*

7. If a rib is to be tied in, place the tip of it just rearward of the lead wire and wrap the thread back over the ribbing material until the thread has reached the appropriate rearward position (standard or extended). When you've finished wrapping the thread rearward, the dubbing will be up against the hook and ready to be

wound on to form the abdomen. This step also secures the tailing material with another layer of wraps.

Speed Tying Tip: This thread handling technique not only saves time but cuts down on the number of thread wraps that are added to the fly. In addition, leaving bare thread next to the hook makes it easier to spin on the dubbing. Some tiers wind all the way to the rear of the hook and then try to spin on the dubbing, but in this position, the hook and vise get in the way and cause no end of frustration. Or the tier might spin the dubbing down on the thread and then push it up to the hook, in which case the dubbing gets loosened.

8. If no rib is to be added, simply wrap the thread back to the rear position to bring the dubbing wick up against the body.

9. Wrap the dubbing forward to form the abdomen. The tapered wick of dubbing will form a nicely tapered body, thin at the rear and fatter toward the midsection. To decrease the fullness of the body, keep each wrap barely touching the preceding one. To increase the fullness of the body, crowd the wraps tightly so that they overlap a bit. The abdomen should finish at the mid-point of the shank. The tapered end of the dubbing will allow you to wrap up onto the lead wire without producing a large bump in the front part of the abdomen (*Figure 4-10*).

10. Pre-trim the end of the clump of herl (page 22) and using the pinch technique, tie it on top of the hook immediately in front of the abdomen. Position the herl so that it covers the sides and top of the hook shank; this arrangement will produce a fuller-looking wing case than if the herl

were all tied in directly on top of the shank. In addition, when the herl is pulled forward, it will act as a brace to keep the hair legs

Figure 4-10. *The finished abdomen.*

sticking straight out to the sides. Wind the thread forward to secure the material, then wind it back to the point where the herl is tied in (*Figure 4-11*).

11. Form a dubbing loop (see page 21) and twist dubbing loosely onto one side (I normally apply

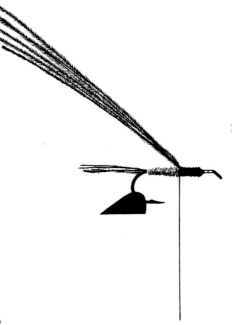

Figure 4-11. *Herl secured at rear of thorax.*

the dubbing to the bottom thread of the loop; (*Figure 4-12* —Note: in Figures 4-12 through 4-18 the herl has not been drawn to length). Push the dubbing up to the very top of the loop. Don't worry, when the loop is twisted tight, the dubbing will be very secure. The finished thorax should be about 1 1/2 times thicker than the abdomen; with a little practice you will easily be able to judge the correct amount of dubbing to use.

Figure 4-12. *Dubbing applied loosely to lower side of loop. Note: Herl not shown to length.*

12. Pluck a cluster of guard hairs from the selected skin. To do this, first bend the hide so that the guard hairs will stick out in an easily grasped position. Place the side of the first joint of the index finger of your bobbin hand under the protruding guard hairs and pinch them tightly with your thumb (*Figure 4-13*). This finger position produces a flattened bunch of hairs that are easily inserted into the dubbing loop. Pull the guard hairs from the hide, and with your materials hand, remove any dubbing fur or basal portions of the guard hairs.

Figure 4-13. *Plucking the guard hairs from the hide.*

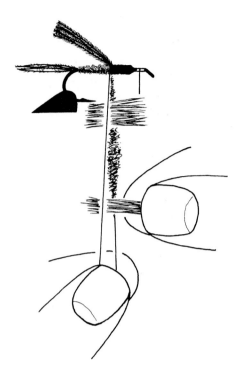

Figure 4-14. *Guard hairs at the top of the closed loop.*

Figure 4-15. *Distributing the guard hairs along the loop.*

13. Keeping the hairs tightly pinched between your thumb and forefinger, insert them into the top end of the dubbing loop (as close to the hook shank as can be easily accomplished). The thread of the loop should bisect the hairs. Close the loop by allowing the thread to slip off the end of your finger and catching it in a pinch between your thumb and finger tip *(Figure 4-14).*

14. At this time, the guard hairs can be distributed along the length of the loop as needed. With the thumb and forefinger of your bobbin hand, grasp the tips of several of the lower-most hairs and gently slide them down the loop to their final position *(Figure 4-15).* Repeat until the guard hairs are distributed as needed. For a size 8-12 fly the guard hairs should be arranged in the upper 2 inches of the loop; for a size 14-16 fly, the guard hairs should be distributed over the upper 1 1/2 inches of the loop.

15. When the guard hairs are in place, twist the loop tight, forming a three-dimensional, hair hackle *(Figure 4-16).*

16. Grasp the end of the twisted loop with a hackle pliers and wind forward over the thorax. After each turn, stroke the guard hairs rearward so they are not wrapped under by the next turn. Continue until the material has been wrapped to the head *(Figure 4-17).*

17. Tie off the material on the underside of the hook shank (and at the rear of the head) and cut away the excess.

Figure 4-16. *The twisted loop with 3-D hair hackle.*

Figure 4-17. *The wrapped thorax.*

Figure 4-18. *Guard hairs pressed out to sides.*

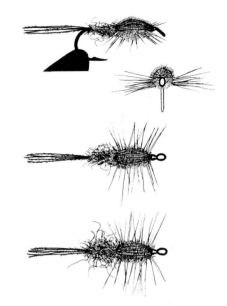

Figure 4-19. *The finished Hair Leg Nymph; side view, front view, top view with lightly brushed abdomen, top view with heavily brushed abdomen.*

18. Using thumb and forefinger of both hands, part the hairs on the top of the shank and press them out to the sides (*Figure 4-18*).

19. Fold the peacock herl forward, tight along the top of the thorax, and, using the pinch technique, secure it on top of the shank at the head. Cut away the excess and form a smoothly tapering head. Tie the finishing knot and cut away the thread.

Speed Tying Tip: Because of its length, you can tie several flies from each clump of peacock herl. Not only that, but when you clip the excess, the end of the clump is pre-trimmed (see step 10) and ready for application to the next fly. Thus after trimming, don't toss the excess away; gently lay it down where it won't be disturbed until you're ready to pick it up for the next fly. Wetting the trimmed end with a little saliva before putting the clump on the bench will help keep the strands of herl in proper alignment.

20. Stroke the hair legs forward so that they stick straight out from the hook shank and cut the legs off the bottom of the fly. If there are too many legs sticking out to the sides of the fly, clip a few away (I like 6-12 on each side, depending on fly size).

21. Using a dubbing brush, tease out the dubbing along the sides of the abdomen to represent the gills. For the crawling and swimming species, the teased out abdomen should be as wide as the thorax. For the clingers, the teased out abdomen should be about 1 1/2 times the width of

the thorax. The teased out fur also gives the clingers a strongly flattened appearance.

22. Apply head cement and the fly is finished (*Figure 4-19*).

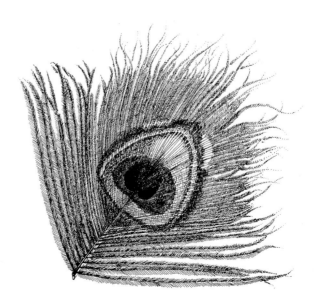

Feather Leg Nymph

Mayfly nymphs that are mature at size 18 or smaller are all of the crawling type and are found principally in four families: Baetidae, Caenidae, Ephemerellidae, and Tricorythidae. Frank Sawyer developed his justly famous Pheasant Tail Nymph (p.t.) to simulate various species of smaller nymphs that he observed on the River Avon in Wiltshire, England, where he was river keeper for most of his adult life. It's a great fly and deserves all the accolades it has received over the years. The p.t. does have three shortcomings, however: (1) it was designed to be fished deep and sinks so quickly that it is of little value when fishing to trout that are nymphing in the film, (2) there's little latitude for color variation, (3) it's difficult to dress effectively in sizes smaller than 20. Thus to imitate the smaller nymphs, I tie the Feather Leg Nymph.

For the tails, I prefer the barbs of the flank feather of mallard, teal, woodduck, or other similarly marked feathers. They are finer than those of the pheasant tail feather, and the delicate speckling of these feathers closely simulates the often-found alternating, dark and light barring of the natural's tails. The barbules are readily apparent and nicely simulate the hairs on the natural's tails. And besides, this easily obtainable material can be dyed any desired color.

When tying these imitations of the smaller mayfly nymphs, I abandon the hair leg technique because suitable-sized hairs are hard to find and hard to handle. In addition, the coarseness and stiffness of hair is not really necessary to create legs in artificials of this size range; barbs from mallard flank feather or other similarly marked feathers produce most suitable legs in these smaller flies.

For the body of small mayfly nymphs, I also use blended furs, both natural and synthetic.

Peacock herl is too bulky to form proportionally correct wing cases on these minute imitations, but to me, the iridescent wing case is an important ingredient in the pattern. So, in place of the herl, I use the iridescent green or blue feathers from the plumage of ring-neck pheasant, mallard, or other easily obtainable skins. To make these relatively small feathers easy to handle, and to prepare them for the tying procedure, I first treat them with flexible head cement. To do this, place a drop of cement on the base of the feather, pinch it between the thumb and forefinger, and stroke it from base to tip. Allow to dry thoroughly. This process narrows and thickens the feather and toughens it considerably. For very small nymphs, I often cut one of these tiny lacquered feathers lengthwise to get a wing case of correct width.

> *Speed Tying Tip:* Don't waste valuable tying time preparing these feathers as you tie. Rather, take time beforehand to prepare several dozen feathers. This not only assures a good supply to choose from, but gives the cement plenty of time to dry.

Like the Hair Leg Nymph, this fly is a necessary part of my angling strategy. Time and time again, it has proved to be the answer for tough fish during heavy hatches. I remember a day on the DePuy water in Montana, fishing with Nancy, Mike Dry, and Tom Travis. They were upstream and taking fish regularly on *Centroptilum* duns, but where I was fishing, the trout wouldn't take the Loop Wing Dun. I watched carefully. Even though they were rising strongly, I couldn't spot a single fish actually taking a fully expanded dun. They had to be eating nymphs. I switched over to the Feather Leg Nymph and fished it just under the film with a Greased Leader tactic; it was just the ticket, and I had a great day.

Feather Leg Nymph: Dressing

Hook: Sizes 18-28, standard shank length (short shank hooks may be substituted for the smaller sizes, see hook discussion in Chapter 14.)

Thread: 8/0, color to match body

Tails: Barbs of flank feather of mallard, woodduck, teal, etc.; dyed to color as necessary; same length as body

Thorax, Abdomen, and Gills: Blended fur and sparkle yarn dubbing, lightly brushed out with dubbing brush; weight thorax with fine lead wire

Rib: None or fine wire

Covert: Iridescent green or blue feather from neck of pheasant or mallard, lacquered

Legs: Mallard flank feather barbs or other similarly marked feathers such as woodduck, teal, and so on, dyed to color

Feather Leg Nymph: Most Used Sizes/Body Color/ Tail and Leg Color/ Naturals Matched (all regions)

Sizes 18-24/Body red brown (BCS 66)/Tail and Legs natural woodduck/Matches nymphs of *Ephemerella* and *Baetis*

Sizes 18-22/Body blend of 50% hare's mask, 25% fur from back of fox squirrel, 25% tan (BCS 61) sparkle yarn, ribbed with fine gold wire/ Tails and Legs natural woodduck/ Matches nymphs of *Centroptilum*

Sizes 18-24/Body blended fur and sparkle yarn, color dark olive brown (BCS 34)/Tails and Legs medium olive yellow (BCS 43)/ Matches nymphs of *Pseudocloeon, Baetis,* and *Caenis*

Sizes 18-28/Body dark brown (BCS 98)/Tails and Legs dyed red brown (BCS 66)/Matches nymphs of *Ephemerella, Tricorythodes,* and dark phase of many other genera

Feather Leg Nymph: Tying Instructions

1. Clamp the hook in the vise and wrap the thread to the standard or extended position.

2. Tie in tails and break away the excess (steps 1-3, page 30).

3. Weight the thorax (steps 4 & 5, page 30).

4. Spin dubbing on the thread and form the abdomen (steps 6-9, page 31).

5. Lay the prepared covert feather over the abdomen with its tip extending about half way forward along the top of the thorax and with the backside of the feather facing up. Gently press the feather so that it curls down around the sides of the abdomen. I normally select a feather that will curl about half way down each side of the abdomen. Secure the feather with a half dozen turns of tying thread *(Figure 4-20)*.

6. Spin dubbing on the thread and wind it onto the shank to form the thorax. The thorax should be 1 1/2 times the width of the abdomen.

7. To form legs on flies size 18 through 22, select three of four barbs of mallard flank feather, and using the pinch technique, attach them to the far side of the fly and just ahead of the thorax. The tips should point rearward and downward to form the legs.

Speed Tying Tip: Don't try to tie the legs at the correct length; rather, tie the barbs near their center with two turns of thread. In this position, it's easy to hold and manipulate them. Once they're in place, grasp the butt ends and gently pull the barbs until the tips form legs of about the same length as the body *(Figure 4-21)*. Add two more tight wraps of thread to lock the barbs in place and cut the waste ends away (don't try to break them).

Figure 4-20. *Iridescent feather tied in at rear of thorax.*

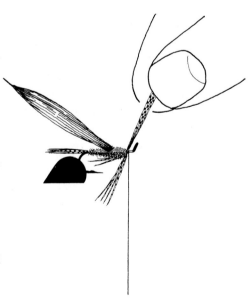

Figure 4-21. *Gently pull the barbs to form legs of correct length.*

8. In a similar fashion, apply legs to the near side of the fly.

9. To form the legs on flies size 24-28, tie in a few mallard flank feather barbs at the throat of the fly. Again, don't try to tie them in to length. Use the pinch technique to secure the barbs, then pull on the butt ends and draw the tips to the correct length.

10. Fold the covert feather forward over the top of the thorax, and using the pinch technique, secure it at the head with several turns of thread. Trim away the excess.

11. Form a smoothly tapered head, tie the finishing knot, cut away the thread, and cement the head (*Figures 4-22, 4-23*).

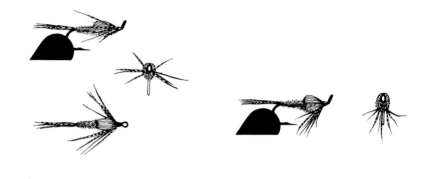

Figure 4-22. *The finished Feather Leg Nymph (sizes 18-22); side view, front view, top view.*

Figure 4-23. *The finished Feather Leg Nymph (sizes 24-28); side view, front view.*

Strip Nymph

The burrowing nymphs of the families Ephemeridae and Polymitarcidae and the pit-dwelling nymphs of Potamanthidae often leave their protective hollows at night and prowl about over the bottom, thus becoming fodder for foraging trout, but it is during the hatch period that they (like other nymphs) are most vulnerable to predation. After leaving their burrows, the nymphs swim to the surface where the dun emerges. They are surprisingly good swimmers, their waving gills and undulating abdomens beating powerfully. It is this snake-like movement that so attracts the trout.

When I began designing a fly to imitate these critters, it was this snake-like movement that I wanted to imitate. A long marabou tail made a good pulsing body, but it lacked the singular up and down undulations of the natural. What to use to simulate this unique movement? The answer came from the same source from which I have drawn a number of the answers to fly tying problems: the creative minds of other tiers. Read everything you can lay your hands

on and never pass up the chance to talk with other tiers and discuss techniques; club meetings and conclaves provide excellent opportunities to discuss and view the methods of others.

In this case, the answer was provided by Royce Dam, a good friend and a gifted, inventive tier. It was the spring of 1976, and we were teaching a fly fishing school in southeastern Wisconsin. After the day's activities were over, Royce tied on a fly and flipped it into the water to show me its action. The fly was a Muskrat Nymph to which Royce had added a wing made of a tanned strip of muskrat hide with the fur still attached (*Figure 4-24*). It was a take off on the Gimp developed by Lacy Gee of Colorado Springs, but what a take off. That strip of hide gave exactly the fluid undulations that I was looking for. Such movement would be a decidedly strong trigger of the trout's predatory instinct. It was an easy matter to replace the marabou tail of my burrowing nymph pattern with a strip of hide, and the Strip Nymph was born. It exceeded my expectations and remains a deadly part of my fly arsenal.

Figure 4-24. *Royce Dam's Strip Fly.*

Because all of the burrowing nymphs are pale in color, I've found that I can get by with one color, dark ecru for the abdomen and one color, fleshy tan for the thorax. In lakes, I fish it with a Strip/Tease retrieve. In streams, I often employ the Leisenring Lift to swim the fly along a natural pathway from the bottom to the surface. For a complete discussion of these tactics and others, see my book "Nymphing."

Here in the Lake States, where *Hexagenia* (The Giant Michigan Mayfly, or Hex) is king, I've

had marvelous days (and nights) with this fly. One trick that I've employed very effectively over the years is to fish the nymph at dawn after a heavy hatch or spinner fall the night before. The trout have had a chance to digest the previous night's meal and are prowling around looking for a hearty breakfast.

One morning, quite early, Phil and Barbara Clarke and Nancy and I pushed two boats out into the mist on Railroad Pond. Massive stumps of long-since-cut white pines had piled up along the shore, and expansive beds of subaquatic plants crowded against them. Spinners of last night's Hex activity were dotted here and there on the lake's gentle swells; it was the ideal setup for fishing the Strip Nymph. We eagerly knotted them to out leaders, and casting tight against the stumps, worked the imitations back over the sunken weeds. It was the right fly in the right place at the right time. The big rainbows and browns came to the fly like children to holiday candies.

Strip Nymph: Dressing

Hook: Sizes 6-12, standard shank length

Thread: 6/0, tan color

Tails, Abdomen, Gills: A strip of tanned hide with the fur intact (page 177); dark ecru color (BCS 55); the strip should be 1/8 to 3/16 inch wide; the hairs of the fur should be about 1/4 to 3/8 inch long; many different furs can be used, if the hairs are too long, simply trim to length; for the giant *Hexagenia* nymphs, the tips of the fur may be colored with a dark gray (BCS 117) permanent marker to more closely simulate the gills

Thorax: Blended fur dubbing, fleshy tan color (BCS 61)

Covert: Peacock herl

Legs: Guard hairs from back of cotton tail rabbit or other similarly colored pelt

Strip Nymph: Most Used Sizes/Naturals Matched, Regions Used

Sizes 6-8/*Hexagenia* (Giant Michigan Mayfly), Northeast, Southeast, Lake States, Pacific

Sizes 8-12/*Ephemera simulans* (Brown Drake), *E. guttulata* (Eastern Green Drake), *E. varia* (Yellow Drake), *Potamanthus* (Yellow Drake), and *Epheron* (White Fly), all regions of U.S.

Strip Nymph: Tying Instructions

1. Clamp the hook in the vise and wrap the shank with thread, ending at the standard position.

2. To prepare the fur strip, pull all the fur from the first 3/16 inch of the head end of the strip; cut this denuded area into a point *(Figure 4-25).*

Figure 4-25. *The prepared fur strip.*

3. Using the pinch technique, tie in the tapered end of the strip as you would tie in a tail. The taper minimizes the buildup of materials at the rear of the hook.

4. Weight the front 2/3 of the shank with lead wire (steps 4 & 5, page 30).

5. Spin dark ecru dubbing onto the thread and wrap it over the rear 1/3 of the shank. With a dubbing brush, roughen the top of the dubbing so the fibers stand up and form a continuum with the fur of the strip *(Figure 4-26)*; this forms the remainder of the abdomen.

6. Finish the thorax and head as described in steps 10-20 for the Hair Leg Nymph (pages 31-33).

7. Cut the fur strip to length; the leather portion of the strip should be as long as the hook; stroke the fur upright so that it's not cut when trimming the hide

to the correct length; the fur will flow rearward when the fly is fished and imitate the tails of the natural *(Figure 4-27)*.

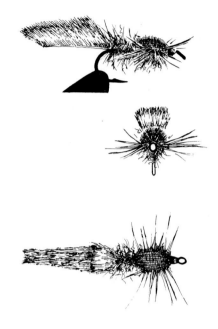

Figure 4-26. *Roughened dubbing blends with fur strip.*

Figure 4-27. *The finished Strip Nymph; side view, front view, top view.*

EMERGERS

When the mayfly nymph is mature, the dun stage of the adult emerges from the nymphal husk. A few species of mayfly nymphs crawl out of the water before the dun emerges. Of these, really only the Gray Drake (both eastern and western; genus *Siphlonurus*) and the Slate Winged Mahogany Dun *(genus Isonychia)* are of much significance to the angler; they create good fishing during the nymphal migrations and during the spinner falls. Duns of the eastern Quill Gordon *(Epeorus pleuralis)* often emerge from the nymphal husk on the river bottom or as the nymph makes its way to the film. The Quill Gordon wet fly is excellent during this hatch.

Most species of mayflies, however, hatch at the surface *(Figure 4-28)*. It is this behavior that so endears them to the hearts of fly fishers. It is

also this behavior that can cause great frustration, because during a heavy hatch, the trout become quite selective. And usually they are selective to the partially hatched adult (the emerger). Trout target the emerger for a simple reason: you can't run with your pants down. The insect in mid-metamorphosis is unable to flee; it's an easy mark for the trout.

Figure 4-28. *Mayfly adult emerging at water's surface.*

I use two styles of emergers: the Parachute Floating Nymph and the Wet/Dry Fly. I use them during heavy hatches of the mid-sized to small mayflies; however, each pattern has a specific application. If there are many cripples floating in the film (as seen very often in the Pale Morning Dun hatch, for example), or if I clearly see a trout take a dun with only partially unfolded wings, then I use the Wet/Dry fly. If there are few or no cripples, and the trout are feeding at the surface but seem to be ignoring the duns, then I'll use the Parachute Floating Nymph.

Parachute Floating Nymph

The concept of the floating nymph is not new. In his book "The Practical Fly Fisherman" (1953), Al McClane describes a particularly successful day that resulted from his accidental discovery of the floating nymph. But other anglers of McClane's time failed to follow his precocious lead. It has only been in the past 10 years or so that fly fishers in general have recognized the importance of such a pattern. This recognition is due, in large part, to the angling observations of the Henry's Fork regulars; most specifically to Rene and Bonnie Harrop, Mike Lawson, and Fred Arbona. I tie my floating nymph much like the one shown in Arbona's book "Mayflies, the Angler, and the Trout."

I can't begin to tell you all the times and places that the floating nymph has been a success for me, so often has it been my fly of choice, but several times it has meant the difference between fish and no fish for scenes in my videos. Gary Glennon, Jason, and I were taping the "Fabulous Bighorn" and had been floating for the better part of the morning, working the banks with a Strip Leech and nymphing the runs with a San Juan Worm. As we drifted past a small stretch of choppy water at the head of an island, I happened to glance over and see several snouts poke out. We beached the boat and crept up on the quite shallow water; it was full of trout, and they were feeding steadily on *Baetis* mayflies. It was a perfect setup for video taping; however, when we got all the equipment set up, the trout politely refused our dun imitations. But they didn't refuse the Parachute Floating Nymph, and we had a field day, trading the rod, video taping, and doing quite a lot of excited angler talk.

Parachute Floating Nymph: Dressing

Hook: Sizes 10-22, standard shank length; 2X long or short shank hooks may be substituted as desired

Thread: 6/0 or 8/0, size depends on hook, color to match body

Tails: Cock hackle barbs

Body: Blended fur and sparkle yarn dubbing, color to match natural

Emerging Wings: Ball of dubbed fur blended with sparkle yarn filaments

Hackle: Dark dun cock hackle, wound one turn parachute style

Parachute Floating Nymph: Most Used Hook Sizes/Body Color/Naturals Matched (all regions)

Sizes 12-22/Body red brown (BCS 66)/ Matches *Ephemerella, Baetis, Paraleptophlebia*

Sizes 12-22/Body blend of 50% hare's mask, 25% fur from back of fox squirrel, 25% tan (BCS 61) sparkle yarn/Matches *Ephemerella, Callibaetis, Stenonema, Centroptilum, Epheron*

Sizes 14-24/Body dark olive brown (BCS 34)/Matches *Baetis*, some *Ephemerella*, and dark phases of other species

Parachute Floating Nymph: Tying Instructions

1. Clamp the hook in the vise and wrap the shank with thread, ending at the standard position.

2. Tie in a clump of hackle barbs for the tail; use 4-12 barbs depending on hook size; cut away the excess.

3. Spin dubbing on the thread and wrap it over the rear 3/4 of the shank to form the body.

4. Spin a short, thick wick of dubbing on the thread, taper both ends; leave about one inch of thread between the hook shank and the dubbing *(Figure 4-29)*. This dubbing will be used to form a ball that represents the unfurling wings. The amount of dubbing will depend on fly size; the finished ball should be about 1 1/2 times the diameter of the thorax. With a little experimentation you will readily learn the correct amount.

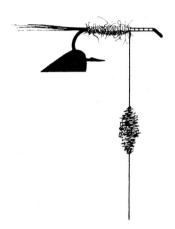

Figure 4-29. *Form a short, thick wick of dubbing.*

5. Using the bare thread between hook shank and dubbing, tie in a hackle feather just ahead of the body; use a hackle one size smaller than normal for the hook being used (see Speed Tying Tip, page 53).

6. Hold the thread straight up and keep it under tension by pulling gently with the bobbin hand. Pinch the thread between the thumb and forefinger of the materials hand and slide them down, compressing the dubbing against the top of the hook shank and forming it into a ball *(Figure 4-30)*.

7. Compress the dubbing once more, and keeping it compressed, pinch it firmly. Maintaining a

tight pinch on the dubbing, wrap the thread twice around the shank and tight against the front of the dubbing ball; release the ball of dubbing and wrap the thread twice around the shank and tight against the rear of the dubbing ball; repeat with two more wraps just ahead and two more just behind the ball.

8. Wrap the thread four to six turns around the base of the dubbing ball to tighten the material and prepare it for receiving the parachute hackle *(Figure 4-31)*.

Figure 4-30. *Compress the dubbing to form a ball.*

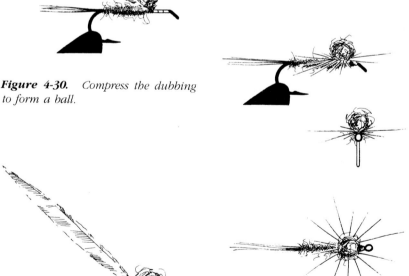

Figure 4-31. *Wrap the thread around the base of the dubbing ball.*

9. Make one full turn of the hackle *around the base of the dubbing ball;* tie off the hackle in front of the ball and cut away the excess (because only one turn is needed, a single hackle feather can be used to tie several flies).

10. Spin a tiny amount of dubbing on the thread and wind it figure-8 fashion under the hackle barbs and in front and behind the dubbing ball, and then wind forward to finish the thorax; this dubbing can be omitted on sizes 16 and smaller.

11. Tie off the thread and cut away the excess.

12. Cement the head of the fly and place a drop of flexible head cement on the dubbing ball (it will soak in and toughen the fly considerably; Figure 4-32).

Figure 4-32. *The finished Parachute Floating Nymph; side view, front view, top view.*

Wet/Dry Fly

It was a fine spring day in 1973 and the fish of the Tomorrow River were rising freely, but not to my fly. Frustrated, and thinking the fish might be taking nymphs just under the surface, I tied on a soft hackle wet fly and presented it to a nearby fish. To my disgust, the fly didn't sink; but then to my amazement, the fish grabbed the floating soft hackle. Two casts and two fish later, I was sure that I was on to something. And that something has proved extremely reliable in the years since. It's saved the day many, many times during heavy hatches when the trout have become selective to the freshly emerged dun. It's often been the secret of my successes on tough waters like Henry's Fork, Silver Creek, and Armstrong Spring Creek.

The Wet/Dry Fly has a short tail of sparkle yarn filaments to suggest the partially cast nymphal husk, a dubbed body of color to match that of the dun, and a soft hackle to imitate the insect's newly emerged legs and wings. The concept of using sparkle yarn to suggest the nymphal shuck was conceived by Craig Mathews and John Juracek and described in their book "Fly Patterns of Yellowstone." The idea of imitating the partially cast shuck is not new, but using sparkle yarn for it made the concept eminently workable. It's the only material that I've used to represent the shuck that really seems to make a difference in the way fish take the fly.

The body of the newly emerged dun is often a shade or two different than the final color the insect assumes. This difference can be significant to the angler. Bob Pelzl had gone to fish the hatch of the Western Green Drake *(Ephemerella grandis)* on Colorado's Frying Pan and found the trout highly receptive to a pale olive fly (BCS 27) he'd purchased locally. During the hatch, he collected some duns but didn't record their sizes and colors until three or four hours later; by that time the duns had become a pale grayish green (BCS 92). That evening he tied grayish green flies for the next day's fishing. The fish steadfastly refused them. When he tried the pale olive flies he'd purchased, the fish took them vigorously. It is important that the body of the Wet/Dry fly is the same color as the recently emerged dun.

While I think the shuck and body are important, it is the soft hackle that makes this fly so successful; its living appearance could be achieved by no other material. In 1857 the Scottish angler W. C. Stewart wrote in his book, "The Practical Angler," that he preferred soft hackles for dressing his wet "spiders," because "...when a spider is made of one of them and placed in the water, the least motion will agitate and impart a singularly life-like appearance to it, whereas it would have no effect on a cock hackle." Soft hackle performs the same when used on a dry fly. The slightest current of wind or water causes the hackle to vibrate and dance on the surface, giving a performance that is most suggestive of the twitching legs and wings of an emerging dun. I am convinced that such movement is one of the reasons for the effectiveness of the European fly "Cul de Canard," which is tied with downy soft hackle from the preen gland of a duck.

For the Wet/Dry Fly I use the marginal covert feathers from the wings of a number of different birds. The barbs of the feather are wide near the stem and thin at the tips. Such a feather provides both support and motion; it also gives the fly the necessary rumpled look. In addition to meeting the other requirements, these feathers can be found in sizes as small as 22. (For a discussion of soft hackles see Chapter 14.)

Wet/Dry Fly: Dressing

Hook: Sizes 14-22, standard shank length

Thread: 6/0 or 8/0, color to match body

Nymphal Shuck: 8-10 filaments of tan sparkle yarn tied in as a short tail—about 1/2 to 3/4 the body length

Body: Blended fur and sparkle yarn dubbing

Hackle: Marginal covert feather of color to match wing of natural

Wet/Dry Fly: Most Used Sizes/Body Colors/Soft Hackles/Naturals Matched, Regions Used

Sizes 12-18/Body red brown (BCS 66)/Hackle, coot or other dark gray feather (BCS 113 or 114)/ Matches *Ephemerella subvaria* (Hendrickson) and *Paraleptophlebia* (Blue Quill), some *Baetis*, and others, all regions

Sizes 14-22/Body olive green (BCS 30)/Hackle, coot or other dark gray feather/Matches *Baetis*, *Pseudocloeon*, some *Ephemerella*, and others, all regions

Sizes 14-18/Body creamy olive (BCS 27)/Hackle, mallard or other dun gray feather (BCS 108/112)/ Matches *Ephemerella infrequens* and *E. inermis*, and several other species known as Pale Morning Duns, Southeast, Northern Rockies, Southern Rockies, and Pacific

Sizes 14-18/Body yellow orange (BCS 51)/Hackle, mallard or other dun gray feather/Matches *Ephemerella dorothea* (Sulphur mayfly), *E. rotunda/invaria* (Light Hendrickson), and others, all regions

Sizes 10-14/Body light olive yellow (BCS 27)/Hackle, coot or other dark gray feather (BCS 113 or 114)/Matches *Ephemerella grandis* (Western Green Drake) and *E. flavilinea* (Small Western Green Drake), Northern Rockies, Southern Rockies, Pacific

Wet/Dry Fly: Tying Instructions

1. Clamp the hook in the vise and wind the thread rearward to the standard position.

2. Tie in 8-10 filaments of tan sparkle yarn (the exact shade of tan is not important) to form a tail about 1/2 the length of the body. End with the thread at the center of the shank.

3. Spin dubbing on the thread, leaving about one inch of bare thread between the hook and the dubbing.

4. Wind the thread rearward to bring the dubbing up into position so it can be wound forward to form the body.

5. Tie in the soft hackle just ahead of the body, ending with the thread at the eye of the hook.

Speed Tying Tip: I prefer to tie the feather in tip first. With this approach the hackle pliers can be fastened to the relatively large-diameter, butt end of the feather shaft. When the small feathers used on this pattern are tied in butt first, the grip of the hackle pliers often breaks off the delicate tip—and of course, this will always happen just as you make the last turn with the hackle. To prepare the soft hackle for use on the fly, first strip off the few, shorter, basal barbs. Then grasp the feather by its tip and stroke the remaining barbs rearward. This action leaves a small triangle of barbs at the tip of the feather; cut this triangle so that it is about 1/16 inch in length *(Figure 4-33)*. Tie in the soft hackle at the point where the terminal triangle meets the reversed barbs *(Figure 4-34)*; wrap the thread two turns. Grasp the feather by the base of the shaft and gently pull the terminal triangle back under the thread until the trimmed tip of the feather is even with the rear of the hook eye *(Figure 4-34)*. Make several more turns with the thread to secure the feather.

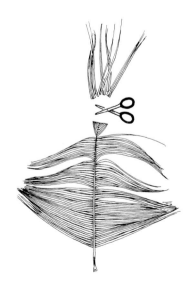

Figure 4-33. *The prepared soft hackle.*

Figure 4-34. *Gently pull the soft hackle into final position.*

6. Wind the soft hackle forward, right up to the eye of the fly. That's right, forget what you were taught in fly tying class, leave no head space. Tie off the feather at the eye *(Figure 4-35)* and clip away the excess. Don't worry if the hackle is sticking out all askew and the fly looks ugly, it's not finished yet.

7. Stroke the barbs of the feather back along the hook shank and hold them there with the thumb and forefinger of your materials hand. Carefully, placing one wrap immediately behind the preceding one, wrap the thread rearward to form a small, nicely tapered head on the fly *(Figure 4-36)*. This forces the hackle into the desired position, sloping slightly rearward.

8. Tie off the thread, cut it away, and coat the head with flexible head cement; add an extra drop of cement and allow it to run back into the base of the hackle to toughen it *(Figure 4-37)*.

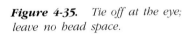

Figure 4-35. *Tie off at the eye; leave no head space.*

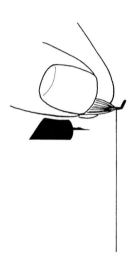

Figure 4-36. *Hold the hackle back and wrap a neat head.*

Figure 4-37. *The finished Wet/Dry fly.*

MAYFLY ADULTS

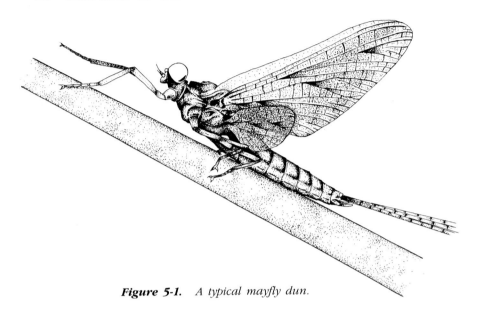

Figure 5-1. *A typical mayfly dun.*

From the days of Dame Juliana Berners, the mayfly adult has been the darling of the fly fisher. More dry fly patterns have been devised to imitate these creatures than any other group of insects. And for good reasons. Mayfly hatches are concentrated affairs that bring on good rises of trout, the insects are relatively large, and they usually hatch at the surface during daylight hours. The characteristically brief life of the mayfly adult has inspired poets for centuries and given rise to the name for the order of these insects, Ephemeroptera ("short-lived wing").

Like the nymphs, mayfly adults come in a wide range of sizes, from the enormous members of the genus *Hexagenia* (1 1/2 inches long) to the ridiculously minute species of *Caenis* and *Tricorythodes* (1/8 inch long). Unlike the nymphs, however, the adults are quite uniform in overall body plan (from the viewpoint of the fly tier). But, there *are* two adult stages: the dun (which emerges from the nymphal husk) and the sexually mature spinner (which emerges from the skin of the dun). The wide range of sizes and the two adult stages present a number of design problems for the fly tier.

DUN

The adult that emerges from the nymphal skin is called the dun *(Figure 5-1)*. In the majority of species, emergence occurs at the surface, and the dun sits on the water until its wings are hardened enough for flight. During this period, the wings are held together and upright over the dun's back. The body normally rests totally or partially on the surface with the feet outstretched for support. Many angling writers have likened the appearance of the dun to that of a tiny sailboat, and a good analogy it is.

From the fish's vantage point, there are several features which must be considered when designing effective imitations of the dun. The first is the upright wing. From below, it is most obvious and can be seen standing high above the surface *(Figure 5-2)*. The experiences of centuries of anglers confirms that it's a definite trigger for the feeding trout. And although many fly fishing authors have written about the importance of the wing in the overall silhouette of a dun pattern, perhaps the most lucid and reasoned arguments were put forth by Vince Marinaro in his book, "A Modern Dry Fly Code" and by John Goddard and Brian Clarke in their remarkable book "The Trout and the Fly." These books contain arguments (and drawings and photographs) that deserve to be read and reread since they accurately and logically establish the need for the dominant, upright wing silhouette in the imitation.

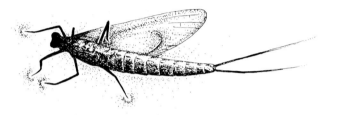

Figure 5-2. *A dun in the trout's window, as seen from underwater.*

When the sun's rays fall on the dun's wings they glisten with specular highlights caused by their corrugated nature (see page 59) and the character and arrangement of the veins. On a sunny day, this sparkling quality can be an important character of the wing, as seen from underwater.

Over the past 30 years, as I've collected data on mayfly adults, I've been impressed with a very noticeable variation of wing length. May-flies with a body longer than about 1/2 inch invariably have a wing 1/16 to 1/8 inch shorter than overall body length. Mayflies from 1/2 to 1/4 inch in length have a wing that is the same length as the body. Mayflies smaller than 1/4 inch usually have a wing length that is 1/32 to 3/32 inch longer than the body. For the larger mayflies, I have not found tiny variations in wing length to change the trout's acceptance of the imitations. But, for adult patterns smaller than 1/4 inch (size 20), wing length can have a dra-matic impact on pattern effectiveness. The reason is simple. A wing that is 1 inch long is only 6 percent larger than one 15/16 inch long. A wing 5/32 inch long, however, is 20 percent larger than a wing 1/8 inch long! Such a dra-matic difference is easily noted by the trout.

Designing a dun imitation with an upright wing dictates the need for a tying method that will keep the wing upright. This can be achieved by techniques that will also simulta-neously imitate the outstretched legs. These tying tactics are considered in the discussions of each of the dun designs.

There are four aspects of the dun's body that must be taken into account when designing imitative patterns. All have to do with the ap-pearance of the body as seen from underwater. First is the overall weight of the insect. The body of a large (heavy) mayfly, deforms the surface of the water considerably more than the body of a small (light weight) mayfly. The deformation caused by a large mayfly is enough to change the refractive angle of the surface and allow a trout to clearly see the mayfly's body even when the insect is well beyond the fish's window of vision *(Figure 5-3)*. For very tiny mayfly duns, the weight of the body is so small that it doesn't deform the surface to any significant degree.

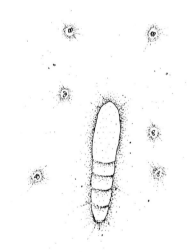

Figure 5-3. *A large dun beyond the trout's window, as seen from underwater.*

And then there's the way the insect holds its body. Often the abdomen is curved slightly upward at the rear, so that only the thorax and a portion of the abdomen are depressing the surface film. Thus, from underwater, the body of a mayfly that is beyond the window appears shorter than it really is. From the angling standpoint, I've only found it important to ape this feature in imitations of the very large mayflies.

Third, in sunshine, the body appears translucent. J. W. Dunne was the first angling writer to treat this quality of the fly with more than a passing comment. In "Sunshine and the Dry Fly" he presented careful arguments on the necessity of translucency in backlit imitations. Certainly on sunny days, the living glow of the insect's body is an important feature. Dunne's flies were tied of lacquered floss over white-painted hook shanks. They certainly glow in strong backlight, but they float abominably and are flat and dull appearing when not strongly backlit. Still, his concept of trying to create a translucent body is one hundred percent on the money.

Fourth, an insect's body is not perfectly smooth, so when it sits down on the water, air is trapped between the insect and the water's surface. This air gives the natural a silvery, glistening appearance when seen from below. Materials used in the construction of the fly's body should produce the same effect. But at the same time, the materials must also be selected to give the fly sufficient buoyancy to keep it afloat without constant applications of flotant or the need for excessive false casting.

The outstretched legs of the mayfly dun depress the surface film and thus alter its light transmitting qualities. When the insect is outside the trout's window of vision, the legs appear as scintillating slashes on the surface. This can be an important trigger for the feeding fish, especially in the smaller mayfly species where the body does not significantly deform the surface.

The fly tier must also consider the enormous size range exhibited by the adults. Such a dramatic variation in size, coupled with the other requirements for a successful pattern, mean that a single design cannot imitate all mayfly duns. I use three patterns to simulate these insects: the Hair Wing Dun, the Yarn Wing Dun, and the Loop Wing Dun.

The Hair Wing Dun

This is my choice for an imitation of the huge duns of the genera *Hexagenia, Ephemera, Potamanthus,* and others. It's easy to tie, sturdy, and well received by the fish; all are attributes that I highly prize in a fly.

Because the very large duns often sit on the water with their abdomens curled upward, I wanted a body material that could be made to conform permanently to this shape and yet meet the other design features discussed earlier. Deer hair proved to be the answer; not spun and clipped, but tied extended-body style. When tied this way and treated with flexible head cement, deer hair makes a most convincing, durable body. And the resultant texture of the body allows it to sandwich air against the water's surface like the natural. Even though deer hair provides only a tiny amount of translucency, these big flies are normally fished at twilight or after dark when this feature is unimportant.

Because the abdomen of the pattern was designed to curve upward, I knew the tails would not be used to help float the fly, but from the aesthetic point of view, I wanted them to look like tails. Little experimentation was needed to convince me that pheasant tail barbs were perfect for the tailing material on this fly.

I wanted to use deer hair for the wing because it holds its shape so well on big flies. In addition, it has a reflective surface; a tuft of deer hair will reflect light much like a mayfly wing. It took me a bit longer to settle on the final wing design. At first I used a clump of deer hair with two hackles parachuted around its base. This made a satisfactory fly, but it had a couple of drawbacks. Because the hackle was parachuted around the base of the wing, and was therefore on top of the rather large-diameter body, the fly would often tip to one side when on the water. The weight of the upright wing would then cause the hackle to collapse, and the fly would fall onto its side. This was especially true after I'd caught a fish or two; the wet, softened hackle could not properly support the fly on the surface.

And that meant tying on a fresh fly. But changing flies after dark, with mosquitoes humming in my ears and large trout crashing around in front of me, is not my idea of relaxation.

So I eliminated the hackle and opted instead for a hair wing that also acted like the hackle, a wing like that of Caucci and Nastasi's Compara Dun. The hairs sticking out to the sides not only give great stability to this pattern but nicely simulate the legs of the dun. This design has been eminently satisfactory. It's taken good fish for me wherever the large mayflies occur, and has provided me with many warm memories. One will always stand out in my mind. Nancy,

Jason, and I had travelled to England, the motherland of fly fishing, and were exploring the river Derwent during hatches of The Mayfly (*Ephemera danica*), which emerges during the midday hours. Jason was fourteen that summer and very proud of his ability to spot trout. He'd located a big fish and called for me to come and cast to it. From his vantage behind the trees he could see it clearly, and offered to help me get the correct drift. As my Hair Wing Dun approached the trout's lie, I tensed, ready for the take, and at the explosive rise, Jason yelled out at the top of his young lungs. I flinched and reared back hard enough to dislocate the neck of a good Hereford bull; even 3X is no match for my power strike!

Hair Wing Dun: Dressing

Hook: Sizes 6-10, standard shank length

Thread: 3/0 or 6/0, depending on hook size, color to match the barring of the natural's body

Tails: A clump of 6-8 pheasant tail barbs

Body: Extended deer hair or other spongy hairs such as elk, antelope, or caribou; color to match body of natural

Thorax: Dubbing to match color of body

Wing: Spongy hair such as used for the body; color to match wing of natural

Hair Wing Dun: Most Used Sizes/Body and Thread Colors/Wing Color/Naturals Matched and Regions Used:

Sizes 6-10/Body yellowish-olive (BCS 37), thread dark brown/Wing natural dun gray deer hair (from back of animal)/Matches *Hexagenia* (Giant Michigan Mayfly),Northeast, Lake States, Pacific; *Ephemera simulans* (Brown Drake), and *E. varia* and *Potamanthus* (Yellow Drakes), all regions

Sizes 8-10/body pale watery green (BCS 12), thread black/Wing natural dun gray deer hair with a few yellow strands mixed in/ Matches *Ephemera guttulata* (Eastern Green Drake), Northeast, Southeast

Sizes 12-14/Body olive green (BCS 20), thread bright yellow (BCS 45)/Wing dark blue gray (BCS 113)/Matches Western Green Drake (*Ephemerella grandis* northern variety), Northern Rockies and Pacific

Sizes 12-14/Body pale olive (BCS 27), thread dark brown/Wing dark blue gray (BCS 113)/Matches Western Green Drake (southern variety), Southern Rockies

Note: The Western Green Drake is of a size that it could be dressed as either a small Hair Wing Dun or a large Yarn Wing Dun (page 52).

Hair Wing Dun: Tying Instructions

1. Clamp the hook in the vise and wrap the thread rearward to the standard position.

2. Cut a clump of 6-8 pheasant tail barbs from the feather. The barbs should be long enough to extend rearward through the center of the extended body and form the tails of the fly.

3. Using the pinch technique, tie the barbs on top of the shank; wrap the thread forward to the head of the fly, securing the tailing material *(Figure 5-4)*.

Figure 5-4. Tailing material in place, thread wrapped to the head.

4. Select a clump of deer hair for the body and cut it from the hide; the hair should be uniform in length and of good quality; do not use hair that is dramatically uneven or has been damaged by excessive heating in the dying process. The size of the clump will vary with the size of the fly; with a little experimentation you will easily learn to gauge the correct amount.

5. Hold the clump in your materials hand, and with a comb or the fingers of your bobbin hand, remove the short, fuzzy fibers of dubbing fur found in the base of the hairs.

6. Continue holding the clump in your materials hand and with the scissors, cut straight across the butts of the hair to even them.

7. Position the clump on top of the hook shank with the squared butt end at the eye of the hook and the tips of the hairs extending rearward.

8. Make two turns of thread at the rear of the head, keeping just enough tension on the thread so it remains in contact with the hair.

9. Smoothly draw downward on the bobbin to tighten the thread; at the same time gently push the clump of hair down so that when the thread comes tight the hairs uniformly surround the hook shank and pheasant tail barbs. *Do not release the clump of hair.* Wrap the thread tightly five or six more turns just at the rear of the head *(Figure 5-5)*.

10. Maintaining your grip on the hair, slide your fingers slowly rearward; as you do so, spiral the thread rearward in open turns much like winding a rib; it should take four to six turns of thread to reach the rear of the hook shank *(Figure 5-6)*.

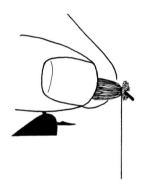

Figure 5-5. Tie in the hair at the rear of the head.

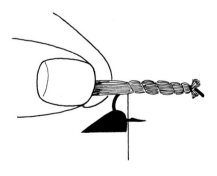

Figure 5-6. The thread is spiralled rearward.

11. When you reach the rear of the hook shank, continue sliding your fingers rearward but also gently lift the hair upward to about 45 degrees from the horizontal; the pheasant tail barbs should be in the center of the clump of hair.

12. Continue to wrap the thread in a riblike fashion around the clump of deer hair, forming an extended body off the hook.

Speed Tying Tip: There are a number of different ways that tiers manipulate the bobbin when tying an extended body. Here's how I do it. I wind the thread over the top of the extended body with my bobbin hand, then, while still keeping the hair pinched between thumb and forefinger, I use the other fingers of my materials hand to grasp the bobbin and complete the turn under the extended body. Once the bobbin has been taken under the body, I again grasp the bobbin with my bobbin hand and continue. It's a very fast way to tie, and the tension on the thread is never compromised.

13. Make the extended portion of the body 2/3 to 3/4 of the length of the hook shank. Wrap the thread five or six turns around the rear-most point of the body *(Figure 5-7)*.

14. Spiral the thread forward, crossing the rearward spiral to form "X's," ending with the thread at a point about 2/5 of the way back the hook shank from the eye.

15. Wrap the thread forward, keeping it very tight and placing each wrap against the previous one. Wrap down an area about 1/8 inch long. This area serves as an anchor point for the wing *(Figure 5-8)*.

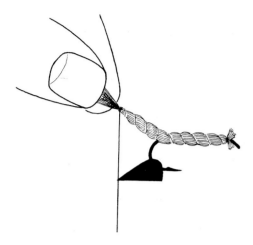

Figure 5-7. *Make several turns of thread at the rear of the body.*

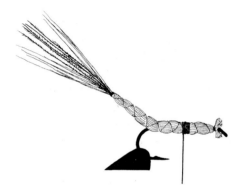

Figure 5-8. *The thread base for the wing.*

16. Cut a clump of hair for the wing. I normally do not stack the hair, preferring a bit of unevenness in the tips. Pinch the clump between thumb and forefinger and tie it in with the tips pointing forward. The length of the wing should be slightly shorter than the overall length of the body. *Do not release your grip on the clump.* Wrap the thread around the clump five or six times to secure it. As you wrap, the tips of the hair will flare a bit.

17. Keeping your grip on the clump, lift the butt portion and cut it off 1/8 inch from the point where it's

tied in. Wrap the tying thread five or six turns *through the butt ends of the hairs*. This maneuver locks the hairs tightly in place *(Figure 5-9)*.

18. Push the wing upright, and if necessary, flare it a bit so that it's spread through a full 180 degrees on top of the fly. Most of the hair should be pointing upward.

19. Spin dubbing on the thread and form the thorax; wind it tightly against the front of the wing to keep it upright.

20. Spiral the thread to the head and tie off. Clip away the thread.

21. Trim away the tips of the deer hair used to form the extended body; 3 to 6 pheasant tail barbs are left to imitate the tails of the natural.

22. Coat the body with water-thin flexible head cement. Place two or three drops of cement into the base of the wing *(Figure 5-10)*.

Figure 5-9. *Wrap the thread through the butt end of the wing.*

Figure 5-10. *The finished Hair Wing Dun; side view, front view, top view.*

Yarn Wing Dun

It's funny how flies evolve. This fly, the Yarn-Wing Dun, began an as outgrowth of the Poly-Caddis. One night, in 1982, as I was doggedly trying to complete some flies for a fishing trip, I lashed the wing onto a Poly-Caddis only to have it stick up at a forty-five degree angle rather than lie down along the back of the fly as it should have. The resemblance to a mayfly dun was immediate and obvious. Only a little trimming of the wing was needed to produce a very good mayfly silhouette. The design seemed like a promising one, so I experimented further.

Several advantages became obvious when I fished with the fly. The Yarn-Wing Dun offers a very good silhouette from the side, from the front, and from beneath. It is easy (and therefore fast) to tie and holds up very well, even after repeated chewings by trout. The single wing causes the fly to be aerodynamically stable; there's no twisting of the leader, as often experienced with double-winged flies. In fact, the wing folds rearward as the fly travels through the air, making it even more aerodynamically stable, and pops up again when the fly drops to the water. The winging material can be any fibrous material from yarn to feathers to deer hair. My preference is sparkle yarn or shiny polypropylene yarn. These materials glint in sunlight like the wing of the natural; they look alive. With a snip of the scissor pliers, the wing can be reduced to a short stub and the fly becomes a floating nymph. Another snip to remove the entire wing and the fly becomes a trimmed-hackle spinner imitation. Such streamside modifications have saved the day for me more than once.

At the same time as I was experimenting with the winging technique, I was working on a method for producing a fan-shaped tail on dry flies. The idea was to produce a tail that gave the type of support offered by a split tail, but which would be easier to tie. I developed several approaches, but none were easy. I mentioned the idea to my long-time friend, Bob Pelzl, from Albuquerque, New Mexico, and he

instantly hit upon the concept that lead to the solution: a small lump of thread formed at the rear of the hook before the tail is tied in. The fan tail was immediately incorporated into the Yarn-Wing Dun, and has since proven effective on all styles of dry flies that require a tail.

Many, many materials have been used for the bodies on mayfly duns. Dunne's lacquered floss, stripped peacock herl (quill body), various feather barbs such as pheasant tail, raffia, tinsel, et al. But for the medium sized duns, I use blended fur and sparkle yarn dubbing. Dubbing is such a versatile material. Since it contains many tiny air pockets, a dubbed body treated with flotant to prevent the filaments from becoming wetted will support the fly extremely well. And dubbing certainly has lifelike properties (page 27). Perhaps the greatest polemist for the dry fly, F. M. Halford, wrote glowingly of the "...transparent, watery, and life-like appearance..." of dubbing and lamented the fact that adequate waterproofing did not exist to make the material suitable for dry flies. If modern fly flotants had been available to Halford, I feel certain that most of his patterns would have been dressed with dubbed bodies.

Dubbing also traps air against the water's surface in the same manner as an insect's body. To emphasize the silvery cushion of air between the surface and the insect's body, I mix undyed sparkle yarn filaments with the dubbing. The filaments not only sparkle but they attract air bubbles from the water which in turn cling to the fly. The effect is most life-like when seen from underwater. This dubbing mix also produces a translucent body which shimmers and sparkles like the exoskeleton of an insect when seen in backlight. Materials such as tinsel, quill, raffia, and so on, just cannot offer the same translucency and other characteristics provided by blended dubbing.

To stabilize the fly in an upright position and simulate the profile of the legs, I use the best quality cock hackle, wound over the thorax and trimmed on the bottom. Because of its stiffness and lifelike translucency, cock hackle is a great material to mimic the outstretched legs of the natural. These qualities have made cock hackle a desirable fly tying material for centuries. In 1624 in Spain, Juan de Bergara published "The Manuscript of Astorga" which contained patterns that used cock hackle (including Andulusian blue dun). How long before 1624 the Spanish had been using hackled flies is speculative, but there must have been a considerable body of working knowledge (developed over an extended period) available to Bergara when he wrote his text. Cock hackle works wonderfully on the Yarn Wing Dun; the fly sits perkily on the surface with the wing upright cast after cast after cast.

It's not the color of the natural's legs that's important in the fly, rather the impression that they create in the surface when seen from below. So instead of using a hackle feather of the color of the legs, I use one of the color of the wing. This emphasizes the upright wing while still producing the necessary leg imprint in the surface.

The yarn wing dun is a simple fly, to be sure, but it has stood the test of the Test, Armstrong Spring Creek, Henry's Fork, Yellow Breeches, rivers and lakes of New Zealand and Alaska, gulper time on Hebgen Lake, and many, many other waters. It has become my standard imitation for duns of the mid-range sizes (hooks 8-16).

Yarn-Wing Dun: Dressing

Hook: Sizes 8-16, standard shank length

Thread: 6/0 or 8/0 (depending on hook size), color to match body of the natural

Tails: A clump of cock hackle barbs, tied fan tail style; tails should be about 3/4 length of body

Body: Fur dubbing blended with 10-15% undyed sparkle yarn

Hackle: One dry fly quality hackle wound X-Wing style over the thorax and trimmed on the bottom only, color to match wing

Wing: Sparkle yarn and polypropylene yarn are easy to find in all the needed colors, but other yarns, deer hair, calftail hair, feather barbs, feathers, or any other suitable winging material can be used with this technique

Yarn Wing Dun: Most Used Sizes/Body Color/ Wing Color/Hackle/ Naturals Matched and Regions Used

Sizes 10-16/Body smokey gray (BCS 108)/Wing medium gray (BCS 109/Hackle medium dun/Matches *Callibaetis* (Speckled Dun), some western *Epeorus,* all regions

Sizes 10-16/Body red brown (BCS 66)/ Wing dark gray (BCS 114)/Hackle dark dun/Matches *Isonychia* (Mahogany Dun); *Ephemerella subvaria* (Hendrickson) and other *Ephemerella* species; *Leptophlebia* (Black Quill); *Stenonema vicarium* (March Brown); *Paraleptophlebia* (Blue Quill); some *Baetis; Rithrogena* spp. (Humpbacked mayflies), all regions

Sizes 14-16/Body creamy olive (BCS 27)/Wing pale blue gray (BCS 105)/Hackle medium dun/Matches *Ephemerella infrequens/inermis* (Pale Morning Duns), Southeast, Northern Rockies, Southern Rockies, and Pacific

Sizes 8-14/Body olive green (BCS 20) with bright yellow thread rib/Wing dark blue gray (BCS 113)/Hackle medium dun/Matches *Ephemerella grandis* (Western Green Drake— northern variety) and *E. flavilinea* (Small Western Green Drake), Northern Rockies and Pacific

Sizes 8-10/Body pale olive (BCS 27) with dark brown thread rib/Wing dark blue gray (BCS 113)/Matches Western Green Drake—southern variety, Southern Rockies, and Pacific

Sizes 14-16/Body yellow orange (BCS 51)/Wing medium gray (BCS 108)/ Hackle medium dun/Matches *Ephemerella dorothea* (Sulphur Mayfly), *E. rotunda/invaria* (Light Hendrickson), Northeast, Southeast, Lake States, South Central

Sizes 12-14/Body creamy tan (BCS 48)/Wing light gray/Hackle light dun/Matches *Stenonema fuscum* and related species (Gray Fox and Light Cahills), all regions

Sizes 12-14/Body white/Wing dark purple gray (BCS 119)/Matches *Epheron* (White Fly), Northeast, Southeast, Lake States, South Central

Note: The above colors and sizes will also match hatches of various other species.

Yarn Wing Dun: Tying Instructions

1. Clamp the hook in the vise and wrap the shank with thread, ending just slightly onto the bend.

2. Form a small lump of thread positioned just at the bend of the hook; the top of the lump should be parallel with the top of the hook shank *(Figure 5-11)*.

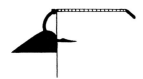

Figure 5-11. *The top of the thread lump is parallel to the top of the hook shank.*

3. Tie the hackle barbs for the tail directly on top of the hook shank and a short distance ahead of the lump of thread. The number of barbs used depends upon the size of the fly. On a size 18, 6 barbs will support the rear of the hook. For a size 8 hook, about 15 barbs are needed. Wrap the thread forward to the midpoint of the hook to secure the tails. Cut away the excess material.

4. To form the abdomen, spin dubbing on the thread, forming a wick that is tapered at each end. Leave an inch or so of bare thread between hook shank and dubbing wick.

5. Wrap the thread to the rear of the shank and *tightly* against the thread ball; this will cause the tails to spread out into a fan shape *(Figure 5-12)* and bring the dubbing up to the hook.

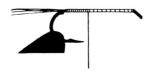

Figure 5-12. *The fan tail; side view, top view.*

6. Wrap the dubbing forward to form the abdomen, ending at the midpoint of the shank.

7. Spin dubbing for the thorax onto the thread, leaving the inch or so of bare thread between hook shank and dubbing.

8. Select a hackle feather of normal size for the hook being used and tie it in just ahead of the abdomen.

Speed Tying Tip: Before nylon tying thread there was silk thread. Silk doesn't stretch; therefore, when using silk, it was necessary to cut the barbs off the base of the hackle rather than stripping them off. This gave the thread a purchase on the hackle stem and prevented the feather from pulling out during the tying operation. Because of the elastic nature of nylon thread (which allows the hackle to be bound very tightly), this procedure is no longer necessary. Rather than cutting, I simply break the hackle shaft at the desired point and strip the barbs off the basal 1/4 inch or so. Much time is saved by this maneuver.

9. Wind the dubbing forward to form the thorax, leaving extra room at the head; the front edge of the thorax should end abruptly and not be tapered (Figure 5-13).

Figure 5-13. *The front of the thorax is not tapered.*

10. Wind the hackle forward to the head, palmer-style in two or three turns *(Figure 5-14)*. Then wind rearward, palmer-style, in

Figure 5-14. *Palmer the hackle forward.*

two or three turns to the rear of the thorax. The forward and rearward wraps should cross and form "X's" *(Figure 5-15)*. This X-Wing style of wrapping points the barbs forward and rearward and provides a very secure platform to support the fly on the water. Finish by winding the hackle forward with as many turns as the feather will allow. Tie off and clip away the waste end.

Figure 5-15. *Palmer the hackle rearward crossing the forward wraps to form "X's."*

11. The yarn for the wing will be tied in just ahead of the thorax. Some experience is needed to determine the amount of yarn to use for the wing; the yarn must be applied rather heavily to get the correct effect. Because twist in the yarn can cause some distortion in the wing, I've found that bulky, single-ply yarns are easiest to work with. If you use a yarn of several strands, be sure the individual plies are rather heavy.

Speed Tying Tip: Bob Pelzl came up with a delightfully simple method for removing the twist in yarns. One day, as he watched his wife Beverly iron a blouse, he was suddenly struck with the idea of ironing the yarn to remove the twist. It works like a charm; after all, the twist is originally set with heat. A steam iron works best; in a few minutes you can iron enough yarn to tie hundreds of flies. (Be careful, too much heat will melt polypropylene.)

12. Using the pinch technique, tie a chunk of yarn just ahead of the thorax. Secure it with six or seven turns of thread. The yarn must extend rearward far enough to form the wing. When finished, the yarn should slope back at about 30 degrees from the vertical *(Figure 5-16)*.

13. Cut away the waste end of the yarn, leaving a short stub. If you wish, you may apply a small amount of dubbing over the thread wraps used to secure the wing. I have not found it necessary to do this.

14. Tie off the head in front of the stub.

15. If necessary (as when using yarn that has not been ironed) separate and flare the fibers of the yarn.

Figure 5-16. *The yarn should slope back over the body.*

16. Form the wing to shape by cutting straight down across it (perpendicular to the hook shank); be careful not to cut the wing too short *(Figure 5-17)*.

Figure 5-17. *Cut straight down to form the wing.*

17. Trim the hackle from the bottom of the fly.

18. Place a drop of flexible head cement on the butt end of the wing and a couple of drops in it's base. Once dry the cement in the wing will permanently keep the fibers in proper alignment. Cement the head *(Figure 5-18)*.

Yarn Wing Dun: Notes on winging with other materials

A clump of hair or feather barbs can be tied in and treated in the same manner as the yarn, producing a most acceptable wing. Two body feathers or hackle points can be paired (with concave sides together) and tied in sloping back over the body—in the same position as the yarn. This wing is trimmed to shape in the same fashion as the fiber wing.

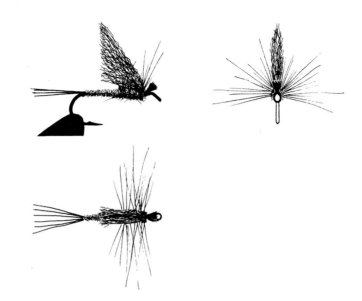

Figure 5-18. *The finished Yarn Wing Dun; side view, front view, top view.*

Loop Wing Dun

A spring creek is a thing of rare and unique beauty. As singular as a jewel among stones. And Idaho's Silver Creek is uniquely singular. It is not only a jewel, but a crown jewel; a stream of such richness and quality that it readily stands out from the rest.

Its hatches of Tricos (*Tricorythodes* spp.) strain the imagination. Equally as astounding is the rise of fish; the noise of their greed masks the quiet murmur of the currents. In this hatch, the trout may not rise in the usual fashion but rather keep their noses poked through the surface and chew at the carpet of insects like Dagwood gnawing at a sandwich. It's the perfect testing ground for new dry fly patterns.

It was 1974, and I had been trying to devise a dun imitation for the tiny mayflies; an imitation that had a strong, upright wing profile and yet was as delicate in appearance as the natural and easy to tie. The single biggest problem with the tiny dun imitations turned out to be achieving the correct profile on such a small hook without adding too much weight to the fly. Minute

mayflies don't weigh very much, and consequently, they sit *on* the surface not in it (as do the large mayflies). It's a real problem. The hooks used to dress the tiny patterns are as heavy or heavier than the exquisite little insects being imitated. Add very many materials to this, and you have a resultant product that sits on the surface like a chunk of lead not like a dainty mayfly dun. True, a full-hackled pattern rides delicately on the surface, but the profile of such a fly is all wrong.

So I'd been trying a series of tying tactics to give a strong dun silhouette with a minimum of weight, and had hit upon the process of using mallard flank feather barbs to form a single, loop wing. These barbs (and those from wood duck, teal, coot, and other species) are long enough to handle easily and thick enough to create a good profile. In addition, the single wing made the fly aerodynamically stable. The hackle used to float the fly also added to the wing's silhouette and gave it the sparkling luster of the natural. This winging technique works well on flies size 16 and smaller, but I rarely use it on flies larger than size 18, preferring to use the Yarn Wing Dun for bigger flies.

Now, I was on Silver Creek to give the pattern a real test in a blanket hatch. Fish were feeding heavily everywhere, but I selected a pod of a half dozen big snouters close in to shore. Not only were they good fish, but the currents were right for a long, drag-free presentation. On the very first cast, one of the big trout sipped the fly. At the hook set, it exploded from the water, spooking the others. Just as quickly, it ran under a bed of aquatic plants and sheared the 7X tippet. But I was delighted. The fly had been a success. The Loop Wing Dun has provided steady action since then, on lakes and streams worldwide.

There was an outstanding, drizzly August day on the Madison Arm of Hebgen Lake with Duane Stremlau. Both the Speckled Dun (*Callibaetis* spp.) and Tricos (*Tricorythodes)* were hatching *en masse* and the gulpers were everywhere. In some areas, the Speckled Duns were very heavy, and the Yarn Wing was the fly of the moment. As we'd move along in our float tubes, we'd suddenly enter a zone where the Tricos were coming off and the Loop Wing was needed. It was spellbinding to see the snout of a gulper getting closer and closer to the distinctively upright wing of the imitation and then confidently suck it in.

Loop Wing Dun: Dressing

Hook: Sizes 18-28, standard shank length

Thread: 8/0, color to match body

Body: Fur dubbing on sizes 18-22; lacquered thread abdomen and dubbed fur thorax on smaller sizes

Tail: Cock hackle barbs

Hackle: Cock hackle wound X-Wing style, trimmed on the bottom

Wing: Mallard flank feather barbs, dyed to color as needed; tied loop-wing style; sparkle yarn may be substituted for the feather barbs

Loop Wing Dun: Most Used Sizes/Body Colors/Wing Colors/ Naturals Matched and Regions Used

Sizes 20-24/Body red brown (BCS 66)/Wing dark gray (BCS 114)/ Matches some *Baetis*, all regions

Sizes 18-20/Body creamy olive (BCS 27)/Wing pale blue gray (BCS 105)/Hackle medium dun/Matches *Ephemerella inermis* (Pale Morning Duns), Northern Rockies, Southern Rockies, and Pacific

Sizes 18-20/Body yellow orange (BCS 51)/Wing medium gray (BCS 108)/ Hackle medium dun/Matches *Ephemerella dorothea* (Sulphur Mayfly), and *Centroptilum*, all regions

Sizes 18-24/Body olive (BCS30)/Wing dark gray/Matches some *Baetis* and *Ephemerella*, all regions

Sizes 22-26/Body grassy green (BCS 19)/Wing smokey gray (BCS 108)/ Matches *Pseudocloeon,* all regions

Sizes 18-28/Abdomen black(BCS 118) or pale creamy gray (BCS 92), thorax black/Wing natural white mallard/Matches *Tricorythodes* (Tricos or White Winged Blacks); all regions

Loop Wing Dun: Tying Instructions

1. Tie in the hackle barbs for the tail. For these small flies it's not necessary to use a fan tail. Form the abdomen on the rear 1/2 of hook (page 53). If you are using dubbing, be *exceedingly sparing* in its application.

2. Spin dubbing for the thorax onto the thread at this time (page 53). Using the pinch technique, tie in the mallard flank feather barbs at the mid-point of the hook (rear of thorax); use 5 barbs for sizes 18-22; 4 barbs for sizes 24-26; 3 barbs for size 28. If sparkle yarn is used for the wing, keep the amount rather sparing.

3. The hackle feather is tied in immediately ahead of the mallard barbs *(Figure 5-19)*.

Figure 5-19. Tie in the mallard flank feather barbs and then the hackle feather.

4. Form the thorax; then wind the hackle X-Wing style (page 54).

5. After the hackle is wound, loop the mallard barbs or sparkle yarn forward over the top of the hackle to the head and tie down with *two turns of thread.* The loop should be as high as the top of the hackle barbs *(Figure 5-20).*

Figure 5-20. The loop should be slightly taller than the body is long.

6. To create the strongest possible wing profile, individual mallard barbs are now grasped at their tips with a hackle pliers and pulled, creating several loops of different sizes. For flies tied on hook sizes 18-22, one barb is pulled to form a loop 1/3 the size of the wing and two barbs are pulled to form a loop 2/3 the size of the wing; for sizes 24-26,

two barbs are pulled to form a loop 1/2 the size of the wing; for size 28, one barb is pulled to form a loop 1/2 the size of the wing. Follow the same procedure if sparkle yarn is used for the wing, pulling several fibers to form each of the smaller loops.

7. Once the loops have been formed, the barbs are secured with two or three more turns of thread, the waste ends trimmed away, and the head finished.

8. The hackle barbs on the bottom of the fly are trimmed off, allowing the pattern to sit on the water like the natural.

9. To strengthen the wing, apply a bit of water-thin, flexible head cement to each loop. Cement the head, then turn the fly upside down and apply a drop of cement to the underside of the thorax *(Figure 5-21)*.

Figure 5-21. The finished Loop Wing Dun; side view, front view, top view.

SPINNER

Once the dun escapes the water, it flies to nearby vegetation or other structures, and there, after a period of a few moments to a day or two, metamorphoses to the sexually mature spinner stage. Wings of the spinner are normally clear and may have a few markings. The body is more shiny than that of the dun and may be a different color or a different shade of color than the dun. The spinners return to the vicinity of the water and carry out their nuptial rites. Afterward, the males fall to the ground or to the water's surface and die. The females lay their eggs and die, dropping on the water in the process. When the spinner fall is heavy, the trout will rise to meet them, providing excellent fishing.

Because the spinners are different than the duns, they present their own separate set of tying requirements. First is the profile. Spinners of a few species will fall to the water and hold their wings upright, at least for a short while. But then they, like all other species, will relax and drop the wings onto the water in the outspread "spent" position *(Figure 5-22)*. From underwater, this cross-shaped profile is very different than that of the upright-winged dun.

Because the spinner is dead, the body lies totally on the surface without the benefit of any support from the legs. The meniscus formed by the body and outstretched wings of the dead insect make the spinner readily visible even when it's beyond the edge of the trout's window. Like the body of the dun, that of the spinner is translucent and traps air against the surface. Consequently, I use the same materials for the body of the spinner as for the body of the dun.

The spent wing has a pronounced effect on the profile of the spinner. Not only is it outstretched and flush in the film, but it changes the refractive angle of the surface, which allows the fish to *see the sky through the wing*. This occurs because the wing is not flat, like a sheet of plastic; rather, it is corrugated. Seen end on, the veins of the wing lie at the top of each ridge and at the bottom of each valley *(Figure 5-23)*. This arrangement produces a very strong structure. In addition to changing the refractive angle of the surface, the corrugated wing may also act like a diffraction grating, breaking up sunlight into its component colors. This is especially true of the wings of tiny mayflies, where the distances between veins are very small. This effect causes the wings to glisten when seen from the angler's point of view; however, this effect is not visible

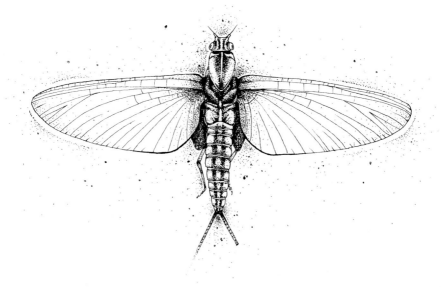

Figure 5-22. *The spent spinner.*

from the fish's point of view. The spent wing also often traps variously shaped and sized bubbles of air against the surface. These bubbles glisten from below and block the view of the sky through the wing. Thus, seen from the fish's vantage point, the wing of the spinner is a mosaic of veins, air bubbles, and sky.

Figure 5-23. *The corrugated nature of the mayfly wing.*

The sky-light effect of the spent wings and the depression of the surface film by the spinner's body can have an interesting influence on the overall coloration of the fly during the evening hours. The light at that time is shifted toward the red end of the spectrum. Consequently, colors that contain red—such as brown and orange—will appear more red than they do under midday lighting conditions. And as John Goddard and Brian Clarke point out in "The Trout and the Fly," in red sunsets, the trout sees the rosy glow of the sky through the spent wings. From underwater, the spinner is no longer the somber color seen by the angler, rather it is afire with the scintillations of a thousand ruby facets. It pays to carry a few fluorescent orange spinner patterns for use during such times (page 63).

I've tried many, many materials to mimic the spent wings of the spinner and am totally satisfied with the effect of good quality, pale watery dun, cock hackle. Hackle not only looks correct from underwater, but is very easy to apply and quite durable, and pale watery dun is translucent—much closer to the qualities of the natural's wing than is white or other pale colors. I tie two, hackle-wing, spinner patterns: the Parachute Spinner and the X-Wing Spinner.

I've tried these patterns with and without egg sacks to represent the ova being extruded by the female. I have not been able to see any difference between the two versions with regards to the numbers or size of fish caught; consequently, I skip the egg cluster and simply tie the fly to match the natural *sans ova*.

Parachute Spinner

This fly originated partially from a need to represent huge mayfly spinners and a need to represent damsel adults (see page 109). It has a very good profile on the water and is quite durable. It has done yeoman work for me over the years. There was the night Nancy and I were on Michigan's Ausable, and I'd had an exceptional evening. The big *Hexagenia* drakes had come first, followed closely by the spinners, and I could do no wrong with the Parachute Spinner. The fine gravel of the bottom had made wading easy, even in the surprisingly strong center currents, and the feeding fish had been out in open water, well away from the cedar sweepers and log jams that line the shore. But Nancy's evening had been different.

I'd put her at the bottom of the pool where I was sure there would be excellent fishing, and when the hatch was over I cut through the woods and came out next to her. She explained that there had only been a few sizable fish working all evening and those so sporadically that it was impossible to raise them. I felt terrible. As we stood there, me apologizing and Nanc being very understanding, a small fish rose about six feet from her. "That small one's been the only fish that's been rising consistently," Nanc said, "maybe I should try for it."

The Parachute Spinner disappeared in a tiny swirl, and Nanc lifted the rod in expectation. In a flash, the line shot to the center of the pool. As the fight dragged on, we realized it's wasn't a little one. She finally worked it close, and I panned its length with my flashlight. It was a monster; nearly twenty-four inches long. It was the biggest trout either of us has ever taken from the Ausable.

Parachute Spinner: Dressing

Hook: Sizes 6-10, standard shank length; 2X long may be substituted for larger sizes (see Chapter 14)

Thread: 3/0 or 6/0 depending on hook size

Tail: Pheasant tail barbs

Body: Deer hair or other spongy hair, tied extended style, lacquered with flexible head cement

Parachute Post: Deer hair or other spongy hair, color to match body, or yarn or other material; pulled forward and tied down at head after hackle is wound

Hackle: Pale watery dun cock hackle wound parachute style

Parachute Spinner: Most Used Sizes/Body and Thread Colors/ Naturals Matched and Regions Used

Sizes 6-10/Body pale yellowish-olive deer hair (BCS 38), thread dark brown/Matches *Hexagenia* (Giant Michigan Mayfly), Northeast, Lake States, Pacific, and *Ephemera simulans* (Brown Drake), North East, Lake States, and Northern Rockies

Note: Sometimes the spinners of The Giant Michigan Mayfly and those of the Brown Drake will alight on the water with their wings upright and struggle as they extrude their eggs. In this case I use the dun pattern and twitch it *very lightly*.

Sizes 8-10/Body natural white deer hair, thread tan/Matches *Ephemera guttulata* (Eastern Green Drake), *Potamanthus* and *Ephemera varia* (Yellow Drakes), Northeast, Southeast, and Lake States

Sizes 12-14/Body dark olive brown (BCS 66), thread dark brown / Matches *Ephemerella grandis* (Western Green Drake—northern and southern variety); Northern Rockies, Southern Rockies, and Pacific

Note: The Western Green Drake is of a size that it could be dressed as either a small Parachute Spinner or a large X-Wing Spinner (page 63).

Parachute Spinner: Tying Instructions

1. Apply the tail and body in same manner as for Hair Wing Dun, but don't curve the abdomen upward, dress it straight; form the thread foundation at the thorax (page 49).

2. Tie in a hackle feather at the thread foundation. The barbs of the hackle should be slightly shorter than the length of the body.

3. To form the parachute post, prepare another clump of deer hair the same size and color as for the body. Trim the butt end of the clump. Position the clump of hair on top of the body with the squared butt end at the front of the thread foundation and the tips of the hairs extending *rearward*. Note: yarn or other material may be used in place of the hair for the post (see discussion of and tying instruc-tions for Braided Butt Damsel, page 111).

4. Take two loose turns of the tying thread over the clump, keeping just enough tension on the thread so it remains in contact with the hair; place these turns just at the rear of the thread foundation (*Figure 5-24*).

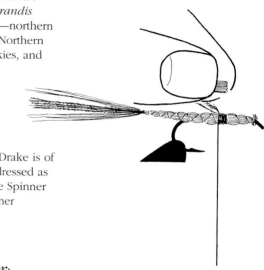

Figure 5-24. *Tying in the hair post.*

5. While holding the clump of hair tightly to keep it from spinning, smoothly draw downward on the bobbin to tighten the thread. The short butt ends will flare. Wrap the thread 6 or 8 turns through the flared butts to lock the hair solidly onto the hook.

6. Hold the clump of hair upright and wrap the thread *around the base of the clump* and as close to the top of the body as possible—5 or 6 turns are sufficient (*Figure 5-25*). This will prepare a base on which the hackle will be wound. Then, wrap the thread around the body just in front of the post.

7. Wind the hackle around the hair post in a clockwise direction (counterclockwise if you tie left handed with eye of the fly facing to the left). Keep the turns as close to the body of the fly as possible. Tie off just in front of the post (*Figure 5-26*).

Figure 5-25. *Wrap the thread around the base of the post.*

Speed Tying Tip: Use a hackle pliers to wind the feather. To tie it off, end with the final turn at the front of the post, then hang the hackle pliers over the near side of the body. The weight of the pliers will hold the hackle in place. With the materials hand, lift the hackle barbs sticking out to the front and take *two* turns of thread around the waste end of the hackle feather. Pull gently on the hackle pliers to draw the hackle tight around the post. Make several more turns of thread to lock the hackle tip firmly. Cut away the waste end.

8. Stroke the hackle barbs that are pointing forward out to the sides, fold the hair post forward over the top of hook shank like the covert on a nymph, and tie it in at the head.

Figure 5-26. *Wrap the hackle around the base of the post.*

Speed Tying Tip: To keep the deer hair of the post from spinning around the head of the fly, first take a loose turn of thread *around the hair only*. This turn should be just tight enough to maintain contact with the hair and should be placed at the point where the hair will be tied in at the head. Then make a turn around both the hair and the hook shank *(Figure 5-27)*. Gently pull the thread tight, drawing the hairs of the clump together and simultaneously binding them to the top of the shank. Make several more turns with the thread to secure the clump to the hook.

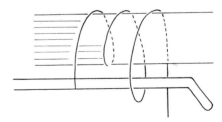

Figure 5-27. *Wrap around the hair and then around the hair and the hook shank.*

9. Cut away the waste portion of the hair post, leaving about 1/8 inch of the ends stick out to form the head of the fly. Tie off the thread at the eye of the hook and clip it away.

10. Stroke the hackle barbs out to the sides and rear to realign them (they get a bit crushed during the tying procedure).

11. Trim away the tips of the deer hair used to form the extended body; 3-6 pheasant tail barbs should remain to imitate the tails of the natural.

12. Coat the body and the folded parachute post with water-thin, flexible head cement *(Figure 5-28)*.

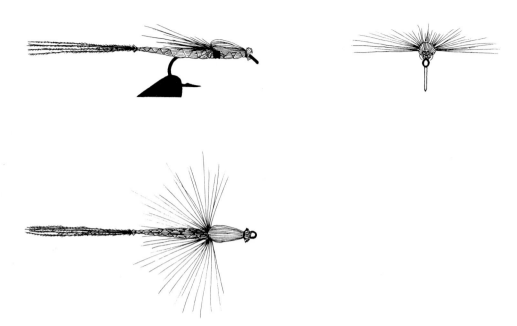

Figure 5-28. *The finished Parachute Spinner; side view, front view, top view.*

X-Wing Spinner

This is the pattern I use to imitate all but the largest mayflies. It's very fast to tie and very effective whenever fish are taking spinners. The wing is hackle wound X-Wing style and trimmed top and bottom. This hackling technique creates a wing shape more representative of the natural than does winding a hackle in the traditional manner. Trimmed hackle wings have always been highly successful for me.

Some of my favorite memories of fishing with spinners are from the early and mid 60's when I was working on my bachelor's and master's degree at Penn State. Waters like Spring Creek, Penns Creek, and Falling Springs were regular haunts back then, and there were wonderful hatches of Sulphurs *(Ephemerella dorothea)* during the end of May, first of June. In late afternoon, the nymphs got very active, and the Feather Leg Nymph produced great fishing. Then came the hatch, and the fish rose in earnest. As the evening light thinned in the west, the spinners fell in abundance. In the gloaming, it was very easy to miss the spent flies and assume the fish were still feeding on the duns. It was a mistake you didn't want to make too often because that overhead stew of spent-wing minutiae could be very thick, indeed, and the big fish would be on the take. I can still feel the pull of a heavy fish that took my fly just above a bridge abutment and parted company with me about four pools down.

X-Wing Spinner: Dressing

Hook: Sizes 8-28, standard length—2X long may be substituted for larger sizes, short shanks for the smaller sizes (see Chapter 14)

Thread: 6/0 or 8/0, depending upon hook size, color to match body

Tail: Pale watery dun cock hackle barbs

Body: Fur dubbing blended with 10-15 percent undyed sparkle yarn (use thread for the abdomen on hooks smaller than 22)

Hackle: Pale watery dun cock hackle wound X-Wing style, trimmed top and bottom; standard size for hooks 10-18, one size larger than standard for hooks 18-28

X-Wing Spinner: Most Used Sizes/Body Color/ Naturals Matched and Regions Used

Sizes 10-24/Body rusty brown (BCS 66)/Matches a whole host of mayfly spinners in *Ephemerella, Isonychia, Paraleptophlebia, Leptophlebia, Stenonema, Baetis, Centroptilum,* and others, all regions

Sizes 8-20/Body dark olive brown (BCS 34)/Matches *Ephemerella grandis* (Western Green Drake), some other *Ephemerella*, some *Baetis*, some *Pseudocloeon*, all regions

Sizes 10-16/Body smokey gray (BCS 108)/Matches *Siphlonurus* (Gray Drakes), *Callibaetis* (Speckled spinner), and some *Epeorus*, all regions

Sizes 18-28/Abdomen black (BCS 118) or pale creamy gray (BCS 92), thorax black/Matches *Tricorythodes* (Tricos), all regions

Sizes 8-28/body fluorescent orange (BCS 77), hackle fluorescent orange/matches all species that fall during the late evening, especially during red sunsets.

X-Wing Spinner: Tying Instructions

1. Follow steps 1-8 for the Yarn Wing Dun (page 53); on hooks smaller than 16, it is not necessary to use a fan tail.

2. Wind the dubbing forward to form the thorax, ending with a taper at the head.

3. Wind the hackle as for the Yarn Wing Dun (page 54).

4. Finish the head and trim the hackle top and bottom *(Figure 5-29)*. Because the spinners of the Gray Drakes (*Siphlonurus* spp.) often fall to the water with wings upright, and then flutter as they lay eggs, I only trim the bottom of the spinner imitation of these mayflies. If a fully spent fly is needed, the hackle barbs can be trimmed from the top of the imitation while you're astream.

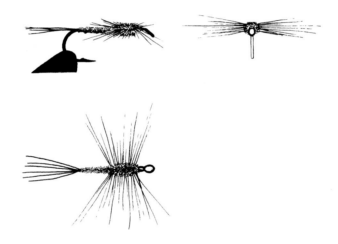

Figure 5-29. *The finished X-Wing Spinner; side view, front view, top view.*

Miscellaneous Notes on Spinners

Fishing tiny flies can be frustratingly delicate work. Frustrating because the fish can so easily shear the tippet or tear the tiny hook free. To counter this, some fly fishers have begun to fish, and quite successfully fish I might note, a double fly pattern. For example, instead of a size 28, they tie a double spinner on a size 18, one on the rear half of the hook, one on the front half. This trick is especially valuable for those species that produce dense spinner falls.

Female spinners of the Blue Winged-Olives (*Baetis* spp.) usually go underwater to lay eggs. They land on objects that stick down into the water (such as your legs) and crawl under to deposit their eggs on subsurface structures (like your waders). As they dive, they carry a silvery bubble of air with them. When they've finished ovipositing, they drift away in the currents, still carrying their trapped glob of air. The fish take them readily. It's hard to imitate this dead, drifting, subsurface spinner because the *Baetis* are generally so small, but its worth a try with a pattern like the diving sedge (see page 90).

STONEFLIES

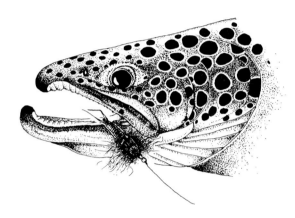

Not every fish that's hooked is landed. Duane Stremlau and I were fishing the Madison and had waded the river to explore the back channels near Slide Inn. We had managed some decent fish, but nothing of gargantuan proportions. And of course, that's what we were looking for. Duane tied on a Golden Mono Stonefly Nymph and headed upriver. In a few minutes he was back, visibly shaken and looking in need of some comforting. Seems that as he'd flipped the nymph into a quiet eddy, the line had tangled around the tip of the rod. As he untangled the line, something grabbed the fly and tore off like an enraged water buffalo, leaving Duane with a shorter leader and a very startled look on his face. Though it happened over a decade ago, it's still one of his favorite stories.

Everyone who fishes with stoneflies has a favorite story like Duane's. And with good reason: a big stonefly nymph is a juicy mouthful for even a ten-pound trout. The adults can also be modest little monsters, bringing every fish in the river explosively to the surface. I remember a soft spring night along Michigan's AuSable in 1988 when the air smelled of sweet vegetation and blackness had closed in like a cloak over the

river. Below me, in the next pool, I could hear a huge fish crashing after fluttering stonefly adults. I waded down, slowly, listening for the brown's position. It was a strange sensation; the utter blackness, the tug of the current, the total stillness broken irregularly by the startlingly loud sound of the rise. After a few exploratory casts, I found the correct drift lane, and the big fish surged up from its lie. I can still feel its sudden, wrenching weight and hear my pulse pounding in my ears. And then it was gone. It had crushed the bend of the hook in its powerful, bony jaws. Everyone who fishes with stoneflies has a favorite story like Duane's.

NYMPHS

Like those of the mayflies, stonefly nymphs come in a wide variety of sizes and colors, but they vary far less in overall body configuration. Oh sure, there are those that are a bit thinner than average and a few that are a bit fatter, but by-and-large, they are quite uniform in anatomical construction (with regard to fly design). They have two conspicuous tails, two visible sets of wing cases, easily seen antennae, and may have filamentous gills at the bases of the tails and legs. Unlike mayflies, they have no gills on the sides of the abdomen *(Figure 6-1)*.

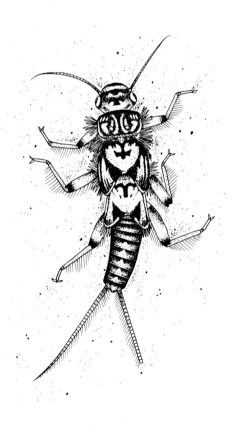

Figure 6-1. *Typical stonefly nymph.*

Some species of stonefly nymphs require only a year to mature, but a number of the larger species may live as long a two and possibly three years. This is good news for the trout and good news for the fly fisher. For the fish, it means that there will be a year-round supply of rather large insects to eat. This food supply is especially critical in the winter months when most other nymphs and larvae are quite small. For the fly fisher, it means that a stonefly nymph is a good pattern to tie on during opportunistic feeding periods. Here in the Lake States, the winter-run steelhead feed on the big nymphs of the *Pteronarcys* stoneflies and are quite susceptible to a large, black, Mono Stonefly Nymph fished dead-drift tight along the bottom.

Stonefly nymphs normally dwell in rather fast currents and so one would think that they would be good swimmers. However, they aren't; in fact, they are quite poor swimmers, if they swim at all. When torn loose from the normal nooks and crannies among the rocks and other bottom debris, they tumble along with legs outstretched, hoping to grasp something solid. The hair leg technique is perfect for simulating these extended extremities. Guard hairs or calf tail hair work very well on these flies. In addition, the dubbing used in the hair leg technique nicely simulates the thoracic gills of the natural.

If you collect a handful of stonefly nymphs and drop them one at a time into moving water, you will note that the drifting insect may wiggle its body slightly, twisting from side to side and perhaps tuck its head under, but that as often as not it holds the body straight and assumes no contorted position. Some tiers dress their imitations on bent-shank hooks to make the pattern appear more articulated. However, I have not found such distortion to increase the fish-catching capability of the dressing; consequently, I dress all my patterns on straight-shank hooks. While dressing them on bent- or curved- shank hooks may not improve their fish-catching ability, neither does it seem to hurt; so if the appearance of such flies is aesthetically pleasing to you, then by all means dress them so.

Since the nymph has its skin on the outside (an exoskeleton—all insects have one) it must change its skin in order to grow. Immediately after molting, the insect enlarges; during this time the new exoskeleton is very soft and pale in color. Patterns have been developed to ape this newly molted, pale nymph. However, for me they have been no more successful, on average, than normally colored patterns. The reason is that the insects molt in hiding where the trout rarely get at them. They are simply opportunistic food items not more nor less attractive than any other stage of the nymph.

Like that of other nymphs, the exoskeleton of the stonefly nymph is a bit translucent. Fur dubbing, therefore, is a good choice to simulate the bodies of these insects, and can, and is, used on patterns of all sizes. In fact, for the smaller species, I simply use the Hair Leg Nymph (page 26) in appropriate colors. But for the very large species (3/4 inch or longer), I form the abdomen with an overbody of flat monofilament or similar material, after the methods of George Grant. I use the monofilament overbody because it very closely simulates the easily seen segmentation of these large insects while simultaneously allowing the fly to sink rapidly and stay down near the bottom where the naturals are found by the trout. In addition, the beautifully translucent look of the monofilament is a great match for the exoskeleton of the insect.

The mono overwrap also allows the tier to create dressings that differ in color on the dorsal and ventral surfaces, an obvious characteristic of several of the large species of stonefly nymphs. This can be done by coloring the top of the underbody with a permanent marker or by adding a feather or feather segment to the top of the fly before the mono is wrapped on. Some anglers have argued that such coloration in the pattern spooks fish, but I have never found this to be true. Plenty of big fish have fallen victim to the Mono Stonefly Nymph, and big fish are the wariest of all.

The argument has been made that fish will hold and chew a soft-bodied nymph longer than a hard-bodied one, and therefore monofilament-bodied flies are poor fish getters. This argument assumes that the fish bites the fly by the sides; if the fish were to bite the fly top to bottom, the hook point would immediately become evident, regardless of the materials used for the body. In fact, many trout hook themselves in this manner. As a fish bites the artificial, the hook point enters the flesh of its mouth. When the fish shakes its head to get rid of the offending morsel, the point only digs deeper. This is the reason that the newer chemically sharpened hooks work so well—they are incredibly sharp.

In addition, the soft-body, hard-body argument assumes that the fish expect to find a soft body *and* will have time to chew on it before the fly fisher detects the strike and sets the hook. But, large stoneflies are not particularly soft; in fact, they're rather tough, and, I imagine, rather crunchy. I can't speak from personal experience, but Jason once ate one out of curiosity and told me it had a nutty flavor and texture. Trout reject our imitations because they don't taste right, not because of their texture; trout will reject a fly of any material, given a moment or two to crunch on it.

Because stonefly nymphs are found in swift water, the trout usually has very little time to grab the imitation as it shoots past in the currents. The fish must move suddenly and quickly, snatch the rapidly moving fly, and dart back to protective cover. Such takes are quite strong and easily felt by the fly fisher. In fact, the angler's response to such takes is often so sudden and violent that the tippet pops. Remember Duane's fish? The Mono Stonefly Nymph was simply lying on the bottom; the fish found it, took it and hooked itself.

In deep water, I usually fish stonefly nymph imitations on a compound tippet (page 77); in shallows I often use the Greased Leader Tactic. For other methods see "Nymphing" or Richards, Swisher, and Arbona's book "Stoneflies."

Hair Leg Nymph For Stonefly Nymphs: Most Used Sizes/Body Color/Guard Hairs for Legs/Naturals Matched and Regions Used

Sizes 8-14/Body red brown (BCS 66) ribbed with black copper wire/ Legs of dark-colored cotton tail rabbit guard hairs/Matches many dark nymphs of such genera as *Capnia, Leuctra, Nemoura, Taeniopteryx,* and others, all regions

Sizes 8-14/Body pale chartreuse (BCS 17) ribbed with olive thread/Legs of light-colored cotton tail rabbit guard hairs/Matches nymphs of genus *Alloperla, Chloroperla,* and *Isoperla*

Mono Stonefly Nymph: Dressing

Hook: Sizes 2-10, 3XL shank

Thread: 3/0 or 6/0, depending upon hook size

Tails: Barbs from leading edge of primary wing feather from goose or other large bird (these barbs are called biots)

Weight: Lead wire tied along either side of hook shank; wire should be same diameter as hook shank

Underbody: Floss or polypropylene yarn; lacquered feather or segment of feather on dorsal surface of abdomen if needed

Overbody: Flat monofilament or similar material

Wing Cases: Section of appropriately colored wing, tail or body feather, lacquered with flexible head cement

Thorax: Fur dubbing mixed with undyed sparkle yarn

Legs: Guard hairs, calf tail hair, or similar material

Mono Stonefly Nymph: Most Used Sizes/Color of Tail/Color of Underbody/Feather Top of Abdomen (if used)/Color of Dubbing for Thorax/ Hairs for Legs/Feather for Wing Cases/ Naturals Matched and Regions Used

Sizes 2-10/Tail black/Underbody black/Thorax and Gills, clumps of black and white dubbing/Legs black calf tail hair, but may use black rabbit on sizes 8-10/Wing cases dark turkey tail/Matches *Pteronarcys* and *Pteronarcella* spp. (Giant Black Stonefly and Giant Salmonfly) and *Acroneuria nigrita* (Black Willowfly), all regions

Sizes 6-10/Tail black/Underbody pale yellow orange (BCS 46) or fleshy tan (BCS 58)/Top of Abdomen, mottled dark browns/Thorax and Gills, clumps of white and pale yellow orange or fleshy tan dubbing (to match underbody)/ Legs black calftail or black rabbit guard hairs/Wing cases dark turkey tail/Matches members of Perlidae especially genus *Paragnetina,* Northeast, Southeast, Lake States, South Central

Sizes 6-10/Tails orangish brown (BCS 63)/Underbody amber (BCS 51) or pale yellowish orange (BCS 46)/ Top of Abdomen, mottled feather dyed with permanent orangish brown marker (BCS 63)/Thorax and Gills, clumps of white and amber or pale yellowish orange dubbing (to match underbody)/ Legs natural cotton tail rabbit guard hairs/Matches species of the genera *Acroneuria, Calineuria,* and *Doroneuria* (Golden Stoneflies), all regions

Mono Stonefly: Tying Instructions

1. Clamp the hook in the vise, wrap to the standard position. NOTE: if the pattern calls for a feather or feather segment on the top of the abdomen, make the tag end of the thread about 6 inches long and allow it to hang out the back of the hook until step 8 below. Form a lump of thread at the rear of the hook.

2. Using the pinch technique, tie a biot on either side of the shank immediately ahead of the thread lump; wrap back against the lump to spread the biots; wrap the thread forward to the center of the hook.

3. Cut one end of the lead wire to a tapering point; tie in the wire on the far side of the hook with the tapered end at the rear of the shank just ahead of the thread lump; wrap the thread forward to secure the lead wire. End the thread wraps about three head spaces behind the eye.

4. Fold the lead wire under the shank and align it along the near side. Trim the rear end to a taper that matches the taper on the far side. Wrap the thread rearward to secure the lead wire. It is usually necessary to hold the lead wire in place as you wrap, otherwise the pressure of wrapping will shift the wire around the shank. When you finish, the thread should be at the rear of the hook and the lead should be along the sides *(Figure 6-2)*.

69

Stoneflies

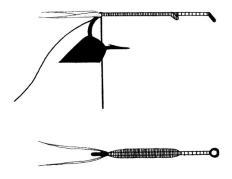

Figure 6-2. *Lead wire in place along the sides of the shank.*

Speed Tying Tip: It is far easier to tie in the lead wire at the center of the shank and wrap it as described above rather than trying to tie it in at the rear of the hook.

5. Tie a piece of flat monofilament on top of the shank with the usable end pointing rearward; the waste end should extend forward to at least the mid-point of the shank. Wrap the thread forward very tightly to secure the mono; end with the thread at the head of the fly.

6. Tie in the floss or polypropylene yarn for the underbody; wrap to the rear of the shank and then wrap forward to the head and tie off. To create a nice taper in the body, slightly overlap the wraps at the front of the body; as you wrap rearward, gradually decrease the overlap until about half way back the wraps are just touching, continue to increase the space between the wraps so that by the time you reach the rear of the hook they form a closely spaced rib. As you wrap forward, gradually begin to close the spacing between the wraps, covering any gaps in the rear portion of the underbody and building a nice taper as you wrap

forward. Taper the forward end of the underbody ahead of the lead *(Figure 6-3)*.

7. After you tie off the underbody material at the head of the fly, spiral the thread back to the center of the body.

8. If a lacquered feather or feather segment is to be used for the back of the abdomen, tie it on top of the underbody with the tip facing rearward and the butt end facing forward; clip away the excess butt end of the segment. The feather or segment should be wide enough to cover the top of the body and extend half way down around each side.

Speed Tying Tip: Lacquer the feather and allow it to dry thoroughly before using (page 34). If a segment is to be used, lacquer the entire feather, allow to dry, and then remove the appropriate-sized piece. If the feather or segment is to be colored, apply the permanent ink marker after the lacquer is completely dry. I normally lacquer an entire feather and color all or a large portion of it so that plenty of material is on hand and ready to use.

9. Use the tag end of the thread left over from step 1 above to secure the feather segment at the rear of the body. To tie off the tag end, take a loop around the index finger of your materials hand and then around the hook shank (as when making a dubbing loop) and tuck the end of the thread through the loop—this will make a half hitch. Pull tight *(Figure 6-4)*. Cut away any excess.

10. Wrap the mono forward to the center of the shank and secure it with a dozen wraps of thread. I normally end with the mono under the body *(Figure 6-5)*.

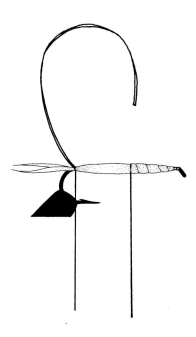

Figure 6-3. *The underbody in place.*

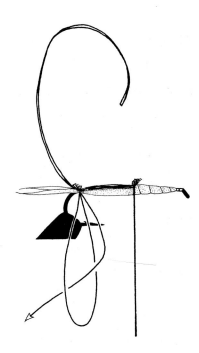

Figure 6-4. *Secure the rear of the feather segment with the tag end of the thread.*

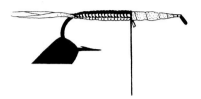

Figure 6-5. *Wrap the mono to the midpoint of the shank.*

Speed Tying Tip: To prevent the mono from pushing the feather segment over the far side of the underbody, maintain only light pressure on the mono as you wrap over the top of the body. Then, pull the mono tight and wrap under the body.

11. Select a segment of feather for the wing cases. The segment should be about 1 1/2 times wider than the underbody. The feather should be well treated with flexible cement and allowed to dry before the segment is removed. This treatment keeps the barbs together during subsequent steps.

12. Tie in the feather segment by its tip on top of the body and immediately in front of the monofilament. Because the segment is wider than the underbody, you should push it down around the sides of the body before tying it in place.

13. Form a dubbing loop at the rear of the thorax.

14. Alternately spin clumps of the two colors of dubbing on the lower thread of the loop *(Figure 6-6).*

15. If calf tail hairs are to be used for the legs, cut them from the tail and insert them into the top of the loop and at right angles to the thread of the loop. Spread them evenly along the loop (page 32). Twist the loop tight.

Figure 6-6. *Alternate the two colors of dubbing on the lower thread of the loop.*

16. Wrap the twisted loop forward over the rear 1/2 of the thorax and tie off. Cut away the excess.

17. To make the first set of wing pads, press the end of the thumbnail of your bobbin hand down against the feather segment at a point about 1/4 of the way back on the abdomen and bend the remaining portion of the segment forward. Your thumbnail acts to crimp the feather. It should bend over neatly at that point *(Figure 6-7).*

18. Tie down the segment at the center of the thorax and then fold it rearward *(Figure 6-8).*

19. Repeat steps 12-17, forming the front half of the thorax: make the loop, add the dubbing and legging hairs, spin tight, and wrap forward to the head; cut away the excess. Crimp the

Figure 6-7. *Use your thumbnail to crimp the feather segment.*

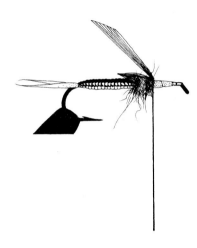

Figure 6-8. *Secure the segment at the center of the thorax and then fold it rearward.*

feather segment with your thumbnail about 1/3 of the way back on the first wing pad, fold it forward to the head and tie off, cut away the excess.

20. Form a smoothly tapered head and tie off the thread and cut it away.

21. Stroke the hair legs forward until they stand out at right angles to the fly and cut off all those on the underside of the thorax.

22. Brush out the underside of the thorax so the filaments will represent the gills.

23. Apply head cement to the head and the wing cases *(Figure 6-9).*

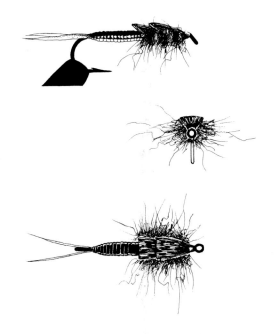

Figure 6-9. *The finished Mono Stonefly Nymph; side view, front view, top view.*

EMERGERS

In nearly all species of stoneflies, the nymphs crawl from the water before the adult emerges. However, there is the occasional individual that will emerge at the surface film. I've seen this in some of the summer hatching species of the Lake States. This phenomenon is too rare to be of importance to the angler. However, Polly Rosborough has noted conclusively that the Golden Stoneflies of the Pacific Coast *(Calineuria californica* and *Doroneuria baumanii)* normally emerge on the stream bottom. The adult then swims rapidly to the surface; needless to say, the fish take them quite strongly. For these insects, fish the adult pattern wet, using a Leisenring Lift to imitate the ascending natural.

Because most nymphs crawl to shore before the adults emerge, the fly fisher should pay very close attention to shoreward waters during the times when such nymphal migrations are occurring. Don't wade out as far as possible and then try to cast as far as possible beyond

that. Rather, sneak along the shore and carefully search likely holding lies; you'll be amazed at the big fish you'll find.

Emergence of the large species in rivers east of the Rockies is basically a night-time phenomenon, and the late twilight hours of evening, the dark hours of night, and the waxing daylight hours of the morning can be good times to find fish actively searching for the migrating nymphs in the near-shore shallows of riffly stretches. In the West, emergence occurs during both the night-time and day-time hours. It's great to fish to big, bank-hugging fish during the daylight hours when you can actually see where you're putting your feet.

Many of the smaller species that hatch during the mid-summer and the mid-winter will emerge during the day. Be especially watchful for this; many trout will be in the shallows, and they're easily spooked by a careless approach.

ADULTS

Stonefly adults fold their wings and hold them along the top of the body when at rest; the order name Plecoptera means folded wing *(Figure 6-10).* In some species the males are wingless. Mating takes place on land and the gravid females fly out over the water, drop to the surface and deposit their eggs. It can be great dry fly fishing if the ovipositing flight is heavy. East of the Rockies, the larger species oviposit at night; smaller species lay their eggs usually in the afternoon or evening. In the West, ovipositing can occur both night and day, although due to the cold nights often experienced at the higher elevations of western trout streams, night-time flights are less common than day-time ones. Talk about exciting dry fly fishing! One of the largest of all trout stream insects flopping to the water in endless hordes has a way of getting both fish and fisher whipped into a frenzy.

When a large female touches down, its body rests in the film, changing the refractive

Figure 6-10. *A typical stonefly adult.*

Adults of the smaller species can be nicely aped by a Poly Caddis (page 88) dressed in appropriate colors. But the sheer size of the larger species (up to 1 1/2 inches in length) presents some design challenges to the fly tier. The major problem is creating a quickly and easily tied body that floats well and yet still imitates the other traits of the natural. Spun and trimmed deer hair makes a good body, but is very time consuming to apply and shape. Dubbing applied in the usual fashion, or spun as a chenille and trimmed, makes a good body, but so much is needed that it too requires a substantial investment in time (not to mention materials).

I solved this dilemma while working on a grasshopper design (page 132); the body uses both deer hair and dubbing. The underbody is deer hair, not spun and trimmed, but tied on like an extended body. This adds the needed bulk and increases floatability. At the same time, the tips of the hair can be used to create the tail of the fly. I know, stoneflies have only two tails and rather small ones at that. But the pattern needs a bushy tail to help keep the rear of the hook afloat (the rear is, after all, quite a bit heavier than the front of the hook). The hair of the tail blends perfectly with the hair of the wing (when seen from underwater) and so is not a distraction to the fish.

Once the underbody is formed, dubbing is spun on the thread and applied over the deer hair. The result is most satisfactory. The body can easily be made any color by blending the dubbing, and 10 to 15 percent undyed sparkle yarn can be added to the blend to suggest the air trapped between the natural's body and the surface film.

For the fluttering-style wing on these big imitations, I like furs like woodchuck or badger because the dubbing fur is very long and can be included in the wing. Coyote, raccoon, dark tan bucktail (not body hair), and any other similarly colored hairs are good alternatives. High quality cock hackle is used to simulate the legs and give the fly a bit of extra support.

angle of the surface and making the insect visible beyond the fish's window; this can be an especially important feature to simulate during the low-light hours of late evening. As with any insect sitting on the surface, the legs are outstretched and the body sandwiches a bit of air against the film, producing random quicksilver highlights. The wings are usually not completely folded, and so I prefer a fluttering-style pattern to imitate this wing position rather than one which tries to imitate perfectly folded wings held closely along the back.

Poly Caddis; Stonefly Version: Most Used Sizes/Body Color/ Hackle/Wing Color/ Naturals Matched and Regions Used

Sizes 10-14/Body dark brown (BCS 98)/Hackle dark brown/Wing smokey brown (BCS 112)/Matches many small dark colored stonefly adults such as those of the genera *Capnia, Leuctra, Nemoura, Taeniopteryx,* and others, all regions

Sizes 10-16/Body chartreuse green (BCS 24)/Hackle yellow or bright chartreuse/Wing pale chartreuse (BCS 17)/Matches adults of genus *Alloperla,* all regions

Sizes 10-16/Body yellow olive (BCS 41)/Hackle olive or dark dun/ Wing pale yellow olive (BCS 38), Matches adults of *Isoperla* and others, all regions

Hair Wing Stonefly: Dressing

Hook: Sizes 2-10, 3XL

Thread: 3/0 or 6/0, depending upon hook size, color to match body

Tail and Underbody: Natural colored deer body hair

Overbody: Fur dubbing mixed with 10 to 15% undyed sparkle yarn; a strand of appropriately colored yarn may be used in place of the dubbing

Hackle: Cock hackle wound over thorax and trimmed top and bottom

Wing: Woodchuck or badger preferred, other similar colored hairs may also be used

Hair Wing Stonefly: Most Used Sizes/Overbody Color/Hackle Color/ Naturals Matched and Regions Used

Sizes 6-8/Overbody pastel orange (BCS 70)/Hackle dark ginger/ Matches Amber Stoneflies and Golden Stoneflies of family Perlidae, all regions

Sizes 2-4/Overbody pastel orange (BCS 70)/Hackle black/Matches Giant Black Stonefly (*Pteronarcys dorsata),* Northeast, Southeast, Lake States, Midsouth

Sizes 2-8/Overbody deep orange (BCS 77)/Hackle black/Matches Salmonflies (*Pteronarcys californica* and *Pteronarcella* spp.), Northern Rockies, Southern Rockies, Pacific

Sizes 8-10/Overbody golden olive (BCS 41)/Hackle dark ginger/ Matches Olive Stoneflies or Willowflies of family Perlidae, all regions

Hair Wing Stonefly: Tying Instructions

1. Clamp the hook in the vise and wrap the thread to the standard position and then wrap back to the head of the fly.

2. For the underbody, use deer body hair that has tan to dark tan tips. Select a clump of hair and stack it to even the tips. Cut the clump to length so that with the butt end at the rear of the hook eye, the tips will extend rearward far enough to form a tail about 1/3 the length of the hook shank.

3. Tie in the clump as for an extended body mayfly (page 49) and spiral the thread rearward. It's

important that the deer hair underbody cover the entire length of the hook shank. Do not extend the body off the hook, however. When you reach the rear of the hook, hold the tips of the hair up and wrap the thread around the body 10 to 12 times to lock the hair securely. The tips of the hair will flare and form a rather bushy tail (*Figure 6-11*).

Figure 6-11. *The deer hair underbody in place.*

4. Spin dubbing rather thickly onto the thread; don't try to spin it all on at once, apply it to the thread in several layers. Note: sparkle yarn may be substituted for the dubbing.

5. Hold the tail up and take the first turn of dubbing under it; this will elevate the tail so that the bottom of it is parallel with the body of the fly. Wrap the dubbing forward to the middle of the underbody, thus forming the abdomen. Keep enough pressure on the thread so that the dubbed body is tight but not so much that you deeply compress the deer hair underbody; this retains the floatability of the hair.

6. Tie in the hackle feathers; use 3 feathers on hook sizes 2 and 4, 2 feathers on smaller sizes.

7. Apply more dubbing and wrap it forward to form the thorax; end about two head spaces behind the eye (*Figure 6-12*).

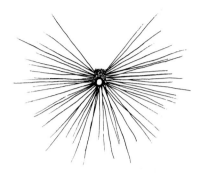

Figure 6-13. *Front view showing the "V" cut in the top of the hackle.*

remove either from the clump. Trim the butt end of the clump so that the final wing length will extend to the tips of the fly's tail.

13. Hold the clump of fur so that the butt end is even with the rear of the hook's eye and tie it in just ahead of the thorax with a dozen

Figure 6-12. *The dubbed overbody in place, hackles ready to be wrapped.*

8. Palmer the first hackle forward in as many turns as possible and tie off at the head and cut away the excess.

9. Wind the second hackle palmer style, but reverse the direction of wrap so that it forms "X's" as it crosses the first hackle. Tie off at the head and cut away the excess.

10. Wind the third hackle, if used, in the same manner as the first.

11. Trim the hackle to form a "V" on top of the fly (*Figure 6-13*); the wing will be supported in the groove of the "V".

12. Select a clump of fur for the wing; both guard hairs and dubbing fur are used in the wing so don't

wraps of thread; this should be about two head spaces behind the eye. Wrap very tightly to compress the deer hair under-body. Compressing the deer hair will cause the butt end of the wing to flare upward and form a hood which simulates the natural's head. Likewise, the wing will flare outward into a fluttering position, filling the groove of the "V" which was cut into the hackle.

14 Tie off the thread at the eye of the hook and cut it away.

15. Trim the hackle off the bottom of the fly, forming a broad "V". Liberally apply water-thin, flexible head cement to the base of the wing, the flared wing butt, the thread wraps holding the wing, and the head of the fly (*Figure 6-14*).

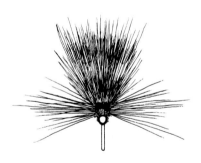

Figure 6-14. *The finished Hair Wing Stonefly; side view, front view, top view.*

CADDISFLIES

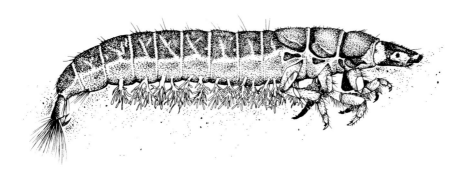

Figure 7-1. *A typical caddis larva showing body proportions.*

We knew they'd come in late afternoon, so we poked along the lake edge, enjoying the softness of a spring day in midsummer. There was the occasional cruiser, mostly rainbows edging along the weeds and watching for stray damsel nymphs or midge pupae. They were easy pickings, and Bob Pelzl and I alternated playing hero and photographer. It was good to be alive and be fishing one of our favorite haunts, the lakes of the Vermejo Park Ranch in northeastern New Mexico. But some of the deep relaxation we should have felt was lost in the anticipation of what we knew was to come.

As the hours crawled slowly onward, we began to get a bit edgy. Not only from anticipation, but because the wind had picked up, and huge cumulo-nimbus clouds were building over Vermejo and Culebra peaks to the North. We did not need a storm now. It was almost time. And then it happened.

Powerful winds roared in off the monstrous storms to the north and the Giant Capering Sedge hatched in numbers beyond counting. Like chunks of driven snow they whipped across the lake and into the trees. They splatted against us and peppered the water like hail. And the fish came to them in what can only be described as a feeding frenzy. The late afternoon sun shown

through the huge waves crashing against our waders, and there in each successive mountain of water was a mass of trout. They were racing around like demons possessed, snatching at the newly hatched caddises. They'd sometimes jump straight out of a wave and land nearly on us. It was insane. We could only cast fifteen or twenty feet into the gale force winds, but that was more than enough. If the fly got onto the water, a fish took it. Such was their lust for the huge caddises, that the trout slammed the fly even on a 2X tippet. We straighted hooks several times trying to horse particularly big fish. We were as frantic as the trout. Two hours flitted past like a moment, and as darkness fell, the wind dropped and the hatch slowed and stopped. That's what it can be like in the time of the caddis.

Caddisflies are enormously abundant in trout lakes and streams around the world. Many places, they are as numerous or more numerous than mayflies. In addition, they splash over the same range of sizes and colors as mayflies and often hatch in intensely concentrated numbers. Obviously such an abundant, ubiquitous creature is highly significant to the trout. However, they often receive much less attention from the fly fisher than do mayflies because caddises basically haunt the twilight and dark hours of the daily cycle. There are, however, species that hatch in the morning, during the day, or in early evening; these can provide spectacular fishing if the angler is prepared. The first step in that preparation is to understand that unlike mayflies and stoneflies which have nymph and adult stages (incomplete metamorphosis) caddisflies (also called sedges) have larva, pupa, and adult stages (complete metamorphosis). All three stages are important to the fly fisher.

LARVA

The caddis larva is wormlike, but possesses the six legs that characterize insects; the legs, however, are rather short. The well-segmented abdomen of the larva is soft and quite long, relative to the thorax and head; on average, the abdomen makes up about 75 percent of the body length, the thorax makes up nearly 15 percent, and the head only about 10 percent *(Figure 7-1)*.

Caddis larvae are among the best-known, immature aquatic insects because many species build a portable, silken case covered with twigs, sand grains, or other debris. The silk is produced by glands located near the larva's mouth; the name caddis comes from the Old French *cadas,* meaning silk. The case provides camouflage, but more importantly, the insect can beat its gills or wiggle its body and create a strong flow of water through the case. This has permitted caddises to invade slow moving streams and lakes where ambient currents would not provide sufficient oxygen. Most species crawl about, with their head and thorax, and perhaps an abdominal segment or two, sticking out of the case *(Figure 7-2)*. Some lake dwelling species build a case of only silk and use their specially modified legs to swim about among aquatic plants.

Larvae of all species of caddises are vulnerable to predation by trout. Fish scrape the case building forms off the bottom as a matter of course. The bits of twigs and grains of sand often found in a trout's stomach are not accidentally ingested, they are the remains of caddis cases. In addition to grubbing them out of the interstices of the bottom, the trout feed on free-drifting, cased larvae. Called behavioral drift, this drifting phenomenon is believed to be associated with population dispersion. Several species of cased larvae, including the widely distributed American Grannom (*Brachycentrus* spp.) and the western Little Dark Sedge (*Oligophlebodes* spp.) are common participants in behavioral drift. In addition, larvae of the American Grannom often disperse by attaching a silken line to the bottom and letting themselves out slowly in the currents. The behavioral drift of cased caddises is a daytime phenomenon, and anglers fishing appropriate, cased imitations during these times can be quite successful.

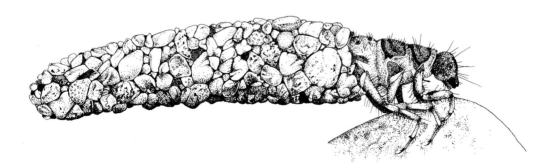

***Figure* 7-2.** *The larva protrudes from the case when drifting or moving about the bottom.*

Some cased caddises leave their cases and drift naked in the currents. For example, as larvae of *Glossosoma* spp. grow, they vacate their cases and build a larger one; when they are out of their cases, these pinkish larvae are highly subject to drifting. During the mid-afternoons of June and July, larvae of the Giant Orange Sedge (*Dicosmoecus* spp.) are an extremely important component of the drift in streams of the Northern Rockies and Pacific region. The huge yellow-orange larvae (up to 1 3/8 inches long) fill the currents with tasty tidbits for even the biggest trout. Gary LaFontaine's book "Caddisflies" presents the best discussion of the drift behavior of this and other species of sedges.

It's a wise idea to carry a pattern like the Peeking Caddis to simulate the commonly found cased larvae. I've used this pattern successfully many times in lakes and streams around the world. In streams, the fly is fished dead drift. I use a four- to five-foot, compound tippet and a strike indicator. The compound tippet consists of two pieces; a 6-8 inch, light-weight, terminal piece attached to a long, heavier piece. For example, if I want to fish the fly on a four-foot tippet ending in 4X, I'll use 3 1/2 feet of 3X and a 6-inch piece of 4X. If needed, shot can be added to the 3X portion just above the knot connecting it to the 4X. The indicator is secured at the point where the 3X is tied to the leader body. This is my standard rig for dead-drift nymphing, and I use it for all types of flies, not just caddises.

In lakes, I normally use the Peeking Caddis when casting to sighted fish. In 1987, Bob and Beverly Pelzl and Nancy and I were fishing in New Zealand. We'd found a lake with some very big fish in it, and as we stalked the edges, I spotted several large, case-building caddises crawling about near the shore. I knotted a suitable imitation to my 3X tippet and continued watching for cruisers. A distinct, slow-moving disturbance of the water about 40 feet out indicated the presence of a fish, and I placed the fly about 15 feet ahead of it. As the disturbance

passed the fly's position, I saw the leader pull under. It turned out to be a 13 1/2 pound brown trout—one of the small ones for that lake. Why is it we always catch the small ones?

The peeking design I prefer is modeled on concepts developed by Rene and Bonnie Harrop, brilliant, master tiers from Saint Anthony, Idaho. Their observations on the feeding behavior of trout, especially on the highly selective rainbows of Henry's Fork of the Snake, have lead to many refreshingly new tying concepts. For the case of their peeking larva, they use an underbody of tinsel chenille with an overbody of dubbed fur. The bits of tinsel stick out through the fur and suggest bits of mica or other flashy materials that caddises often incorporate into their cases. It's a remarkably creative technique. This design is superb for larger hook sizes, but makes a rather bulky body on smaller sizes. For this reason, I have abandoned the tinsel chenille in favor of a pattern that uses the hair leg technique to form the abdomen. In place of the hair legs, however, I substitute short chunks of Crystal Hair, Flashabou, Krystal Flash, metallic sewing thread, or similar material. After twisting the loop tight and forming the abdomen, the flashy "legs" are trimmed to the same diameter as the body. This technique additionally allows the tier to use a wide range of flashy materials in the abdomen.

To get the fly down fast and keep it down where the naturals are normally seen drifting, I weight the case portion of the fly with lead wire. This also causes the fly to ride case down, head up, a position often assumed by drifting larvae.

The "peeking" larva is an important component of the pattern. A small portion of the abdomen along with the thorax and head should be imitated in the finished fly. This design is much more productive than one which simulates only the caddis case. I use dubbing for the "peeking" portion of the insect. Since the legs are so short, they can be adequately simulated by feather barbs at the throat.

Peeking Caddis: Dressing

Hook: Size 2-10, 3XL

Thread: 6/0, black or dark brown

Case: Coarse fur dubbing with guard hairs left in, blended with sparkle yarn, spun on dubbing loop with pieces of Crystal Hair, Flashabou, Krystal Flash, metallic sewing thread, etc., inserted like hair legs; weighted with lead wire; trimmed to shape

Peeking Larva: Fur dubbing blended with sparkle yarn

Legs: Barbs of pheasant tail feather tied in at throat

Peeking Caddis: Most Used Sizes/Case Materials/Materials for Peeking Caddis/ Naturals Matched and Regions Used

Sizes 2-6/Case made from blend of fox squirrel and hare's mask and coarse, tan sparkle yarns to give overall sand color (BCS 61) with bits of gold, pearlescent, copper, or silver flashy material (or a mixture of these)/Peeking larva with yellow-orange abdomen (BCS 47) and brown thorax (BCS 87)/Matches cased larva of the Giant Orange Sedge (*Dicosmoecus* spp.), Northern Rockies, Pacific

Sizes 2-10/Case as above/Peeking caddis with bright green abdomen (BCS 19) and black thorax, or peeking larva with watery tan abdomen (BCS 91) and dark red-brown thorax (BCS 66)/These two colors match a wide range of larvae that build sand grain cases, all regions

Sizes 2-10/Case made from blend of dark brown mink, coarse olive brown yarn (BCS 31) and coarse black sparkle yarn or any other blend to give a black-olive-brownish mix, with bits of silver, dark green, purple, black, or brown flashy material (or a mixture of these)/Peeking larvae with bright green abdomen (BCS 19) and black thorax, or peeking larvae with watery tan abdomen (BCS 91) and dark red-brown thorax (BCS 66)/These two colors match a wide range of larvae that build plant-fragment cases, all regions

Peeking Caddis: Tying Instructions

1. Clamp the hook in the vise and wrap the thread to the standard position.

2. Weight the rear half of the hook shank with lead wire and wrap over it with the tying thread (page 30); finish with the tying thread slightly behind the standard position (*Figure 7-3*).

3. Form a dubbing loop and spin the dubbing for the case onto one side of the loop.

4. Insert pieces of flashy material into the loop at right angles to the thread and spread them out along the length of the loop (page 32). I normally use pieces about 3/4 inch long—they're easy to handle. Don't use too many pieces—6 to 12 are all

that's necessary. Remember, each piece has two ends and so will show up twice in the finished case.

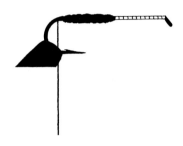

Figure 7-3. *The rear half of the hook is weighted.*

5. Twist the loop tight and wind it forward over the rear 3/5 of the hook shank; secure it with the tying thread and cut away the excess.

6. Form the peeking abdomen. It should cover 1/2 of the remaining hook and should be about 3/4 of the diameter of the finished case.

7. Form the thorax; it should be of the same diameter as the abdomen and should cover the remainder of the hook; the eye of the hook represents the natural's head.

8. Tie in the pheasant tail barbs at the throat (page 37).

9. Tie off the thread and cut it away. Cement the head.

10. Roughen the case with a dubbing brush and then trim the case to shape (*Figure 7-4*).

Figure 7-4. *The Peeking Caddis; side view, front view.*

In addition to the case building caddises, there are stream species that do not build a case (free-living) or which build a permanently stationary home attached to a silken net (net-builders). The net sieves food from the currents. The best known free-living caddis larva is the Green Rock Worm (*Rhyacophila* spp.). This bright green insect lives in fast currents and lacks gills *(Figure 7-5)*. The net builders fall into several groups, but by far the most universal are those of the family Hydropsychidae. These have prominent gills along the undersides of their abdomens (see Figure 7-1). Their nets are found attached to rocks in the swift flowing portions of streams across North America *(Figure 7-6)*. This is perhaps the most important family of caddisflies because these insects are frequently the most abundant caddises in any given stream. Both free-living and net-building caddises have large anal hooks that they use to help them cling tightly to the bottom.

Trout feel quite comfortable about eating a free-living caddis larva that's been spotted crawling about in the stones of the bottom or a net-building larva out harvesting the food from its silken meshwork. Imitations of these insects are a great choice when fishing riffle water. And, like the case-makers, there are several species of these naked larvae that participate in behavioral drift. Trout feed on them regularly. In fact, anglers of the Lake States frequently employ, with great success, the bright imitations of the Green Rock Worm during fall and spring steelhead and salmon runs.

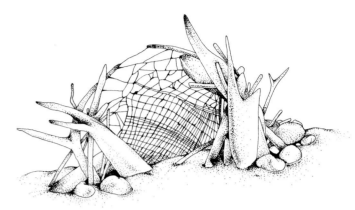

Figure 7-6. *Larvae of the Hydropsychidae make nets to strain the currents for food.*

For free-living and net-building larvae, and for cased larvae that are drifting without the case, I use the Fur Caddis Larva: a dubbed fur pattern ribbed with wire. It's an easy matter to brush out the abdomen to simulate gills or leave it unbrushed to represent species without gills. Uncased larvae normally assume a somewhat curved position; the head is tucked under and the end of the abdomen curved slightly. The anal hooks are extended ready to grasp any object they contact. For this reason, I tie the Fur Caddis Larva on a curved hook or carry the body onto the bend of a standard hook.

I normally fish this design dead drift on a four- to five-foot compound tippet with a strike indicator. In rivers like the Bighorn and Bow, where caddisflies are legion, this simple design has yielded many exciting hours. For taking BIG trout on an insect imitation in North America, Gary LaFontaine rates as his number one choice the huge, yellow-orange-bodied imitation of the drifting larvae of the Giant Orange Sedge (*Dicosmoecus* spp.).

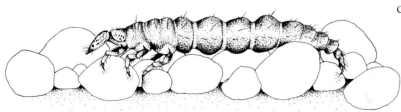

Figure 7-5. *The larva of the Green Rock Worm.*

Fur Caddis Larva: Dressing

Hook: Sizes 2-16; curved larval hook or English bait hook; if a standard hook is used, begin the abdomen at the extended position

Thread: 6/0, same color as thorax

Abdomen: Fur blended with sparkle yarn; weighted with lead wire if desired (the wire rib adds a bit of weight); brushed out on underside to represent gills if necessary

Rib: Fine wire (30 or 32 gauge)

Thorax: Peacock herl

Legs: Pheasant tail barbs tied in at the throat

Fur Caddis Larva: Most Used Sizes/Colors of Abdomen and Rib/ Naturals Matched and Regions Used

Sizes 2-16/Abdomen orange (BCS 70), rib gold or copper/In sizes 2-6 matches free drifting larvae of the Giant Orange Sedge (*Dicosmoecus* spp), Northern Rockies, Pacific; in smaller sizes represents a number of widespread genera in families Philopotamidae and Polycentropodidae, all regions

Sizes 8-16/Abdomen bright green (BCS 19)—fluorescent if possible/ Rib silver/Matches the Green Rock Worm (*Rhyacophila* spp.), all regions

Sizes 8-16/Abdomen olive brown (BCS 33), rib silver; or Abdomen pale gray (BCS 116), rib silver; or

Abdomen blended fur from hare's mask, rib copper/Matches various genera of Hydropsychidae (these are by far the most widespread non-cased caddis larvae), all regions

Sizes 12-16/Abdomen pinkish tan (BCS 72)/Rib copper/Matches free drifting larvae of *Glossosoma* spp., all regions

Sizes 8-16/Abdomen pale watery tan (BCS 91)/Rib copper/this pattern really matches the larvae of many cased species, and although the fish rarely see them uncased, they take this fly very well (perhaps also as a horsefly larva or other similar appearing creature), all regions

Fur Caddis Larva: Tying Instructions

1. Clamp the hook in the vise and wrap the thread to the rear of the hook.

2. Tie in the wire rib on top of the shank; extend the butt end of the rib forward to the front of the abdomen (3/4 of the length of the hook). Wrap the thread forward to the front of the abdomen to secure the end of the wire rib.

3. Weight the front half of the abdomen with lead wire, if desired; secure it with the tying thread (page 30), and end with the thread at the rear of the hook. If no lead is added, simply wrap the thread back to the center of the shank.

4. Spin dubbing for the abdomen onto the thread and then finish wrapping the thread to the rear of the hook (page 31).

5. Wrap the dubbing forward to form the abdomen over the rear 3/4 of the hook shank.

6. Tie in 1 to 3 pieces (depending upon hook size) of the best peacock herl you have; wind forward to form the thorax and tie off at the head. Clip away the excess.

7. Wrap the rib forward over the abdomen *and* thorax and secure at the head of the fly. Cut away the excess. Winding the rib over the peacock herl of the thorax greatly strengthens this material.

> *Speed Tying Tip:* I love wire ribs. The wire not only toughens the fly and adds weight, but it doesn't have to be tied off. When you get the rib to the front of the thorax, just wrap several turns tightly around the shank (like it was the tying thread). Then cut away the end.

8. Apply a throat of 6-8 pheasant tail barbs to suggest legs (page 37).

9. Finish the head, cut away the tying thread, and apply head cement *(Figure 7-7)*.

Figure 7-7. *The finished Fur Caddis Larva; side view and front view.*

PUPA

Caddis larvae normally live a year. When mature, the cased forms seal themselves in their cases and transform to the pupa. Uncased forms build a pupation chamber. Nancy and I have kept an artificial stream aquarium (a fluvarium) and watched in fascination as free-living larvae sealed themselves against the glass and metamorphosed into pupae. Not much happens the first few days, but then a wondrous process takes place. The abdomen shortens, the legs lengthen, wing pads sprout and grow, and almost invisible antennae extend enormously. Three week later the fully developed pupa cuts its way out of the case *(Figure 7-8)*.

Some species head to shore before the adult bursts out of the pupal skin, but many make this transformation at the water's surface. To assist themselves on the ascent from bottom to surface, most species pump air between the pupal husk and the adult within. During this time the pupa drifts along the bottom of the stream. Once buoyant, the insect heads for the film, the legs of the pupal shell beating swiftly, crewed by the adult within. When this pharate adult, as it is correctly called, reaches the surface, the pupal shuck pops open between the shoulders, and the winged adult hops out, shakes itself off, and darts away. And the trout? They're going crazy, rushing about snatching the drifting pupae near the bottom, grabbing the ascending insects in midwater, or lunging at emergers in the film.

Often the rush of its desperation carries the trout into the air in a splashy, awkward jump.

The behavior of the pharate adult is an obvious trigger to the feeding trout, but so is its rather unique appearance. The air inside the pupal skin masks the wing pads and gives the dual creature a gleaming aurora through which the body of the adult shimmers like a desert mirage. The elongate, wildly pumping legs and flowing antennae impart a definite sense of frantic motion to the darting insect. The trout become fixated on these most obvious characteristics.

For well over a century, the English have used soft hackles to mimic the flailing legs of the pharate adult on its way to the film. The first really influential fly fishing literature that discussed soft hackle flies was Charles Cotton's addendum to Walton's 1676 edition of "The Compleat Angler." However, it wasn't until 1857, when the Scottish angler W. C. Stewart wrote "The Practical Angler," that using soft hackles on flies became recognized as a distinctive and separate tying style. Most wet flies of Stewart's time used cock hackle (either as a hackle or as legs), but for dressing his "spiders," Stewart eschewed the stiff hackles and chose hen hackles, or more preferably, the body feathers of a variety of small, wild birds. He preferred these feathers because of their softness, and because they came in a wide variety of colors (see Chapter 14). He was convinced that the soft hackle imparted a moving, lifelike quality that no cock hackle or hen hackle could provide (page 41).

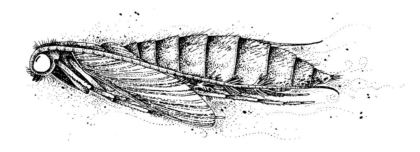

Figure 7-8. *The mature caddis pupa is dramatically different than the larva.*

There was a gap in Stewart's understanding, however. He felt that his soft-hackle patterns most likely represented the arachnid for which he named them: spiders. But one of Stewart's most dedicated disciples, T. E. Pritt (who lived in the north country of England), clearly understood the reason for the appeal of these flies to the trout. "Trout undoubtedly take the (soft) hackle fly for the insect just rising from the pupa in a half-drowned state; the opening and closing of the fibers of the feathers give it an appearance of vitality, which even the most dexterous fly fisher will fail to impart to the winged imitation." Clearly, Pritt was using the soft-hackle fly as an emerger.

Pritt built directly from Stewart's work, employing the same angling tactics but expanding the fly selection to match the naturals. The body was of silk thread (occasionally of dubbing or herl). Hackle selection was considered critical, and Pritt's pattern list reads like a who's who of the bird world. These classic soft-hackle patterns have continued to be wonderful imitations of emerging aquatic insects. For a good discussion of the flies, the tying techniques, and the fishing methods, see Sylvester Nemes' books, "The Soft-Hackled Fly" and "The Soft-Hackled Fly Addict."

The first soft-hackle advocate of note in this country was Jim Leisenring. Leisenring had studied the works of Stewart and Pritt and was convinced of the power of soft hackle flies. In "The Art of Tying the Wet Fly" he parroted his mentors' findings: "...the wing is the least important part of the fly....I could always, and still can, catch more fish on a wingless imitation.... Therefore, the careful fly tier will select his hackle according to its ability to *act* and *look* alive." Nor did Leisenring use any old soft hackle for his patterns. Like Stewart and Pritt, he was very picky about the feathers he chose. He carried a notebook with feathers taped in it so he could observe their colors under streamside light.

Some of the flies Leisenring tied were fashioned directly after Stewart's, but most were dressed to mimic the insects Leisenring collected along his favorite streams. Rather than use a simple, silk thread body on his flies, Leisenring preferred delicate, fuzzy bodies dubbed of various types of furs. He explained, "...bodies of artificial flies are most deadly when, in addition to color, they imitate the texture, translucence, and flash of the natural fly as much as possible."

Dubbed furs have been the choice of many tiers since Leisenring's time. In "How to Take Trout on Wet Flies and Nymphs," Ray Ovington describes pupal designs originated by his friend Ed Sens. To simulate the gasses in the pupal shuck, Sens dubbed on a delicate overbody of gray muskrat fur and brushed it out well, nicely suggesting the expanded, gleaming exoskeleton. Larry Solomon and Eric Leiser also recommended dubbed fur pupae in their book "The Caddis and the Angler."

But pupal designs took a leap forward when Gary LaFontaine first described the marvelous properties of Dupont Antron (commonly called sparkle yarns) in his benchmark book "Caddisflies," a compendium of careful observations and thoughtful fly designs. At the time of Gary's book, Bob Pelzl and I were examining the behavior of midge pupae, both when we fished together on the Vermejo lakes and when we independently fished other waters. We compared notes and chattered excitedly about each new observation and potentially useful design. Needless to say, sparkle yarns gave us cause for excitement. We tried LaFontaine's folded yarn technique on midge pupa, but the resultant imitation was too bulky. A technique more like that of Sens seemed a logical choice. It made a fine fly, but somehow still didn't satisfy my wants. As we continued to experiment with midge pupae designs, I stumbled onto a process that yielded the look I wanted. It's so simple that I'm amazed it took me so long to think of it. After a thin abdomen is applied, a robust thorax is created with sparkle yarn dubbing. The filaments of this dubbing should be twice the length of the hook. The thorax is then brushed out so the sparkling filaments trail back around the abdomen. It's proven a most successful design for midge pupae.

It also makes a highly effective caddis pupa. Not only does the sheer negligee of sparkle yarn reflect light in the same fashion as the air inside the pupal husk, but the filaments wave and pulse, adding additional, lifelike motion to the fly. After the body is formed, a soft hackle is wound in place at the head of the fly to simulate the legs and antennae of the pupa.

The Leisenring Lift was developed to simulate the bottom drifting/rapid ascent of the pharate adult and is still the best way to seduce stream trout that are feeding on the naturals. In stillwaters, the fly is very successful when fished with the Strip/Tease tactic (slowly strip the line while vibrating the rod tip). This method causes the soft hackle to vibrate dramatically.

Caddises smaller than size 18 are collectively called the microcaddises. They're stream insects that can produce some of the most confounding hatches of any insect. The fish's feeding behavior is strongly suggestive of a midge hatch, often duping the angler into selecting the wrong pattern. Watch carefully for the tiny adults before diving into the fly box. If the fish do seem to be selecting microcaddises, try the pupa fished just under the film, either dead drift or with a down and across presentation.

Sparkle Caddis Pupa: Dressing

Hook: Sizes 4-24, standard shank length, 3XL may be substituted in larger sizes.

Thread: 3/0 to 8/0, depending upon hook size

Abdomen: Blended fur and sparkle yarn or just sparkle yarn, dubbed

Thorax: Dubbed sparkle yarn cut twice length of hook shank; weighted with lead wire; on sizes 8 and larger, sparkle yarn is spun in a dubbing loop

Hackle: Appropriately colored soft hackle (see Chapter 14 for listing and possible substitutions)

Sparkle Caddis Pupa: Most Used Sizes/Color of Body/Hackle/ Naturals Matched and Regions Used

Sizes 10-24/Body bright green (BCS 18)/Hackle mottled grouse feather/Matches American Grannom (*Brachycentrus* spp.),

the Tan Sedge (*Glossosoma* spp.), White Miller (*Nectopsyche* spp.), some Microcaddises (family Hydroptilidae), all regions

Sizes 10-24/Body yellow (BCS 49)/ Hackle mottled grouse /Matches a host of caddises in families Lepidostomatidae, Helicopsychidae, Hydropsychidae, Hydroptilidae, Leptoceridae, Limnephilidae, Polycentropodidae, and Psychomyiidae, all regions

Sizes 10-24/Body olive green (BCS 20)/Hackle coot, dorsal marginal covert feather /Matches various species of Hydropsychidae, Hydroptilidae, and Leptoceridae

Sizes 10-18/Body light brown (BCS 100)/Hackle chukkar, dorsal marginal covert feather/Matches species in families Hydropsychidae, Lepidostomatidae, and Limnephilidae, all regions

Sizes 8-14/Body orange (BCS 73)/ Hackle rusty pheasant rump in larger sizes, woodcock ventral coverts in smaller sizes/Matches species of the families Polycentropodidae, Limnephilidae, and some Phryganeidae, all regions

Sizes 14-18/Body black/Hackle crow or jackdaw dorsal marginal covert feather/Matches species of families Hydroptilidae and Psychomyiidae, the Black Dancer (*Mystacides* spp.), and the Little Black Sedge (*Chimarra* spp.), all regions

Sparkle Caddis Pupa: Tying Instructions

1. Clamp the hook in the vise and wrap the thread to the center of the shank.

2. Weight the front 1/4 of the hook shank with lead wire and secure with the thread (page 30).

3. Apply dubbing for the abdomen and finish wrapping the thread to the standard position at the rear of the hook (page 31).

4. Wind the dubbing forward to form the abdomen, ending at the rear of the lead wire. Keep the abdomen relatively narrow in diameter.

5. Cut a chunk of sparkle yarn twice the length of the hook shank; use these filaments to form the thorax. The finished thorax should be 1 1/2 to 2 times the diameter of the abdomen.

6. For hook sizes 10-22, spin the dubbing onto the thread in the normal fashion and wind it on to form the thorax.

7. For hook sizes 4-8, form a dubbing loop and insert 25 to 30 sparkle yarn filaments in it and spread them out, as if using them for hair legs (page 32). Twist the loop tight and wind on to form the thorax.

8. Brush out the filaments of the abdomen to give it a fuzzy appearance, and then brush out the filaments of the thorax such that they flow back around the abdomen to the rear of the hook. The filaments of the thorax must be twice as long as the hook so that they remain attached after being brushed out.

9. Apply the soft hackle as for the Wet/Dry Fly (page 42).

10. Finish the head, tie off the thread, cut it away, and apply cement (Figure 7-9).

Figure 7-9. *The finished Sparkle Pupa; side view and front view.*

ADULTS

Caddis adults are quite easy to recognize. On the wing, they look like tiny moths; at rest they hold their wings tentlike over their abdomens *(Figure 7-10)*. The wings are clothed in tiny hairs (hence the name of the caddis order, Trichoptera, "hair wing"). Adults live an average of a month, feeding on plant nectar and other liquids. They return to the water on a daily basis to drink, and females may mate and lay eggs several times. Thus it is that fish see adult caddises on a very regular basis. An adult caddis imitation, therefore, makes a good searching pattern during opportunistic periods.

Nuptial flights occur near or over the water. The female may lay eggs by alighting on the surface and extruding them. In some instances, especially in stillwaters, the female may run over the surface to scatter the eggs. Most commonly, however, the female goes underwater and deposits the eggs directly on the bottom. To do this, the female either crawls underwater or dive bombs into the stream or lake and swims to the bottom. Often in the dive-bombing species, the females will fail to get through the surface and

will flutter about, a bit stunned, before trying again. The fish are extremely alert to this behavior.

The submersed insect carries a bubble of air with it and can stay down an hour or more, crawling about over the bottom and sticking its eggs to rocks and other items. The bubble of air is held beneath the wings and over the surface of the thorax, creating a distinct, silvery sheath around the body of the ovipositing female. Such flashy dress makes the females easily seen by foraging trout.

Because caddises can be both emerging and ovipositing during the twilight of dawn and dusk, there can be some rather confusing feeding behavior on the part of the trout. The fly fisher must be very alert and willing to change flies often, first trying pupa, then emerged adults, then the diving female patterns. Once you unlock the puzzle, however, the fishing can be astounding.

By-and-large, caddis adults are rather mobile critters. They fly extremely well and, as mentioned, are very active when egg laying. Thus, fly designs of the adults must reflect the need to make presentations that include active

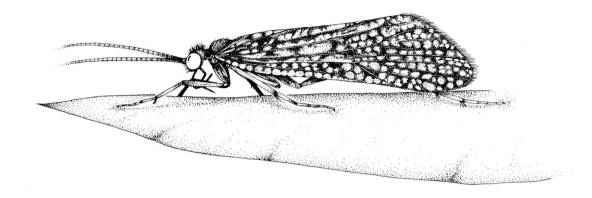

Figure 7-10. *The appearance of the adult caddis at rest is diagnostic.*

retrieves. I dress three patterns for the adults. The Devil Bug is a great all around pattern that can represent an emerging or egg laying caddis (both on the surface and underwater). The Poly Caddis mimics the fully winged adult and is also a good choice for egg laying insects. It can be dressed in considerably smaller sizes than the Devil Bug. The Diving Caddis is specifically designed to imitate the underwater, egg-laying female.

Devil Bug

The Devil Bug had its beginning in desperation. It was 1976 and Bob Pelzl, Nancy, Jason, and I were teaching fly fishing schools at the Vermejo Park Ranch. I had ordered 12 dozen Humpies for the students to use during the daily hatches of the Giant Capering Sedge (*Banksiola crotchi*); the flies didn't arrive. So, the night before our first instructed fishing day, we were tying flies like crazy people. About 11 pm, I decided to tie a hackleless version of the humpy modelled after an eastern brook trout pattern called the Cooper Bug. However, I modified the design to give the fly more buoyancy and to keep it from diving under when stripped over the surface. I started tying it with a thread underbody, but Bob suggested we add dubbing to increase the color range and provide the extra measure of life. And so it was. It proved to be the perfect design for the big caddises. Not only

was it the ideal shape for the emerging caddis, but it was perfect for the egg laying female. The fish went crazy for it, and students that had never caught a trout suddenly found themselves attached to 2-4 pound fish with regularity. In fact, the fly was so good, we began teasing about it being "the ol' Devil Bug," and the name stuck. Soon, we were tying it to imitate smaller caddises we saw on the lakes, and the next year we were using it to imitate stream caddises. It's been highly effective, taking big trout across North America and other waters around the globe.

When Jason and I were planning and taping "The Fabulous Bighorn" video, we decided that the ending should be a grand finale with one fish after another coming to net. We knew the caddises would be hatching and that diving females would be egg laying in late afternoon, and so we began watching for big, rising fish. We found a spot with deep, slick water next to shore filled with 15- to 23-inch trout feeding eagerly. The trout took the Devil Bug so well that we would pick out a fish, get the cameras ready, make a cast or two, and get the action we wanted. It was every fly fisher's and every cinematographer's dream rolled into one fabulous event.

While the Bighorn's fish wanted the Devil Bug presented dead drift, in other situations the trout may want it fished quite actively. This is especially true when the trout are rigorously pursuing diving females. In slow-moving water, a tiny microshot can be added ahead of the fly to make it dive when the line is stripped. In riffles, the shot can be omitted and the fly delivered down and across so that the swinging line will pull the fly under and work it at the same time. As the fly submerges, the clump of deer hair at the head catches a bubble of air which forms around the body of the diving fly. The effect is most lifelike.

Mike Dry and I were fishing Canada's Bow River and stumbled into an astonishingly heavy flight of caddises just at dusk. The fish rose in numbers that stupefied us. But the Devil Bug came through. At first we just let drag have its way with the fly and took whatever fish came along. But soon big snouts were poking out in the near-shore shallows, and we began hunting individual fish. The best of the evening came to Mike's fly—24 inches of heather-hued brown trout. Not bad for a size 14 fly.

Although it's a simple, rather funny-appearing fly, it's so successful as a dry fly because it nicely simulates what the trout sees when it's looking for emerging or egg laying caddises. Gary LaFontaine has a wonderful description of a trout's-eye view of the adult caddis in his encyclopedic book "Caddisflies." Anyone interested in these insects (meaning all fly fishers) should study this book with utmost care. Gary discovered that the trout keys in on the width of a stationary adult; from the edge of one trailing wing to the edge of the other. Thus, to the trout, the caddis looks quite bulky. The folded deer-hair body of the Devil Bug nicely simulates this perceived bulk. In addition, he found that when an egg-laying female runs over the surface, the moving legs and the tips of the wings (which drag in the water) cause twin streaks of light on the surface. These scintillating slashes on the film are a strong trigger to a trout that is hunting active caddises. The deer hair body and tail of the Devil Bug create a definite light slash when the fly is moved over the surface. In addition, the tail may suggest the partially cast husk of an emerging insect. The clump of deer hair at the front of the fly keeps the moving fly riding high like the natural; it also simulates the partially unfolded wings of an emerger.

Devil Bug: Dressing

Hook: Sizes 8-18, standard shank length

Thread: 6/0 or 8/0 depending upon hook size; color to match dubbing

Body: Deer body hair for tails, underbody, and back; dubbing for body, colors to match naturals

Devil Bug: Most Used Sizes/Hair Color/ Dubbing Color/ Naturals Matched and Regions Used

Size 8-18/Natural dark gray brown deer hair/Dubbing bright green (BCS 18)/In larger sizes matches Giant Capering Sedge (*Banksiola crotchi*) of western lakes; in smaller sizes matches American Grannom (*Brachycentrus* spp.), the White Miller (*Nectopsyche* spp.), the Green Rock Worm (family Rhyacophilidae), and others, all regions

Sizes 10-18/Dark gray (BCS 114) deer hair/dubbing olive green (BCS 20)/Matches various genera of the families Hydropsychidae, Leptoceridae, Rhyacophilidae, and the genera *Psilotreta* and *Wormaldia*, all regions

Sizes 10-18/Natural gray brown deer hair/dubbing yellow (BCS 49)/ Matches a host of caddises from various families: Lepidostomatidae, Helicopsychidae, Hydropsychidae, Leptoceridae, Limnephilidae, Polycentropodidae, Psychomyiidae, and others, all regions

Sizes 8-14/Rusty brown deer hair (BCS 63)/Orange dubbing (BCS 73)/ Matches various species in families Polycentropodidae, Limnephilidae, and Phryganeidae, all regions

Sizes 14-18/Black deer hair/Dubbing black/Matches some Hydroptilidae and Psychomyiidae, the Black Dancer (*Mystacides* spp.), and the Little Black Sedge (*Chimarra* spp.), all regions

Devil Bug: Tying Instructions

1. Clamp the hook in the vise and wrap the thread to the standard position and then back to the front of the hook; end about two head spaces behind the eye.

2. Select a clump of deer hair for the body; the size of the clump will depend upon hook size; for a size 10 hook, the clump should be about 1/2 the diameter of a pencil. With a little practice you will quickly learn the correct amount for all hook sizes. Since the hair will be folded twice over the top of the hook, be sure it's long enough for this purpose. For hook sizes 8-12, I do not stack the tips of the hair, but for smaller sizes, the tips should be evened in a hair stacker.

3. Position the clump on top of the hook so that the tips of the hair extend rearward and form a tail about 3/4 the length of the hook shank.

4. Secure the clump tightly at the front, spiral the thread rearward, and secure the hair at the rear of the hook with 6 or so turns of thread *(Figure 7-11)*.

5. Apply the dubbing rather heavily to the thread, leaving an inch or two of bare thread between the dubbing and the hook.

6. Grasp the butt ends of the deer hair with the materials hand and fold the hair tightly back over the top of the body—do not release the butt ends.

7. Keeping the hairs tightly folded against the top of the body, secure it at the rear of the hook with 6-10 turns of thread; this will bring the dubbing up against the body *(Figure 7-12)*.

8. Retain your grasp on the butt ends of the deer hair and wrap the dubbing forward, keeping the turns tight, but not so tight as to totally compress the deer hair underbody.

9. Fold the deer hair forward over the top of the body—like a shell—and secure it at the head. Secure the hair with 6-8 turns of thread.

Speed Tying Tip: To keep the deer hair from spinning around the hook shank when it's being tied down, first wrap the thread around the hair and then around the hook (page 61).

10. Tie off in front of the butt ends of the hair, and cut away the thread.

Speed Tying Tip: Here's a chance to practice tying the finishing knot with your middle finger while holding materials out of the way with your index finger and thumb (page 23).

11. Clip the butt ends of the hair, leaving a clump equal to 1/3 the length of the hook shank.

12. To finish the fly, give the back a thorough saturating with water-thin, flexible head cement. When that's dry, coat it again *(Figure 7-13)*.

Figure 7-12. *Fold the deer hair back and secure at the rear of the hook.*

Figure 7-11. *Spiral the thread rearward.*

Figure 7-13. *The finished Devil Bug; side view, front view, top view.*

Poly Caddis

The Poly Caddis was developed before the Devil Bug. I designed it in 1972 as a take-off on Al Troth's justly famous Elk Hair Caddis. I was looking for a substitute for hair that would allow me to not only increase the range of colors but to easily tie the fly in sizes smaller than an 18. The properties of polypropylene dubbing had recently been introduced to fly tiers by Doug Swisher and Carl Richards in their book "Selective Trout," and it seemed to me it would also make great winging material. Macrame was in vogue then, and it was an easy matter to find polypropylene cording. The coarse fibers made great wings. Slightly kinky, translucent, and available in a spectrum of colors, it nicely suggests the delicately haired, membranous wing of the natural. It has the correct shape when seen from underwater. It's a great fly to simulate the fully emerged adult or a female that is laying eggs at the water's surface. When pulled underwater, it catches a bubble of air and carries it down, just like the natural.

Brian Clarke and I were fishing England's Test and enjoying a fruitful day of hunting rising fish. We took them on a wide variety of patterns, from Loop Wing Duns to Para-Ants. At six o'clock we paused for a light supper of french bread, tomatoes (that's toe-mot-toes), cheese, and Harp lager.

"It's been a wonderful day," I told Brian, "thanks for letting me share it with you."

"Just wait," he replied, "the best is yet to come." "The sedges will appear just about dark and there'll be a heavy rise of fish."

True to Brian's prediction, the caddises filled the evening air. At the last rays of the setting sun, the gravid females began diving into the film while simultaneously other caddises began emerging. Absolute shoals of trout in the one-to four-pound range were coursing around the head of the pool I had selected, slashing at the flies and often leaping clear of the water. At first, I tried to cover individual fish, but did poorly because they were moving so quickly. But then I simply cast the Poly Caddis down and across and let it drag. It was a bit like shooting fish in a barrel and a bit like the lottery. A fish on nearly every cast and with just as much chance for a big one as for a small one. I was ever so grateful to Brian for the opportunity to fish the Test, but Oh! I didn't want to leave when the appointed hour came.

The Poly Caddis is a great imitation for the delicate little microcaddises. Over the last two decades it has provided me with many wonderful memories, like the time five of us caught and released over 500 trout from the Yellowstone River in one incredible day's fishing. The trout were feeding on size 18-20 sedges when we arrived at 7 am and were still feeding on them when we left at 9 pm. It was a good thing we had a well-equipped fly tying case with us because we lost more than our share of flies that day.

Poly Caddis: Dressing

Hook: 8-24, standard shank length

Thread: 6/0 or 8/0 depending upon hook size, color of wing

Body: Fur dubbing blended with 10 to 15% undyed sparkle yarn

Hackle: Cock hackle wound over thorax X-Wing style; same color as wing; trimmed top and bottom

Wing: Polypropylene yarn tied in down-wing style

Poly Caddis: Most Used Sizes/Body Color/Wing Color/Naturals Matched and Regions Used

Sizes 10-24/Body bright green (BCS 18)/Wing tan (BCS 59)/Matches American Grannom (*Brachycentrus* spp.), the Tan Sedge (*Glossosoma* spp.), some Microcaddises (family Hydroptilidae), all regions

Sizes 10-24/Body yellow (BCS 49)/ Wing speckled brown (if mottled yarn unavailable, mark tan yarn with dark brown permanent marker)/Matches a host of caddises in families Lepidostomatidae, Helicopsychidae, Hydropsychidae, Hydroptilidae, Leptoceridae, Limnephilidae, Polycentropodidae, and Psychomyiidae, all regions

Sizes 10-24/Body olive green (BCS 20)/Wing dark gray (BCS 114)/ Matches various species of Hydropsychidae, Hydroptilidae, and Leptoceridae

Sizes 10-18/Body light brown (BCS 100)/Wing medium brown (BCS 103)/Matches species in families Hydropsychidae, Lepidostomatidae, and Limnephilidae, all regions

Sizes 12-16/Body bright green (BCS 18)/Wing white or ecru (BCS 120)/Matches White Miller (*Nectopsyche* spp.), all regions

Sizes 8-14/Body orange (BCS 73)/ Wing rusty orange (BCS 73)/ Matches species of the families Polycentropodidae, Limnephilidae, and some Phryganeidae, all regions

Sizes 14-24/Body black/Wing black/ Matches species of Hydroptilidae and Psychomyiidae, and the Black Dancer (*Mystacides* spp.) and the Little Black Sedge (*Chimarra* spp.), all regions

Poly Caddis: Tying Instructions

1. Clamp the hook in the vise and wrap the thread to the standard position.

2. Dub on the abdomen, covering the rear half of the hook shank.

3. Tie in the hackle.

4. Wind the thread forward to form the thorax.

5. Apply the hackle X-Wing style (page 54).

6. Trim all the hackle off the top of the hook.

7. Tie in the poly yarn at the head of the fly; apply it rather thickly. The yarn should lie tight against the top of the body.

8. Tie off in front of the wing butt; cut the thread away.

9. Trim the butt end of the wing to form a small clump.

10. Cut straight down across the wing to trim it to a length slightly longer than the hook; the end of the wing may be shaped to more closely imitate the natural if desired—I've never found it necessary.

11. Trim the hackle from the bottom of the fly, forming a broad "V".

12. Apply cement to the head, the clump formed by the wing butt, and the base of the wing. Turn the fly upside down and place a drop or two of head cement on the underside of the thorax to strengthen the hackle (*Figure 7-14*).

Figure 7-14. *The completed Poly Caddis; side view, front view, top view.*

For the very large adult caddises of the families Limnephilidae (the Giant Orange Sedge and others) and Phryganeidae (the Giant Rust Sedge, genus *Ptilostomis*) I revert to a hair wing pattern because poly yarn is too soft for the long wings needed on these imitations. Flies such as the Bucktail caddis have successfully matched these huge insects for many years. I tie mine like the Hair Wing Stonefly, using bucktail (not deer body hair) for the wing. Two colors dressed on 3XL hooks in sizes 4-8 will match the most encountered species of the giant sedges:

1. Rusty brown body (BCS 63), brown hackle, and rusty brown wing

2. Light ginger body (BCS 56), ginger hackle, and ginger wing.

Diving Caddis

When diving adults are egg laying, the Poly Caddis or Devil Bug works wonders, but when the adults are crawling underwater, I prefer to fish an adult imitation dead drift close to the bottom. Georges Odier has discussed the dead-drift, bottom-dredging tactics for fishing diving caddises in his book "Swimming Flies."

Since the fly is fished like a nymph and does not necessarily catch a bubble when it goes under, the angler must rely on the materials in the fly to suggest the air bubble. Undyed sparkle yarn is perfect for this purpose. Because it is the flash of the air bubble that is so important in this fly, I've only found three body colors necessary for the majority of my fishing.

Diving Caddis: Dressing

Hook: Sizes 10-16

Thread: 6/0 or 8/0, depending upon hook size, color to match body

Body: Peacock herl ribbed with fine silver wire or sparkle yarn dubbing, either yellow (BCS 49) or bright green (BCS 18); weighted with lead wire

Wing: Undyed sparkle yarn

Legs: Pheasant tail barbs tied in as a throat

Diving Caddis: Tying Instructioxns

1. Clamp the hook in the vise and wrap the thread to the standard position.

2. Weight the center portion of the hook shank with lead wire and secure with the thread (page 30).

3. Form the body, ending at the head.

4. Tie in a clump of 6-8 pheasant tail barbs at the throat to suggest legs.

5. Tie in a clump of sparkle yarn on top of the hook shank to form a wing. Tie off in front of the wing. Trim the butt end of the wing to form a short clump.

6. Trim the wing to length as for the Poly Caddis.

7. Cement the head and the butt end and base of the wing *(Figure 7-15)*.

Figure 7-15. *The completed Diving Caddis.*

DIPTERANS

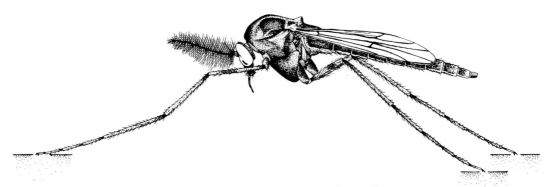

Figure 8-1. *An adult Chironomidae midge.*

Dipterans are the "two-winged" insects that include houseflies and horseflies, craneflies and blackflies, mosquitoes and midges. Dipterans, like caddises, have a complete life cycle: larva, pupa, and adult. Dipterans are also extremely abundant. In fact, aquatic systems are jammed with them. In any given lake or stream, at least fifty percent of the insect species will be dipterans; larval numbers can exceed 50,000 per square yard! This abundance means that every trout knows these insects, and that their importance to the fly fisher cannot be over emphasized. Some dipterans, like the craneflies are quite large, but the vast majority are the tiny midges.

MIDGES

Fly fishers use the term midge as a nontechnical one encompassing all the small aquatic dipterans. In terms of abundance and distribution, "midge" usually means members of the family Chironomidae *(Figure 8-1),* although other families of dipterans can also produce significant "midge" hatches. Midges are in all water systems, but are especially prevalent where the bottom is silty and where there are aquatic plants. These flies hatch in astounding numbers all season long—even if the season runs right through the winter.

Fly fishers should avoid midge hatches because: (A) big fish won't eat such small fare, or (B) there's little chance of a fish taking the fly, or (C) it's too difficult to land a good fish on delicate tackle, or (D) all of the above. Actually the correct answer is (E), none of the above. Big trout do eat midges, they will take your fly, and they can be landed. For example, a friend, Jim Sellers, who lives in Greensboro, North Carolina, took a 26 1/8-inch rainbow (yes, 1/8 inch) from a stream in his area on a size 26 Sparkle Midge Pupa—on a 2-weight rod. The fish was released in excellent condition, but three years later Jim is still coming down from the adrenaline high he experienced that day.

The chances of hooking a fish feeding on midges are far better than hooking one feeding on larger insects. Why? Because the trout has to feed so many more times when eating midges. A trout that requires 250 medium-sized mayflies for dinner will need 2500 midges to feel as full, and that's 2500 chances you have of getting the fish to take your fly; and sometimes taking it more than once.

In 1977, Nancy and I took Jason on his first trip to Nelson's Spring Creek in Montana. We arrived at 7 am to find an excellent midge hatch in progress, and I took several fine trout early on. At noon, there was a changing of the guard; Jason had fished with Nancy in the morning, and now I took him in tow. As we walked along the stream, I pointed to a rock where I'd taken a trout. And there, as we watched, was a ring on the water. Inching closer, we saw a rainbow feeding in the same place as one I'd taken earlier. The midges were still emerging; perhaps it was the same fish, lured back to feeding by this extremely abundant fare.

"Come on, Jason," I whispered, "you try him." Several times the trout rose close to the artificial. Then, there it was, backing downstream under the fly and examining it closely. We could only watch, holding our breaths, as if exhaling would somehow spook the trout. But the fly and the timing were right, and the rainbow took the tiny imitation.

The big trout tumbled into the air and dashed about the pool in wild-eyed abandon. Jason, though only eight years old, had been fishing since he was two and one-half and was a seasoned angler. He played the fish skillfully (despite my excited coaching), and the long rushes and wild leaps were replaced with a dogged swimming, then surrender. It *was* the same fish that I'd caught earlier; a missing, right maxillary flap and uniquely scarred fin were our confirmation. Trout and midges, they're a great combination.

Midge Larva

Midge larvae are quite wormlike in appearance. This stage is eyeless, and its body is soft, segmented, and lacks jointed legs (although small, fleshy prolegs can be seen on some species) *(Figure 8-2)*. In addition to looking like worms, many species also act like worms, burrowing into the bottom of a lake or slow-moving pool or crawling about in dense mats of algae or other aquatic plants. Others, however, like the larvae of blackflies prefer the swiftest of streams, attaching themselves to rocks with a suction disk. By-and-large, midge larvae are small; most are 1/8 to 3/8 inch long, but there are always those who have to do things differently: the larvae of some species of lake midges in the family Chironomidae may be as much as 1 1/4 inches in length! Normally, midge larvae crawl about like earthworms, but they are capable of twitching and flailing swimming motions to help them move.

Regardless of species, midge larvae that burrow in muddy bottoms (where oxygen is low) contain high levels of hemoglobin to increase oxygen uptake, and are thus bright red. These "bloodworms" are found in streams and lakes everywhere, and an appropriate imitation, fished dead drift near the bottom, can be very successful. Other important larval colors are rusty brown, yellow, gray, or creamy white.

Like some mayfly nymphs and caddis larvae, midge larvae may participate in behavioral drift. This is especially true for larvae of the blackflies (Simulidae) which drift during the day. The blackfly larva also lets itself out into the currents on a silken thread, in a fashion similar to that of the *Brachycentrus* caddis. This is a daytime activity, too. In addition, non-drifting midge larvae that live in bottom vegetation may

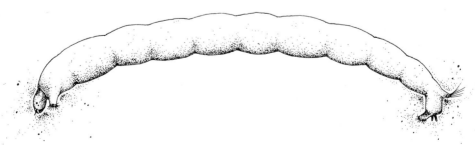

Figure 8-2. A Chironomidae midge larva.

be caught in the currents and carried away. During behavioral drift or accidental drift, the larvae may assume a slightly curved position, may remain rather straight, or may wiggle a bit.

The huge lake midges are widely distributed in warm-water lakes around the world, but occur in cold-water trout lakes in only a few places. They're found in abundance in the trout reservoirs of England and Southern Africa and in the lakes of the northern Rockies and Pacific Northwest. Brian Chan, Senior Fisheries Biologist for the Thompson-Nicola Region of British Columbia, has carefully documented the behavior of the huge Chironomidae that live in the lakes of that area. He notes that the larvae leave their bottom burrows in late fall and migrate to deeper water to avoid winter's near-shore ice. In the spring, just after ice out, the larvae twitch and wiggle their way back to the near-shore waters. Normally the larvae hug the bottom, but if the wind comes up, wave action carries these frail swimmers up into the mid-waters, and the trout feed heavily on them. A larval imitation fished on a floating line that is allowed to drift in the wind can be a trout magnet.

For the fly tier, then, the task is to create a well-segmented, worm-like imitation in a range of sizes and colors. And if possible, especially in the larger sizes, the imitation should show some action in the water. To achieve a notion of motion in the big larval imitations, I use a curved shank hook (like an English bait hook) or bend a straight-shank hook laterally in a couple of places. The bent shank concept was developed by George Anderson from his observations on the spring creeks just south of Livingston, Montana. The curved shank or the bent shank causes the imitation to twist when drifting, giving the appearance of a twitching natural. I use two patterns to mimic midge larvae: the Brassie and the Fur Midge Larva.

These patterns are best fished on a long tippet with a strike indicator. Many fly fishers are reluctant to fish a size 16 to 20 nymph pattern,

but I can assure you, when the fish are feeding on midge larvae, the fishing can be superb. I also enjoy fishing these tiny flies to fish I've spotted, either in streams or in lakes. The little patterns are presented several feet ahead of the trout, and the fly fisher watches for the "wink underwater"—the white interior of the trout's mouth as it opens and closes to take the fly.

Brassie

Actually this fly is my mistaken interpretation of the original dressing of the South Platte Brassy. In 1971, I read an article by Ed Marsh describing how to tie the Brassy, and I went into my tying room and dressed some for on-stream trials. However, I forgot to add the thick, cigar-shaped underbody of thread; I simply wrapped the shank with a single layer of bright copper wire and added a throat of pheasant tail barbs. The next summer I was fishing Armstrong Spring Creek and having a slow day. As I rummaged around looking for something, anything, to try I spotted the little copper flies. From then on I could do no wrong. I quickly lost or gave away the dozen in my box, but after a few minutes at the van with my portable tying kit there were plenty more ready to go. This fly has caught fish in lakes and streams everywhere (it's even taken steelhead).

It works because the wire body provides a strongly segmented appearance and because the bright copper produces an attention-getting flash. The copper color also suggests a rusty brown larva and may hint at the red color of a bloodworm. In addition, I use fluorescent red thread when dressing the fly, and I'm sure that spot of red strengthens the suggestion of a bloodworm. I've dressed this pattern in every imaginable shape and form; with a thorax, with a tail, with legs, with a sparkle yarn husk, with a wing, with a soft hackle, with a stiff hackle, and so on. They all catch fish, but not anymore than the simple body and throat. So I've stayed with my original, mistaken design.

Brassie: Dressing

Hook: Sizes 14-20, standard shank

Thread: 6/0 or 8/0 fluorescent red

Body: Bright copper wire wound in a single layer; 24 to 32 gauge depending upon hook size

Throat: Pheasant tail barbs, tied short

Brassie: Tying Instructions

1. Clamp the hook in the vise and wind the thread to the standard position.

2. Beginning at the rear of the hook, wind a single layer of bright copper wire along the length of the hook, ending at the head. Keep the wraps tight against each other. Trim off the ends of the wire.

3. Wind the thread forward to the head, placing the turns in the grooves between the wraps of wire.

4. Tie in several pheasant tail barbs for a throat (page 36); they should be about 1/2 the length of the hook shank.

5. Tie off the head, cut away the thread. Coat the head and body with water-thin flexible head cement; this will keep the body bright for several seasons *(Figure 8-3).*

Figure 8-3. *The finished Brassie.*

Fur Midge Larva

This fly, like the Brassie, is so simple that it seems almost a crime to catch fish on it, almost. It's nothing but a dubbed fur body with a wire rib and short throat of feather barbs. Although I tie this pattern in red, yellow, gray, and white, I find myself reaching first for the red one. Call it confidence in the fly, call it a Pavlovian reflex, but it's certainly proven itself to me. The white one has done well for me also, probably because it's not really white, the body is undyed Antron with a copper rib. I've had some great days nymphing the riffles of western spring creeks with this fly, and have used it many times to take lake cruisers.

Fur Midge Larva: Dressing

Hook: Sizes 14 to 22 standard shank; larval hooks or English bait hooks may also be used in appropriately substituted sizes; for the huge lake midges, sizes 8 to 12 English bait hook.

Thread: 6/0 or 8/0, depending upon hook size

Body: Blended fur and sparkle yarn or pure sparkle yarn, dubbed to form a relatively thin body

Rib: Wire, 24 to 32 gauge depending upon hook size

Throat: Pheasant tail barbs (or others) tied short

Fur Midge Larva: Most Used Sizes/Dubbing Color and Rib (all regions)

Sizes 14-22:

Dubbing scarlet red (BCS 85) with copper rib

Dubbing undyed Antron with copper rib

Dubbing gray (BCS 109) with silver rib

Dubbing pale yellow (BCS 42) with silver rib

Dubbing reddish brown (BCS 66) with copper rib

Fur Midge Larva: Most Used Sizes/Dubbing Color and Rib, (Matches jumbo lake midges in Northwest)

Sizes 8-12 English bait hook:

Dubbing deep red (BCS 86) with copper rib

Dubbing olive green (BCS 30) with silver rib

Dubbing black (BCS 118) with silver rib

Fur Midge Larva: Tying Instructions

1. Clamp the hook in the vise and wind the thread to the extended position on a standard hook or onto the rear bend of a larval or English bait hook.

2. Tie in the wire rib; extend the tag end forward along the top of the shank to the head (this prevents any unevenness in body diameter and adds a bit of weight); end with the thread at the center of the shank.

3. Spin dubbing onto the thread, wrap the thread to the rear to bring the dubbing up to the hook, wrap the dubbing forward to form the body.

4. Wind the rib forward, keeping the turns rather close, secure at the head and cut away the excess.

5. Add a short throat of pheasant tail barbs (page 36).

6. Form the head, tie off, cut away the thread. Apply head cement.

7. Brush the body lightly with a dubbing brush *(Figure 8-4)*.

Figure 8-4. *The finished Fur Midge Larva.*

Midge Pupa

Most midge larva mature in several weeks to a few months; thus, there are often two or more broods per year. The very large lake midges, however, require a full year to fully develop. Once mature, the larva pupates. The blackfly larva seals itself in a silken case, and some others crawl from the water and pupate in earthen burrows. Many, however, have an actively mobile pupa which is quite capable of swimming, and often does. The pupa has a readily recognizable and well-segmented abdomen, robust thorax, and head. There are wing pads on the sides of the thorax and often puffy, white gills on the thorax and on the tail end of the abdomen *(Figure 8-5)*. The pupal stage lasts a week or two as the adult develops within. Pupal colors match those of the adult rather than reflecting larval tints.

Blackfly adults emerge underwater and rise to the surface in a bubble of air, but for most midges, the pharate adult (as the mature pupa is correctly called) migrates to the surface where the husk splits and the adult eases out. Ascension is aided by gasses in the skin (page 81) which effectively blur the finer details of the pupal structure. Trout feed heavily on the pharate adults near the bottom and in midwaters, but especially as they hang in the film. The fish's rise is deliberate and its snout often breaks the surface as the mouth opens to take the tiny insect. Such feeding activity can be quite confusing. The question always arises: is the fish eating the pharate adult just under the surface or taking the fully emerged adults off the top? Watch closely. If the trout is taking adults, you'll see the insects on the surface and you'll see the fish take them. If the adults are not being taken, it's pupa time!

Figure 8-5. *A Chironomidae pupa.*

To suggest the inflated husk of the pupa, I use the sparkle yarn pattern discussed in chapter seven (page 82). It's a disarmingly simple fly to dress, but oh, so effective. Jason and I were fishing Colorado's South Platte and encountered a superhatch of bright green midges just at the end of a good Trico hatch. Jason grabbed a 2-weight rod and headed upstream for a pool that we knew contained some good fish while I decided to try to stalk individual rainbows in a shallow riffle. Jason looked like a fishing machine: cast, set the hook, play the fish aggressively, release it, repeat the performance. I could see he was determined to give me a good drubbing—which he did. But I enjoyed a different type of excitement: spotting 15- to 22-inch rainbows and watching them take the size 16 fly as casually as if sucking in the real thing. We've had the same quality of fishing with the Sparkle Midge Pupa many, many times in lakes and streams worldwide.

Sparkle Midge Pupa: Dressing

Hook: Sizes 14-28, standard shank length

Thread: 8/0, color to match body

Abdomen: Dubbed sparkle yarn, thin

Thorax: Dubbed sparkle yarn; filaments twice length of hook shank; well brushed out to form pupal shuck around abdomen; weighted with lead or copper wire

Sparkle Midge Pupa: Most Used Colors (all regions)

Gray (BCS 109)

Golden Olive (BCS 40)

Bright Green (BCS 19)

Yellow (BCS 49)

Black (BCS 118)

Sparkle Midge Pupa: Tying Instructions

1. Clamp the hook in the vise and wrap the thread to the center of the shank.

2. Weight the front 1/2 of the hook shank with copper wire and secure with the thread (page 30).

3. Apply dubbing for the abdomen and finish wrapping the thread to the standard position at the rear of the hook (page 31).

4. Wind the dubbing forward to form the abdomen, covering the rear 3/4 of the hook shank. Keep the abdomen relatively narrow in diameter.

5. Cut a chunk of sparkle yarn twice the length of the hook shank; spin these filaments onto the thread and form the thorax. The finished thorax should be 1 1/2 to 2 times the diameter of the abdomen.

6. Brush out the filaments of the abdomen to give it a fuzzy appearance, and then brush out the filaments of the thorax such that they flow back around the abdomen to the rear of the hook. The filaments of the thorax must be twice as long as the hook so that they remain attached after being brushed out.

7. Finish the head, tie off the thread, cut it away, and apply head cement *(Figure 8-6)*.

Figure 8-6. *The completed Sparkle Midge Pupa.*

Jumbo Lake Pupa

The English have studied the huge lake midges extensively. Frank Sawyer wrote of his frustrations during the evening hatches of the big "buzzer" flies until he began using pupal imitations rather than adult patterns, and John Goddard gives an excellent account of these insects in his book "Trout Flies of Stillwater." Both stress the need to simulate the inflated husk and the large, plumose gills at the head of the pupa. Brian Chan's flies also reflect this attention to imitating the gills. I use a clump of sparkle yarn tied in like stubby spinner wings to simulate the gills. The abdomen of dubbed sparkle yarn is brushed out to suggest the translucent reflectivity of the inflated pupa skin with the adult inside.

The pupa can be designed to be fished deep along the bottom or hanging in the film. The mature pupae usually rise a foot or two and then settle back to the bottom, repeating this performance several times before beginning the final ascent to the surface, and the trout often stay down to feed on these indecisive insects. So, if the hatch is in progress and few fish are seen feeding at the surface, the fly is fished deep. Because the pupae can be found in water as deep as 25 feet, I rib the imitation with Crystal Flash or other highly reflective material that not only suggests the loosened husk but reflects what little light is available at that depth, and so makes the pattern more noticeable.

To fish it deep, anglers of the desert lakes of British Columbia, Washington, and Oregon often use very long leaders—up to 25 feet in length—with a floating line. The fly is allowed to sink, and the line is retrieved very slowly. The end of the line is used as a strike indicator. Another unique tactic is tube jigging. The fly fisher anchors a float tube in 10 to 25 feet of water and presents the imitation on a fast sinking line and normal leader. The length of the cast equals the depth of the water. When the cast has sunk completely, and is hanging directly down from the rod tip, the fly fisher slowly jigs the rod tip up and down. If there's wave action, the rod is held stationary, allowing the swells and troughs to do the jigging. Rather than jigging the fly, the angler may slowly strip in the line, retrieving the fly straight up, thus suggesting as ascending pupa. Either way, it's great fun when a big trout nails the pupa.

If the trout are feeding at the surface, then the fly fisher uses the suspender version of the pupa with the Greased Leader tactic.

Jumbo Lake Pupa, Sinking Version: Dressing

Hook: Sizes 8-14, 3XL shank

Thread: 6/0, color to match body

Anal Gills: Undyed sparkle yarn, tied short (optional depending upon natural)

Abdomen: Dubbed sparkle yarn

Thorax: Peacock herl; weighted with lead wire

Rib: Crystal Hair, Flashabou, or Krystal Flash

Shuck: Sparkle yarn filaments of abdomen, brushed out

Thoracic Gills: Undyed sparkle yarn, tied like stubby spinner wings

Jumbo Lake Pupa, Sinking Version: Most Used Body Colors and Rib

Black with a pearlescent or silver rib

Orangish brown (BCS 63) with copper rib

Olive green (BCS 20) with pearlescent or silver rib

Note: A large Brassie with peacock thorax and sparkle yarn gills can also be very good.

Jumbo Lake Pupa, Sinking Version: Tying Instruction

1. Clamp the hook in the vise and wrap the thread to the extended position.

2. If anal gills are present in the natural, tie in a clump of undyed sparkle yarn as a short tail to represent these structures.

3. Wrap the front 1/2 of the shank with lead wire and secure with the thread; end with the thread at the middle of the shank.

4. Spin the dubbing on the thread, leaving an inch of bare thread between hook and dubbing. Use the bare thread to tie in the rib (wrap rearward). This will also bring the dubbing up to the hook.

5. Wrap the dubbing forward, covering the rear 3/4 of the shank.

6. Tie in 2 or 3 pieces of peacock herl and wrap forward to form the thorax, ending at the head.

7. Brush out the filaments of the abdomen to give it a fuzzy appearance.

8. Wind the rib forward over the abdomen and thorax and secure in front of the thorax.

9. Using a figure-8 wrap, tie in a clump of undyed sparkle yarn crosswise of the hook, like short spinner wings; these will represent the thoracic gills.

10. Finish the head, tie off the thread, and cut it away (Figure 8-7).

Figure 8-7. *The completed Jumbo Lake Pupa, Sinking Version.*

Jumbo Lake Pupa, Suspender Version

This pattern is tied in the same sizes and colors as the sinking version, but the lead wire is omitted. In addition, a chunk of white foam plastic is tied in at the head before the remainder of the fly is dressed. This piece of foam should be about 1/2 the length of the hook shank and about 1/8 inch square in cross section. It should point forward and slant upward at a 30 to 45 degree angle (*Figure 8-8*). The foam represents the partially emerged adult, suspends the pattern at the surface, and allows the angler to see the fly. This design also works to simulate emerging mayflies and caddises.

Midge Adult

Adult midges vary in shape, from the Chironomidae which tend to be slender of body and long of leg (Figure 8-1) to the robust bodied, stubby legged blackflies (*Figure 8-9*). The trout don't seem to mind, however; they eat them all, without prejudice. It's hard to believe that truly large trout will feed on the smallest of midges, but they will.

Figure 8-8. *The completed Jumbo Lake Pupa, Suspender Version.*

In the early 1960's I spent many days on the Fisherman's Paradise water near Bellefonte, Pennsylvania. Big trout were common in that stretch of Spring Creek, but they were highly conditioned by the crush of fly fishers who frequented that then-unique, catch-and-release area. I'd stalked a particularly large trout for weeks, but it refused everything, feeding steadfastly on midges twice as small as any hook I had. But then I located a single, dusty box of gold-plated, size 28 hooks hidden away in a local sports shop. It was the smallest hook I'd ever seen, but I knew it was right. The huge brown sucked in the tiny fly without reservation, and fortune smiled on me as I played nearly 28 inches of trout to net.

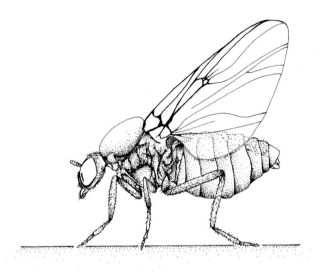

Figure 8-9. *The adult blackfly.*

In addition to delicately sipping single adults, trout often get a chance to gulp midges by the clump. This happens because midges frequently mate on the surface. Several males will cluster around the receptive female. The clump of single-minded insects is a churning, milling ball of legs and wings and contorted bodies. This activity is highly attractive to the trout. I've seen rafts of mating midges an inch or two deep extending hundreds of feet along the shores of streams such as New Mexico's San Juan and Montana's Bighorn. Chunks of such rafts frequently break loose and drift into the currents where the trout quickly vacuum them up. It sounds like science fiction (or maybe just a typical angler's tale); it's one of nature's phenomena that must be seen to be truly comprehended.

To simulate both the single adult and the clump, I use the Griffith's Gnat. I first learned of the fly in 1973 from Ernest Schwiebert's richly informative book, "Nymphs." Developed by George Griffith, founding father of Trout Unlimited, this design is without a doubt the single-best, all-around, adult midge pattern ever developed. George began fishing his first version of the Gnat in 1936, and he reckons that a size 16 is almost universally applicable, regardless of the size of the insect. Though my two decades of experience with this fly fall far short of George's 50-plus years, I would add my voice to his. Why does this size serve so well? Because if the midge is as large as a 16, the fly works to represent a single adult. If the naturals are smaller, the fly simulates a clump. In addition to the 16's, I also carry a few 18's through 28's (to mimic smaller species) and a few 14's and 12's (to ape a big clump or a huge lake midge).

The Griffith's Gnat looks precious little like a midge—at least when held in the hand. Remember though, that it's the fish's view that's important. The adult chironomid midge stands well up off the water, the ends of its lanky legs creating sparkling points of light where they depress the rubbery surface film. Even the stubby legs of the blackflies are long enough to hold the body well above the water. And that's exactly what the hackle of the Griffith's Gnat does; it keeps the body well off the water and creates a distinctive pattern of light flashes in the underside of the surface. The hackle barbs sticking above the body of the fly suggest the wings of a single fly or legs and wings of a clump.

Sometimes the trout won't take an imitation of the pupa or the fully developed adult. This happens because the fish are locked into the emerger. Ernest Schwiebert recommends clipping the Griffith's Gnat either on the bottom or on both top and bottom so it rides awash in the film—like the adult struggling out of the pupal fetters. It's sage advise that has worked numerous times for me.

Griffith's Gnat: Dressing

Hook: Sizes 12-28, standard shank length

Thread: 6/0 or 8/0, depending upon hook size, color to match body

Body: Original dressing is with peacock herl body; for other colors use blended fur and sparkle yarn or sparkle yarn

Hackle: Good quality cock hackle, palmered

Griffith's Gnat: Most Used Body Color and Hackle (all regions)

Peacock herl with grizzly or black hackle

Bright Green (BCS 19) with pale dun hackle

Yellow (BCS 42) with ginger hackle

Gray (BCS 109) with grizzly hackle

Griffith's Gnat: Tying Instructions

1. Clamp the hook in the vise and wrap the thread to the standard position.

2. Prepare a hackle feather and tie it in.

3. Form the body; either tie in the herl and wind forward or apply a dubbed body.

4. Wind the hackle forward like a rib (palmer style) and tie off at the head—use at least five turns of hackle.

5. Form the head, tie off, and cut away the thread.

6. Apply head cement *(Figure 8-10)*.

Figure 8-10. *The completed Griffith's Gnat.*

While I rely on the Griffith's Gnat for the vast majority of my adult midge fishing, I've also used the Poly Caddis quite successfully on occasion; especially when the occasion is that I'm out of Griffith's Gnats. It's a substitution that should be kept in mind.

CRANEFLIES

These are the largest of the aquatic dipterans and can be of considerable importance to the fly fisher. They occur in heavy numbers in some eastern streams, but are especially prevalent in waters of the West. Popular rivers like the Madison, Bighorn, Beaverhead, South Platte, and Bow, as well as lesser known rivers and lakes, have heavy concentrations of these "giant mosquitoes," and angling authors that write knowingly of western streams and lakes—Schwiebert, Mathews and Juracek, Hafele and Hughes, Rosborough, Whitlock, and others, describe patterns to match larval and adult stages.

Cranefly Larva

The cranefly larva is often called a "water worm." These larvae of the dipteran family Tipulidae can be rather huge, over 3 inches long, but some are as small as 1/2 inch. By and large, the larvae live for a year, occupying just about every known aquatic habitat, from swampy lake edges to rapids. Likewise they may be herbivores, carnivores, omnivores, or cannibals. Many have a darkened area at the anal end of the abdomen that sports fingerlike gills; the anterior end of the larva may be darkened also, then again they may be uniformly colored. The actual head is quite tiny and can be retracted into the body *(Figure 8-11)*. The craneflies are an extremely diverse group with a large number of individual species. Fortunately, most of the significant trout-stream larvae are one of four basic colors: olive, gray, dirty tan, or dingy orange.

Cranefly larvae present the same basic problems for the fly tier as the big midge larvae. Cranefly larvae can move by whipping the body back and forth and are clearly segmented. To help suggest movement in the water, I dress these flies on curved-shank, English bait hooks, weighting them so they'll sink deep and stay there. The fly fisher could dress imitations of the huge larvae, but as Craig Mathews and John Juracek point out, such big flies are no more successful than smaller versions. And, the smaller flies are much easier to cast.

Here's a chance to get away from dubbing and use yarn for the body. Yarn is great for many flies and can be substituted whenever the fly is big enough or yarn of a suitable diameter can be found. I especially like mohair and fuzzy acrylic yarns because they have a translucence that other materials often lack. In addition, the yarn can be twisted very tight before it's wrapped on in order to give a definite, segmented look to the fly. It can also be roughed up nicely with the dubbing brush. I use a wire rib to augment the segmented look and add additional weight. The fly is actually dressed in reverse on the hook; a short peacock thorax and a few pheasant tail barbs suggest the darkened anal region and gills.

Fur Cranefly Larva: Dressing

Hook: Sizes 6-10, English bait hook or other similarly curved hook

Thread: 6/0, color to match body

Body: Mohair or sparkle yarn well brushed out and trimmed; blended fur and sparkle yarn dubbing may be used if yarn of proper color cannot be located; weighted with lead wire

Rib: Wire of appropriate color

Head: Peacock herl to represent darkened anal segments

Gills: Pheasant tail barbs tied short

Fur Cranefly Larva: Most Used Sizes/Body Color/ Rib and Regions Used

Sizes 6-10/Body dingy orange (BCS 60)/Copper rib, Northeast, Southeast, Lake States, South Central

Sizes 6-10/Body dirty tan (BCS 104)/ Copper rib, all regions

Sizes 6-10/Body olive (BCS 30)/Silver rib, all regions

Size 10/Body gray (BCS 109)/Silver rib, all regions

Fur Cranefly Larva: Tying Instructions

1. Clamp the hook in the vise and wrap the thread rearward onto the rear curve.

2. Tie in the wire rib as for the midge larva (page 95).

3. Tie in a piece of yarn; extend the tag end forward along the top of the shank to the thorax of the fly—this prevents non-uniformity in body diameter.

4. Make one turn of the yarn around the hook shank and then twist the strands of the yarn very tight and continue wrapping. Be sure the yarn wraps stay tightly twisted, this will produce a segmented body. Secure at the rear of the thorax. The thorax should be relatively short—about 3 normal head spaces.

5. Tie in 2 or 3 strands of peacock herl and wrap forward to form a short, robust thorax that represents the darkened anal segments of the abdomen.

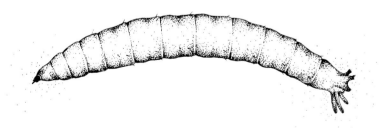

Figure 8-11. *A typical cranefly larva.*

6. Wrap the wire rib between the yarn segments and through the peacock thorax; secure at the head.

7. Tie in 6-8 pheasant tail barbs as a throat; they will suggest the anal gills.

8. Brush the abdomen thoroughly to really tease out the filaments. Trim to a uniformly rounded shape. In the water the trimmed fibers produce a distinctive halo around the fly, suggesting the exoskeleton and watery appearance of the body itself (*Figure 8-12*).

Figure 8-12. *The completed Fur Cranefly Larva.*

Cranefly Pupa and Adult

At maturity the cranefly larva crawls from the river and burrows into the wet soil of the bank. There it pupates; thus the pupa and emerging adult are unavailable to the trout. The adult looks like a huge mosquito with long, easily broken legs (*Figure 8-13*). Mating occurs over the stream or lake, and the female then flies along over the surface, dipping her abdomen into the water periodically to lay eggs. Often the legs trail in the film as the female whirs along just above the surface. On streams, this activity occurs near shore, especially in places where vegetation grows close to, or overhangs, the water. If there is any depth to the stream in these places, you can be sure that trout will be there, feeding on the egg-laying females. The

fish must be quick to grab the hovering adult, and the rise is easy to see! Craneflies are also lake creatures; the natural adult is used for blow line dapping in Scotland, and in "Trout Flies of Stillwater" John Goddard reports excellent fishing with adult imitations in such famous English reservoirs as Blagdon and Chew.

There are several approaches to imitating the adult. One is the ultra-realistic approach, designing a fly with six lanky legs and stubby body and wings. Such flies have never done well for me. They don't hold their shape for more than a cast or two, and besides, that's not the form that the fish sees. From underwater, the egg-laying adult is a blur of wings, dragging legs, and dipping abdomen—the perfect combination to be matched by Hewitt's Skater Fly, or better yet, Al Troth's elk hair Skater. Al is an amazingly creative fly tier living in Dillon, Montana. He's fished the Beaverhead extensively and knows its cranefly hatches as well as anyone alive. His simple fly is easy to tie, durable, made of readily available materials, and catches fish like there's no tomorrow. Everything I love in a fly. I always keep a couple of these huge flies in my vest when fishing in the Rockies; they've provided me with some exceptionally exciting fishing, not only during cranefly ovipositing flights, but as an attractor pattern during opportunistic periods.

There are a couple of ways to fish the pattern. One is to cast the fly, hold the rod very high to keep the line and leader off the water, then gently work the pattern back with short strips. This action keeps the pattern dancing on

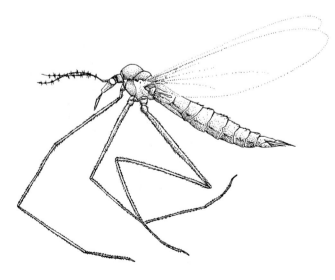

Figure 8-13. *A typical cranefly adult.*

the surface very nicely. It's a great tactic for lakes and slow moving stretches of stream. It can also be employed in a downstream direction along the edges of streams. Another stream tactic that I like is to tie a heavily weighted nymph to the point of a three-foot tippet and tie the skater to a short dropper made from the blood knot where the tippet is tied to the leader body. This combination is cast down and across stream and the rod held high as the currents push the flies toward shore. The sunken nymph acts like a sea anchor, allowing the fly fisher to dap the skater up and down on the surface by lifting and lowering the rod tip. When the fly is hanging straight downstream, the angler strips the fly back and continues to dap the fly. What a response this action can elicit! As Troth says, "I dig my toes into the gravel awaiting the savage strike this fly usually brings."

Troth Skater: Dressing

Hook: Sizes 6-10, standard shank length

Thread: 3/0, orange

Body: Tying thread

Hackle: Two, tied fore and aft, twice length of hook shank; made from elk body hair; deer or other similar hair will work, too

Troth Skater: Tying Instructions

1. Clamp the hook in the vise and wrap the thread to the standard position.

2. To form the rear hair hackle, select a clump of hair about the diameter of a pencil and stack it to even the tips.

3. Holding the butt ends of the hair in the materials hand, secure the clump at the rear of the shank with several turns of thread so that the tips are twice the length of the hook shank. The tips should flare and spin around the shank. Do not release the butt end of the clump.

4. Hold the butt end of the clump up at a 45 degree angle to the hook shank and cut it off about 1/8 inch from the thread. Wrap the thread through the butts three or four turns to secure them.

5. Wrap the thread forward in *close* turns, *through the flared tips*. This causes them to flare and spin further, distributing them evenly around the shank *(Figure 8-14)*.

6. Wind the thread forward to a point about three head spaces behind the eye and form another hair hackle.

7. Form the head, tie off the thread, cut it away.

8. Place several drops of water-thin, flexible head cement into the base of each hair hackle to strengthen it *(Figure 8-15)*.

Figure 8-14. *Wrap through the tips to form the rear hair hackle.*

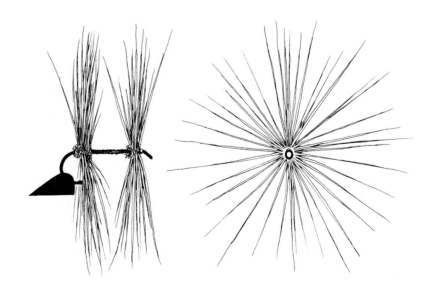

Figure 8-15. *The completed Troth Skater; side view, front view.*

OTHER DIPTERANS

The larvae of some species of horseflies and deer flies (family Tabanidae) occupy the swift water reaches of streams, and several species of them occupy the quiet waters along lake edges (Figure 8-16). Everyone knows the adults of this family. Additionally, the larvae of the snipe flies (family Rhagionidae) are found living in streams *(Figure 8-17)*. The adults look much like house flies. The female lays eggs on a branch or other structure (such as a bridge) overhanging the water and dies, still attached to the eggs. Others usually lay eggs nearby. In this manner, a great mass of dead flies can accumulate. The dirty white to fleshy tan colored larvae of these two families creep about in the detritus and are occasionally numerous enough to form an irregular addition to the fish's diet. Because these creatures are only incidental in the fish's day to day feeding pattern, imitations of them are used during opportunistic feeding periods. And rather than design a specific imitation, I simply use a size 12 or 14 white Fur Midge Larva. This is one of my favorite imitations when fishing in lakes for cruising trout, and I've done well with it fishing in those areas of a stream where I've seen the masses of dead snipe fly adults.

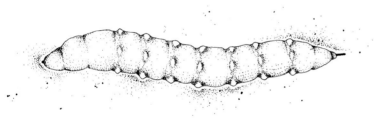

Figure 8-16. *A typical horsefly larva.*

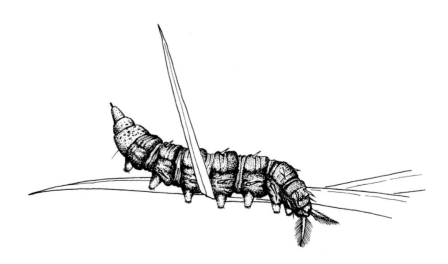

Figure 8-17. *A snipefly larva.*

DAMSELS AND DRAGONS

The "big four" stream insects are mayflies, stoneflies, caddisflies, and midges. But in stillwaters, stoneflies are almost non-existent, and their role is usurped by the Odonata: the damselflies and dragonflies. In some lakes, damsels and dragons can be the most important food insect for trout. Thus for stillwaters, the "big four" become mayflies, damsels and dragons, caddisflies, and midges.

Not only do the damsels and dragons fill the stillwater niche left open by the stoneflies, but they share other characteristics as well: the Odonata are mostly large insects, they have an incomplete life cycle with only nymph and adult stages, and the adults emerge on shore. The two types of Odonatan insects are separated into their own suborders. The damsels are placed in Zygoptera (meaning "yoke wing," referring to the narrowed wing bases) while the dragons are separated into the Anisoptera (meaning "unequal wing," referring to the different-sized forewings and hindwings).

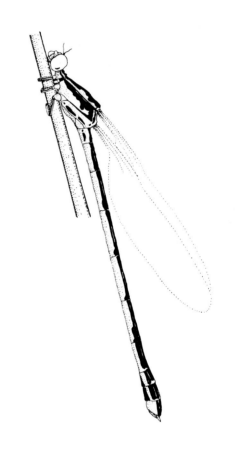

Figure 9-1. *Damsel adults are often seen clinging to near-shore plants.*

DAMSELS

Damselflies are well-known insects; on bright summer days the colorful adults *(Figure 9-1)* can be seen fluttering clumsily along the shore or clinging to nearby vegetation. These creatures are widespread in lakes and streams around the world. In the vast majority of streams, damsels haunt the weedy shallows close to shore and are only occasionally available to the trout. In some slow-moving streams, where mats of floating aquatic plants undulate gently in the currents, nymphs and egg-laying adults can be prevalent enough to induce feeding by trout. However, such situations are highly localized, and only anglers who fish such special places need carry imitations of these insects.

But stillwaters are an entirely different story, especially in the West. The numbers of damsels in the lakes of that region can be astounding. They produce exciting fly fishing from Arizona and New Mexico all the way north into Canada. And depending upon elevation, they can be found emerging in huge flights from May through August. Eastern trout lakes do not support the dense damsel populations found in the West; never-the-less, their large size makes them important even where they occur in only modest numbers. Stillwater anglers who don't carry imitations of damsels are asking for some mighty frustrating summer days.

Damsel Nymphs

The nymphs are aquatic and easily recognized by the presence of three paddle-shaped gills at the end of the long, thin abdomen. The stocky, foreshortened thorax bears wing pads and long, slender legs, and the bulging compound eyes make the stubby head wider than the thorax (Figure 9-2). Nymphal color is variable, not only from species to species and from watershed to watershed, but to some degree for any individual. Like a chameleon, the insect can alter its body color to somewhat match the background; most nymphs are shades of olive, olive brown, tan, or purplish brown.

Although they are perfectly capable of crawling or swimming, and often do, they normally sprawl on plants or in the bottom trash and wait for their prey. Damselfly nymphs are not the dainty feeders that their name might suggest; in fact, they are fierce predators, attacking and devouring small species of insects, worms, mollusks, and crustaceans. Their mouthparts are elegantly specialized for this raptorial existence. The lower jaw is much elongated and strongly toothed at the end (hence the name Odonata, "a tooth"). This device is hinged in the middle so that at rest it can be folded back under the head. When a food organism comes within striking range, the toothed jaw shoots forward to grasp the victim and then draws it back to the mouth.

Most damselflies have a one-year life cycle, but in the very abundant Blue Damsels of the western genera *Enallagma* and *Ischnura*, there can be two or more broods per summer. At maturity, the nymphs leave their protective cover and head for shore, swimming along near the surface. This migration usually occurs in mid to late morning. They use their big gills to aid in propulsion, wiggling their bodies in a most minnow-like fashion. Their long legs are folded into various configurations depending upon the individual insect, but some part of the flexed appendage is held out to the side as the organism swims (Figure 9-3). The nymph moves a foot or so and then stops and rests for a few moments before repeating the process. The wiggle must be most provocative to the trout, for the fish often roll and splash as they rush to grab the migrating nymphs. This behavior can be confusing, since in their excitement the fish give the appearance of chasing a fast-moving prey. The presence of the migrating nymphs, which by the way do look a bit like tiny, slow-swimming minnows, should be your clue.

For the fly tier, the problem is not to create a three-tailed pattern with bugling eyes and long, straight body. Rather, the task becomes one of producing a swimming fly; one that looks like the wiggling damsel that the trout sees. A decade and a half ago, when Bob Pelzl and I first fished the immense damsel hatches on the Vermejo lakes, we were unprepared for the degree of sophistication shown by the trout. Sure, we caught fish on all manner of olive brown flies, but we also spooked a lot of fish or simply couldn't interest them in our patterns. So we began dressing experimental flies and trying them on the toughest trout on the ranch. The first pattern of promise had a marabou tail, elongate ribbed abdomen, and hair legs. It caught fish, and plenty of them. It was successful enough that I included it in "Naturals"; however, there were still fish that would turn it down with only a glance. It looked good in the vise, but when we investigated more closely, we noted it didn't look entirely right in the water. It didn't swim like the real thing. We had to have a

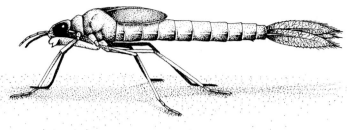

Figure 9-2. *The paddle-shaped tails of the damsel are diagnostic.*

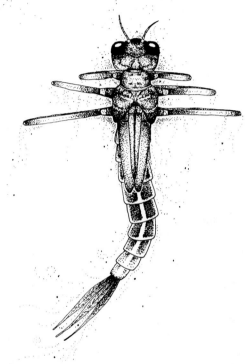

Figure 9-3. *The swimming damsel wiggles its abdomen strongly.*

fly whose design was coupled not only to the features of the natural but to its behavior, and that meant having a fly designed to be fished with a specific retrieve. We had to couple fly design with angling tactic. We knew the retrieve we wanted to use: the Strip/Tease. With this tactic the line is stripped a foot in three or four seconds while the rod tip is teased in a vibrating fashion up and down or side to side. The strip moves the fly, the vibrations cause it to twitch. Since this was the tactic I used for the Strip Nymph in stillwater, we decided to try a similar imitation to suggest the swimming damsel nymph. In place of the fur strip, we used a tail of marabou plumage. To accentuate the swimming action, we weighted the thorax region with lead; this causes the fly to jig when presented with a Strip/Tease retrieve. A dubbed body of marabou, a peacock herl wingcase, and hair legs completed the fly.

The waving, pulsing marabou tail was a good suggestion of the natural's whipping abdomen and tails. The marabou body added to the suggestion of life, as did the peacock herl wingcase (page 28). The legs also proved significant. In the natural, the folded, partially outstretched legs stabilize the thorax so it remains on a more-or-less straight course as the abdomen flails back and forth. These appendages are easily seen in the swimming natural, and hair legs provide a excellent counterpart in the artificial.

The Marabou Damsel was an instant success, and ten years later, it continues to take fish as regularly as clockwork. It wasn't the three tails, the linear profile, or the bugling eyes of the natural that were important. It was the living, behavioral characteristics that were so important. Because the nymphs are rather variable in color, we've found that either an olive brown or a purple brown pattern works for nearly all lakes. We've had mornings during the peak of the damsel migration when we've taken fifty trout of two to four pounds in fifty casts. How? We saw every fish because they were right in next to shore grabbing the undulating nymphs.

Marabou Damsel Nymph: Dressing

Hook: Sizes 10-14, standard shank length

Thread: 6/0 olive or brown

Tails: Marabou barbs same length as hook (these represent the tails and part of the abdomen of the natural); don't use too many or the tail won't pulse correctly and will look too thick

Abdomen: Dubbed marabou barbs, over rear 1/3 of hook shank

Thorax: Dubbed marabou barbs or fur dubbing covering front 2/3 of hook shank; weighted with lead wire

Legs: Guard hairs

Covert: Peacock herl

Marabou Damsel Nymph: Most Used Colors (all regions)

Tail 4-6 brown marabou barbs (BCS 87) on top of 6-8 pale, olive yellow marabou barbs (BCS 37)/ Body a mix of these two colors/ Legs pale olive yellow

Tail 6-8 brown marabou barbs (BCS 87) on top of 4-6 purple marabou barbs (BCS 127)/Body a mixture of these two colors/Legs brown

Marabou Damsel Nymph: Tying Instructions

1. Clamp the hook in the vise and wrap the thread to the standard position.

2. Weight the front 1/2 of the shank with lead wire and secure with the thread (page 30). End with the thread at the rear of the lead.

3. Select a clump of marabou barbs of the bottom color. Cut or strip them from the feather shaft and tie in by the butt ends to form a long tail. Wrap the thread rearward over the marabou and end at the standard position.

4. Select a clump of marabou barbs of the top color. Cut or strip them from the feather shaft and tie in (by the butt ends) on top of the first clump. Wrap the thread forward over the marabou and end at the rear of the lead.

5. Break the tail to length (as long as the hook—from the front of the eye to the bend). DO NOT CUT the marabou barbs. Rather, pinch them at the correct length between the thumb and forefinger of the *bobbin hand (Figure 9-4)*, and with the materials hand, tear off the remainder of the barbs. This leaves the ends somewhat uneven and thus gives a more natural look than does a square cut made with a scissors.

6. Don't try to save the torn off tips of the marabou for use in making more tails: they're too fragile. Rather, use them to form the dubbing for the abdomen. Tear the barbs into segments 1/2-inch long and spin onto the thread, leaving an inch or so of bare thread between the hook and the dubbing. Wrap rearward to the standard position to bring the dubbing up to the hook, then

wrap the dubbing forward over the rear 1/3 of the hook shank.

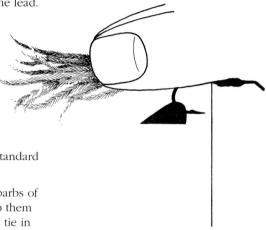

Figure 9-4. *Pinch the marabou tail with the bobbin hand.*

7. Finish the thorax as for the Hair Leg Nymph, using either marabou dubbing or fur dubbing (steps 10-22, pages 31-33) *(Figure 9-5).*

Figure 9-5. *The completed Marabou Damsel Nymph.*

Damsel Adult

When the nymph reaches shore, or any protruding object such as a boulder, stump, or emergent vegetation, it crawls stiff-legged from the water, and in preparation for emergence of the adult, fastens its feet to any handy, vertical surface. Many times, I've had them climb out and hatch on my vest. The newly emergent adult is soft and golden tan colored. By the time its wings have expanded and dried, the body is brownish. This teneral adult flies awkwardly away to the protective cover of nearby vegetation. Strong winds during the emergence period often dash the tenerals to the water where the trout seize them readily. After several hours, the body hardens and takes on full adult coloration. Males are often bright: emerald green with black wings, bright blue with clear wings, red with red wing bases, and so on. Females are usually dull colored: olives, browns, tans, pale yellow, and others.

Adults have long slender abdomens. At rest, most species hold the wings slanting back along the top of the abdomen. The legs are adapted for clutching, not walking, and the insect must rest on small stems. Almost without exception, adult damsels are on the wing only during sunny periods (usually in the afternoon) and then only in sunlit areas. If a cloud should cover the sun, they disappear rapidly. They are weak fliers and are normally seen fluttering about close to the water.

Mating occurs on objects near the water, and eggs are injected into the submersed portions of aquatic plants or deposited into the water over sunken vegetation. The male grasps the female just behind the head and the two of them fly in tandem to a suitable egg-laying site. The male hovers, and the female dips its abdomen beneath the surface. In some species, the male releases the female and she crawls beneath the surface to lay eggs.

Either way, this is a dangerous time for the adults. Being, at best, fitful fliers, they are easily cast onto the water's surface by a gust of wind.

Trapped in the film, they struggle weakly. The forewings are often outstretched like the spent wings of a mayfly. The hind wings point back along the abdomen in an inverted "V" shape *(Figure 9-6)*.

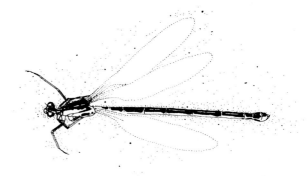

Figure 9-6. *The damsel adult on the water's surface.*

Trout feeding on the mired insects rise very deliberately. Females that crawl beneath the surface are taken as they clamber about and as they float back to the surface. Regardless of their gender and egg laying modes, adult damsels are very nicely mimicked by the Braided Butt Damsel.

Behavior of the adults, however, dictates three basic angling approaches. When the naturals are lying on the film, the artificial should be fished with the Heave and Leave method. Cast to the place where fish are cruising and just let the fly sit there; several minutes if necessary. If you see a rising fish, cast ten feet or so ahead of it and allow the fish to come to the fly. To simulate diving females, cast, pull the fly under, and work it back with short pulls punctuated with pauses. This is an especially good technique next to weed beds. If the fish are jumping for hovering adults, the Scottish loch method of blow line fishing is deadly. Since most fly fishers, including myself, don't normally carry such gear, the best solution is to try to hit the fish on the head. As soon as the fish jumps, cast the fly hard onto the water right into the ring of the rise.

Adult damsels are of occasional significance to eastern stillwater anglers, but it is the huge hatches of Blue Damsels on western lakes that get the fly fisher's pulse pounding. I've seen the air absolutely alive with these insects over the desert lakes in Washington, Henry's Lake in Idaho, the Vermejo lakes in New Mexico, and many other stillwaters in Arizona, British Columbia, California, Colorado, Montana, Nevada, Oregon, and Wyoming.

Anglers unfamiliar with the heavy flights of damsel adults can sometimes be a bit skeptical about the importance of these insects, but I can assure you, there are no doubting Thomases among the trout, nor among serious stillwater anglers. In lakes, the damselfly hatch offers the best chance of taking a really big trout on a dry fly.

The first time we fished the Vermejo lakes, it was late afternoon. Nancy tied on a parachute pattern of the Giant Michigan Mayfly and started catching fish left and right. We didn't know why, but we quickly joined her. The next day we saw the damsels and understood. From there, Bob Pelzl and I quickly developed a spent-wing adult with an extended deer hair body and white calf-tail wings. It was a great fly except on days

when the water was very calm. Then it was too evident as a fraud. The white of the wing was too bright and looked too bulky. So, I switched to a Parachute Spinner style, using dun hackle for the wings. It was a needed improvement. The hackle gave the pattern a delicate, realistic touch not evident with the hair wings. Then in January of 1985, Bob and I went to New Zealand to video tape "South Island Sampler." While there, we saw an adult damsel pattern that used braided monofilament for the abdomen. It looked so real. We were certain it would be easier to use than extended deer hair and would be a great deal tougher; we had to have it on our design. Back home, while I edited the video, Bob got busy and found some process-blue, permanent marking pens to dye the braided monofilament and then tied up some flies for the next season. These Braided Butt Damsels were exactly right in all regards: easy to tie, very realistic when seen from underwater, and extremely durable. We dress a mustard colored one to mimic the teneral (and some females) and a bright blue one to simulate the fully developed adult.

Braided Butt Damsel: Dressing

Hook: Sizes 10-12, standard shank length

Thread: 6/0, color to match body

Abdomen: Braided monofilament (leader butt), 0.050-inch diameter, dyed with permanent markers

Thorax: Fur and sparkle yarn dubbing

Hackle Post: Yarn, color to match body

Hackle: Cock hackle, wound parachute style

Braided Butt Damsel: Most used colors for western Blue Damsel: Abdomen/Thorax/Hackle (Northern Rockies, Southern Rockies, and Pacific regions)

Abdomen blue (BCS 136) with black bands (use process-blue colored marker to dye mono; wait one hour and add black bands)/ Thorax blue (BCS 136)/Hackle dun

Abdomen mustard (BCS 57) (dye monofilament with Berol brand mustard color permanent marker)/ thorax yellow olive (BCS 43)/ hackle pale ginger

Braided Butt Damsel: Tying Instructions

1. Clamp the hook in the vise and wrap the thread to the *low water position.*

2. Form a small lump of thread at the low water position.

3. Cut the braided butt material to length and heat seal one end. The finished segment should be 1 1/4 inches long.

Speed Tying Tip: It's much faster to prepare a whole series of abdomens at one time. First, dye three or four feet of mono; then, cut it into 1 1/4-inch long segments. To give control when melting one end, use a pair of hemostats (a pair of forceps or pliers works also). Grasp the braided mono about 1/16 inch from the end. Flame the end to melt the mono back to the jaws of the hemostat.

4. Fray about 1/4 inch of the unsealed end of the mono abdomen. Tie in the frayed end just ahead of the thread lump. The separated ends of the braided mono should surround the hook shank; this prevents a lumpy body and simultaneously secures the material very tightly, preventing the mono from slipping onto the side of the hook. Wrap forward to completely cover the frayed ends, then wrap rearward, ending with the thread immediately ahead of the thread lump *(Figure 9-7)*. The thread lump holds the abdomen up away from the shank and prevents the abdomen from tangling around the hook bend during casting.

5. For the hackle post, I use 3-ply, medium weight, acrylic yarn. This is doubled to form a loop, and the loose ends tied in on top of the shank just ahead of the thread lump. Secure the yarn by

wrapping forward to the eye and then back to the post. To prevent an uneven body, stagger the ends of the yarn slightly when tying in *(Figure 9-8)*.

6. Select a hackle feather (the barbs should be the same length as the abdomen), prepare it, and tie in just ahead of the yarn post.

7. Wind the hackle 5-6 turns around the base of the yarn post, tie off, and cut away the excess.

8. Spin dubbing onto the thread and wrap forward to the head to form the thorax.

9. Part the barbs pointing to the front and spread them to the sides. Fold the yarn post forward, tight against the top of the thorax, and secure at the head.

Figure 9-8. *Slightly offset the ends of the yarn loop.*

10. Cut away the excess yarn, leaving the trimmed ends about as long as the hook eye. These ends suggest the head and buggy eyes of the natural.

11. Tie off the thread ahead of the yarn clump and cut it away.

12. Straighten the hackle barbs so they lie in more-or-less one plane.

13. Apply water-thin, flexible head cement to the head and the entire top of the thorax *(Figure 9-9)*.

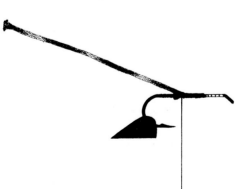

Figure 9-7. *Abdomen in place on the Braided Butt Damsel.*

Figure 9-9. *The completed Braided Butt Damsel; side view, front view, top view.*

DRAGONS

If any insects ever deserved the name of "dragon," these creatures are surely the ones. The adults of some species are truly huge; they are far and away the largest aquatic insects. At rest, they hold the wings outspread *(Figure 9-10)*. Powerful fliers, they dart about or hover with all the dexterity of the most agile bird. Their insatiable appetites drive them to attack and devour any insect smaller than themselves; there is even a species that specializes in eating Giant Michigan Mayflies. Two separate times I've had these brutes swoop down and intercept my dry fly as it dropped to the water. They held fly and leader aloft as they tried to kill and eat the artificial, finally releasing it when they realized it was a sham. I think these incidents say more about the nature of the dragonfly than about the quality of my flies.

Trout get only very rare opportunities to eat dragon adults, so for all the angling action they provide, tying imitations of these aerial insects is a waste of good effort. The nymphs, however, are another story. Like the adults, these insects are voracious predators. The largest species are, in terms of sheer mass, the top monsters of the deep. Unlike the damsels, the dragons have a robust body; the abdomen is somewhat triangular in cross section (being flat on the bottom) and considerably wider than the thorax. The long legs are quite stout *(Figure 9-11)*.

They don't breathe fire, but they can become jet propelled. The nymph's gills are located in its rectum (maybe this is the reason for the dragon's nasty disposition), and by rapidly expelling water through their terminal opening, they can shoot along in quick, little pulses, whether pursuing their hapless prey or trying to escape the jaws of a big trout. Like the damsels,

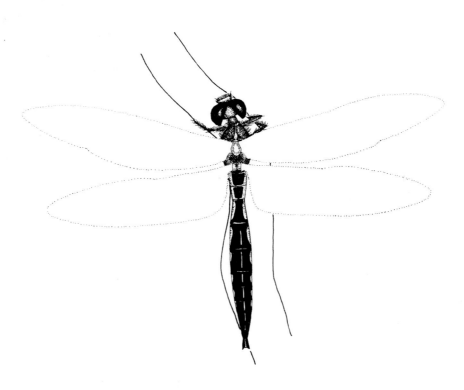

Figure 9-10. *The adult dragonfly at rest.*

they have a front-end-loader jaw that mercilessly snares the prey, including minnows and small trout.

Some species are stream denizens, sprawling in vegetation at the edges or venturing out to hug the bottom of pools and riffles. These open-water species can be quite abundant in trout streams, and fly fishers should carry imitations of them. These are flies for big trout. Charlie Brooks, who specialized in fishing for the largest trout, knew the value of these insects to opportunistically feeding fish in rivers of the West. In "The Trout and the Stream" he stated that 95 percent of the fish he had taken on his dragonfly

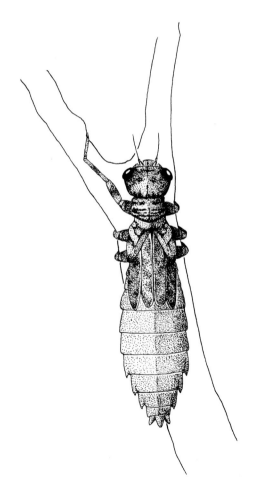

Figure 9-11. *A typical dragonfly nymph.*

nymph imitation were 15 inches or longer! In addition to using dragon nymph patterns in the West, I've used them very successfully here in the Lake States and in the East. You must have a dragon nymph pattern.

Like the damsels, most species of dragons are creatures of stillwaters. There they terrorize the weed beds, sprawling motionless in wait for their victims, or jetting about like some ancient machine of destruction. The nymphs live a year, perhaps two, and at maturity head to shore where the adults emerge. These migrations are rarely as concentrated as those of the damsels, but you don't need too many of these migrating monsters to get the trout excited. If there seems to be a fair number of adults around, or if you see the nymphs coming ashore, put on a stout leader and start chucking a big dragon nymph imitation; you could be pleasantly surprised.

The biggest design problem in creating an effective dragon nymph imitation is to create bulk; bulk that has some action; bulk that looks alive as the fly is retrieved on short, quick pulls. The Cary Special and Muskrat Nymph are two general patterns that very nicely suggest the jetting dragon nymph. Charlie Brooks' Assam Dragon is a great fly, designed specifically to mimic these robust insects; it's tied by wrapping a fur strip on the hook and finishing it with a large, soft hackle. The fur stands out at right angles to the shank, making a soft, highly active pattern. I use a very similar fly: the Fur Chenille Dragon. It's tied with a dubbing loop which allows the use of synthetic fibers, any type of fur or hair, or a combination of these. The loop is made of yarn, which not only adds bulk, but can be of a different color than the fur and thus can help give the fly a mottled appearance. For those who prefer to shape the fly more like the natural, the chenille is easily trimmed with scissors. I've not found a shaped fly to be any more effective than an unshaped one, however. To increase the active appearance of the fly, the marabou fluff is left on the soft hackle. The fly is fished with one- to two-inch long pulls, pausing occasionally.

Fur Chenille Dragon: Dressing

Hook: Sizes 2-8, 3XL

Thread: 3/0, color to match body

Body: Fur chenille made on a dubbing loop of thread and/or yarn; weighted with lead wire

Hackle: Pheasant rump feather, or other suitable feather, basal marabou fluff left on

Fur Chenille Dragon: Most Used Colors of Body and Hackle (all regions)

Body dark brown fur (BCS 129) spun in a loop of brown yarn (BCS 97)/ Hackle rusty brown rump feather

Body natural cottontail rabbit spun in a loop of bright green yarn (BCS 19)/Hackle rusty brown rump feather

Body olive (BCS 30) spun in a loop of pale olive yarn (BCS 28)/Hackle bluish or olive rump feather

Fur Chenille Dragon: Tying Instructions

1. Wrap the shank with thread, ending at the standard position.

2. Wrap the center 1/2 of the hook shank with lead wire and secure with the thread (page 30); end with the thread at the rear of the shank.

3. Form a dubbing loop, then wrap the thread to the head of the fly. There are two ways the loop may be formed:

    A. A piece of fuzzy yarn is tied in, a standard thread dubbing loop is formed, and the yarn is laid along one side of the thread loop; use this for larger sized yarns.

    B. A piece of thin yarn (crewel weight) is formed into a loop and the loose ends tied in at the rear of the hook shank.

4. With a spring-backed paper clamp, grasp the tip half of a 1/8 to 1/4 inch wide section of the selected fur; cut the fur from the hide *(Figure 9-12)*.

Figure 9-12. Use a spring-back paper clamp to hold the fur.

5. Holding the clamp in the bobbin hand, insert the fur into the dubbing loop at right angles to the material of the loop *(Figure 9-13)*.

6. Close the loop and then release the clamp.

7. Twist the loop, forming the fur chenille.

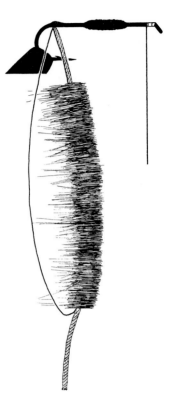

Figure 9-13. The fur is placed into the loop at right angles to the material of the loop.

8. Wrap the chenille forward to form the body; with your materials hand, brush the fur rearward after each turn to prevent it being covered by the next turn.

9. Secure at the head and cut away the excess.

10. Select a hackle feather with the non-marabou barbs as long as the hook. Cut off the basal end of the feather shaft so that the part bearing the marabou fluff is as long as the part bearing the non-marabou barbs *(Figure 9-14)*.

11. Tie the feather in by the basal end and wrap the thread to the *eye of the hook*—leave no head space.

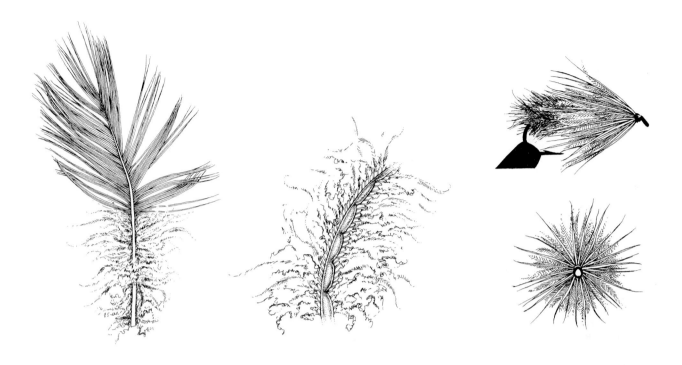

Figure 9-14. *There should be as much basal fluff as there are regular barbs.*

Figure 9-15. *Crimping the basal portion of the feather shaft.*

Figure 9-16. *The finished Fur Chenille Dragon; side view, front view.*

12. Wrap the hackle forward to the eye; use up the whole feather. Secure at the eye.

Speed Tying Tip: To make the heavy basal area of the feather shaft easier to tie and wrap, crimp it sideways between your thumbnail and forefinger. The thumbnail should crimp against the side that will be wrapped against the shank *(Figure 9-15)*. When wrapping, hold the hackle in your fingers for the first two or three turns, then attach the hackle pliers and finish winding the hackle. This method helps prevent the tip of the hackle from breaking while being wound.

13. Stroke all the barbs of the soft hackle rearward and hold them there with the materials hand. Wrap the thread rearward, keeping each wrap tight against the last one and form a head. This will force the hackle into a swept-back position.

14. Tie off the thread, cut it away, and coat the head with cement. Allow a couple of drops of cement to flow back into the base of the hackle to reenforce it *(Figure 9-16)*.

Another design that nicely mimics the dragon nymph is a Strip Leech (page 154) with the tail cut off. Rather than tie this fly in the bob-tail form, simply save any that lose the tail during fishing. All three leech colors (black, olive, and brown) can be used to suggest dragon nymphs.

Wooly worms and aquatic bugs

Wooly worms

Originating in bogs and spring ponds of the Wisconsin Highlands, the streams wind their way north to the shores of Superior. Cutting through ocher clays of the Gogebic Range, they flow swiftly down riffles dappled by the shadows of black spruce and towering white pines or pause momentarily in deep holes that shelter the scarlet-flanked brook trout. It was here in the early 1970's that I discovered the secret of the wooly worm.

Wooly Worm Larvae

My sampling nets revealed large numbers of huge black stonefly nymphs, squat dragonfly nymphs, and long, strongly pincered larvae that I recognized from my youth as something akin to the Hellgrammite (larva of the Dobsonfly). The insect key revealed them to be fishfly larvae *(Figure 10-1)*. Other samplings turned up Hellgrammites (which look like large fishfly larvae with more bushy abdominal filaments) and larvae of the Alderflies *(Figure 10-2),* aquatic beetles *(Figure 10-3),* and aquatic moths *(Figure 10-4)*. In addition to the usual compliment of six legs, all these larvae sported a series of lateral abdominal appendages. Though from different insect orders, there was a common thread: these larvae all looked like wooly worms.

Never present in numbers that could rival the "big four" stream insects, these ancient wooly worm larvae are, never-the-less, collectively abundant enough to form a regular part of the trout's menu. And, they're widespread; not only in stillwaters and streams of North America, but around the world. Charlie Brooks wrote of the Riffle Beetle larva in his fine books, and British anglers such as Kingsley and Skues have written glowingly of the Alderfly for over a century. In New Zealand, which pulled away from Australia before the evolution of mammals, the huge fishfly larvae are a staple of the big browns and rainbows. When caught in the currents, the wooly worm larvae may drift with the body straight or slightly curved. The legs and lateral filaments often twitch or move rhythmically. When seen against the light, the semi-translucent exoskeleton creates a halo around these larvae. They definitely look alive.

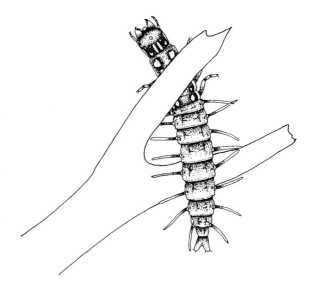

Figure 10-1. *A typical fishfly larva.*

The conventional Wooly Worm fly, with peacock herl or chenille body and palmered hackle is a good design to suggest the elongate body, obvious segmentation, and numerous appendages of these insects. But when I first discovered the abundant fishfly larvae in northern Wisconsin streams, I was experimenting with the hair-leg technique and decided to use it to create an imitation of these insects. The Hair Leg Wooly Worm has been a staple in my fly boxes ever since. To mimic the fleshy, glistening body and lateral appendages, I use brushed out mohair or a blend of sparkle yarns and coarse fur. A wire rib augments the segmentation and toughens the body, and palmered legs of calftail hair or guard hairs complete the fly. Even though some of the wooly worm larvae get to be three inches long, I've never found a need to tie the imitation larger than a size 2, 3XL.

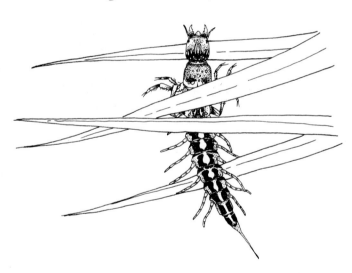

Figure 10-2. *The Alderfly larva.*

In addition to representing various larvae, the Hair Leg Wooly Worm is also a passable imitation of a large stonefly nymph. Two colors, dark brown (BCS 129) (or black) and dark tan (BCS 61) have filled the bill, no matter where I've fished. I've never found trout feeding selectively on any of the wooly worm larvae, so I use the imitation during the opportunistic periods between hatches, swinging it deep with a sinking line and the Brooks Method, dribbling it dead

drift along the bottom with a floating line and split shot on the leader, or in stillwaters, working it along weed edges on a floating or intermediate line.

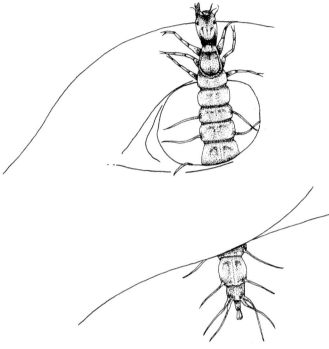

Figure 10-3. *A beetle larva with abdominal filaments.*

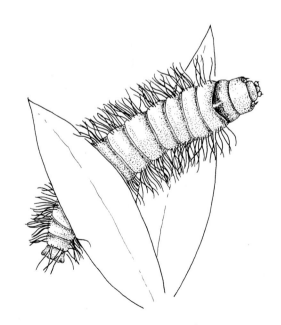

Figure 10-4. *A common aquatic moth larva.*

Hair Leg Wooly Worm: Dressing

Hook: Sizes 2-12, 3XL

Thread: 3/0 or 6/0, depending upon hook size, color to match body

Tail: Short tail of calftail hair or guard hairs, color to match body

Body: Mohair yarn or blend of sparkle yarn and coarse fur; weighted with lead wire; brushed out at sides

Rib: Wire, 24 or 26 gauge

Legs: Calf tail hair or guard hairs spun in a loop, hair leg style

Hair Leg Wooly Worm: Most Used Colors of Body/Rib/Tail and Legs (all regions)

Body dark brown (BCS 129) or black (BCS 118) mohair or blend of sparkle yarn and mink with guard hairs left in/Rib silver/Tail and Legs of black calf tail hair

Body blend of 25% dark tan sparkle yarn (BCS 61), 25% fur from back of fox squirrel, 50% hare's mask; or body of dark tan mohair/Rib copper/Tail and Legs of guard hairs from back of cottontail rabbit

Hair Leg Wooly Worm: Tying Instructions

1. Clamp the hook in the vise and wrap the shank with thread; ending at the standard position.

2. Tie in the tail; it should be 1/2 to 1/3 the length of the hook shank.

3. Weight the front half of the hook with lead wire and secure with the thread (page 30), ending with the thread at the rear of the lead *(Figure 10-5).*

Figure 10-5. *Tie in the tail and secure the lead.*

4. If using dubbing, spin it onto the thread, leaving 1 1/2 to 2 inches of bare thread between the shank and the dubbing.

5. Cut a six-inch length of wire for the rib and lay one end along the top rear 1/2 of the shank (butting up against the lead).

6. Secure the wire by wrapping rearward over it with the thread; this will also bring the dubbing up against the shank in preparation for forming the body.

7. If you wish to use yarn for the body, secure the wire rib as above, then lay one end of the yarn on top of the shank and extending forward to the lead. Secure by wrapping the thread forward. For most mohair yarns, one strand is sufficient. but if the yarn is thin, it may have to be doubled—use your judgement.

8. Wrap the body material forward over the rear 3/4 of the hook shank. If using yarn, tie off but do not cut away the excess.

9. Wind the wire rib forward and secure in front of the body (page 80).

10. Form a thread dubbing loop and apply dubbing to one side. If yarn is being used, it may be laid along one side of the loop. On larger sizes, the free end of the yarn may be looped back and

tied in to form the dubbing loop. A thread loop is not necessary in this case.

11. If guard hairs are used for the legs, pull them from the hide, insert them in the loop, spread them out, and spin the loop tight (page 32).

12. If the legs will be simulated by calf tail hairs, cut a clump from the tail (the hairs should be about 3/4 the length of the hook shank), insert them in the loop, spread them out, and spin tight *(Figure 10-6).*

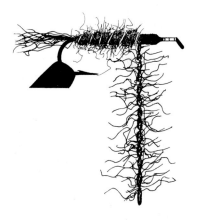

Figure 10-6. *Prepare the hair hackle in the usual manner.*

13. Form the thorax by winding the twisted loop forward to the head. After each turn, brush the hair legs back out of the way so they're not trapped by the next turn. Secure at the head and cut away the excess.

14. Form a smooth head, tie off, cut away the thread, and apply head cement.

15. Brush out the abdomen to give it a fuzzy appearance *(Figure 10-7).*

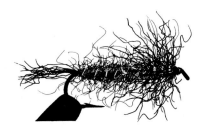

Figure 10-7. *The finished Hair Leg Wooly Worm.*

Wooly Worm Adults

Wooly worm larvae live from one to four years. At maturity those of the order Megaloptera ("large wing," Dobsonfly, fishflies, and Alderfly) and those of the order Coleoptera ("sheath wing," beetles) crawl from the water and pupate in chambers of the stream or lake shore. The aquatic moths (order Lepidoptera, "scale wing") pupate on the stream bottom, and the adults emerge there and swim to the surface. The adult Megalopterans and moths can be of occasional significance to the fly fisher. I've never seen trout feeding actively on adult *aquatic* beetles (terrestrial beetles are another matter).

Adult Alderflies look like husky bodied, gray-brown caddises *(Figure 10-8)* and can be nicely imitated with a size 12 Poly Caddis in smokey gray (BCS 108). In addition, this same-sized Poly Caddis in dark tan (BCS 61) apes the adult aquatic moths. Like the caddis, adult aquatic moths also often crawl underwater to lay eggs. Adult fishflies may be black or tan; they superficially resemble large stoneflies. The Tan Fishfly occurs in the Pacific region and is usually on the wing at dusk, but the widespread Black Fishfly frequently flutters about on bright sunny days. Aside from the coloration, they can be separated from stoneflies by the resting wing position: the fishflies hold theirs in a more tentlike fashion *(Figure 10-9)*. The Dobsonfly closely resembles the Tan Fishflies, but is larger and has more robust mandibles. Dobsonflies are prevalent in rocky areas of smallmouth bass streams and are occasionally found in trout waters. I've found them significant when fishing those transition areas between bass and trout waters. Fishflies and Dobsonflies can be imitated very nicely with a Hair Wing Stonefly of tan or black color. I've

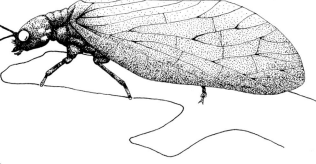

Figure 10-8. *The adult Alderfly looks like a husky caddis.*

used these adult imitations quite successfully in the Lake States and in the West Coast rivers of New Zealand's South Island.

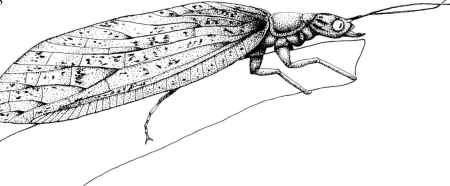

Figure 10-9. *The tentlike wing position of the fishflies is an easy way to separate these insects from the stoneflies.*

AQUATIC BUGS

In the common vernacular, the word "bug" can denote any and all insects. But to the entomologist, a bug is a member of the order Hemiptera ("half wing," referring to the forewings which are thickened on only the basal half). Bugs have an incomplete life cycle. That is, from the egg hatches a nymph. It looks like a miniature adult; however, its wings are not developed. As the insect grows, its wing enlarge. When mature the bug is fully capable of flight. Terrestrial bugs are extremely numerous, but there are only three aquatic bugs that are of significance to the fly fisher. In order of importance they are the Waterboatman, Backswimmer, and Giant Water Bug.

Waterboatman

These members of the family Corixidae inhabit lakes and ponds and the quiet-water edges of streams. In such places, I've seen them in absolute clouds, dashing this way and that among the weeds, or darting for the cover of the bottom at the approach of a fish. For trout of stillwaters, the Waterboatman can be a truly significant food source, and anglers fishing such areas should carry reliable imitations of this odd little creature.

Odd because first of all, it does not have gills to extract oxygen from the water. It must rise to the surface periodically to capture a bubble of air that it then carries with it when diving. Odd because its back legs are modified for rowing: elongate, paddle shaped, and heavily fringed with hairs *(Figure 10-10)*. Using these modified appendages, the insect oars itself about in a jerky fashion like a child who has just taken up rowing.

The pattern design must be linked to the angling tactic. The imitation works best when fished with a series of short, jerky movements.

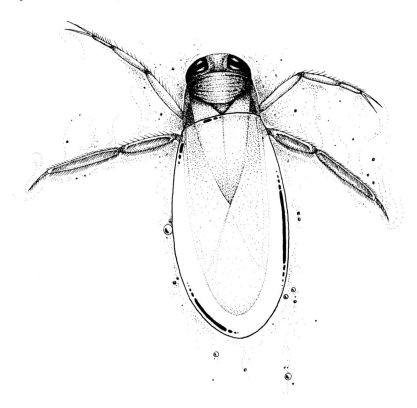

Figure 10-10. *The Waterboatman rows about with its long hindlegs.*

Either the Strip/Tease tactic or the Short Pull method works very well. When moved in this manner, the fly should show plenty of motion. In addition, it should glisten like the silvery air bubble carried by these gray to gray-brown insects. I've tried all manner of shell back patterns that use various materials for the sculling legs, but I've never found any of them as effective as a standard, soft hackle fly. That's because the trout doesn't see a motionless bug with rear legs outstretched and looking exactly like a pinned museum specimen. The trout sees a sculling, glowing caricature, not detail. Before the development of sparkle yarns, I simply used a Muskrat Nymph. Now, I use a size 12-16 Sparkle Caddis Pupa dressed in smoky gray (BCS 108). It's been very successful. To increase the motion of the imitation, the soft hackle can be prepared and wound as for the Fur Chenille Dragon (page 114) *(Figure 10-11)*.

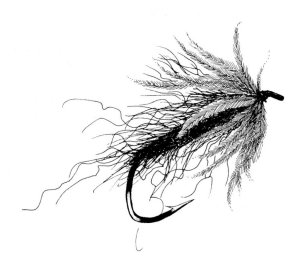

Figure 10-11. *The Sparkle Boatman.*

This Sparkle Boatman has produced some exceptional catches for me when the trout are foraging in the shallows. I've used it on shy,

crimson-sided brookies in the spring ponds of the Lake States, slow water reaches of streams in the Rockies, and in lakes across North America and other countries. Others who have written of stillwater fishing rate the Waterboatman highly. John Goddard notes the importance of these insects to the British reservoir angler in his book "The Super Flies of Still Water," Steve Raymond relates his most satisfactory experiences with Corixidae in "Stillwater Trout" (edited by John Merwin), and Donald Roberts cautions against discounting the importance of the bugs in his book "Flyfishing Still Waters."

Because the Waterboatman is usually a creature of water less than three feet deep, the Sparkle Boatman is one of my favorite selections when I'm stalking cruising trout in lake-edge shallows. Knowing the habits of these bugs paid off for me on a New Zealand excursion. My friend, Mike Allen, and I had spotted a number of large browns cruising very close to shore in the shallows at the head of a lake. We knew how spooky they were and how carefully we'd have to approach them, and we knew they'd be picky about what they were eating. As we watched from our position behind some matagora bushes, I saw a particularly good fish tip sideways and dart forward a bit to grab something. Mike and I had been good-naturedly giving each other a hard time about our respective angling skills, and I saw a chance to count coup. "I'll bet I can take two of those fish in less than five minutes," I remarked offhandedly.

Unable to resist, Mike snatched up the gauntlet, "OK, you're on. I could use a good laugh; loser buys the beer."

"Start timing when I make the first cast," I reminded him.

Using the scattered bushes of cover, I worked close to the edge; sure enough, there were clouds of backswimmers rowing about in the shallows. Rubbing my hands together gleefully and chortling under my breath, I watched the cruising patterns of the fish. A brown approached my position about 15 feet out. The sidearm cast fell perfectly; the fish darted forward. With heavy pressure that strained the limits of my tackle, I landed the fish in less than five minutes. A second fish cruised by about 40 feet out as I straightened from the release of the first fish. It took the fly as confidently as had the first trout.

"Beginners luck," Mike grumbled at the pub.

"Maybe so," I laughed, "but regardless of the skill involved, I think two browns in less than five minutes deserves another Double Brown; somehow they taste better when you're buying."

Like other adult bugs, the aquatic species are fully winged and perfectly capable of flight. The Waterboatman does leave the water to fly to other ponds or streams, but this occurs either at night or so sporadically that an angler could fish a lifetime and never encounter fish keying in on such activity. Thus, carrying a floating imitation is totally unnecessary. And besides, if you ever do stumble onto fish feeding on the "dry" adults, an appropriately sized Devil Bug will match them just fine.

Backswimmers

Looking very much like a large version of the Waterboatman, this bug belongs to the family Notonectidae. It gets it's common name from the uncommon habit of swimming upside down. Also like the far-more prevalent Waterboatman, the Backswimmer must carry a bubble with it as it dives, and trout eating this bug are easily fooled with a size 10 or 12 Sparkle Boatman.

Backswimmers will sometimes migrate from pond to pond, but I've only seen a couple of really good flights in fifteen years of rather intense lake fishing. They came buzzing in and splatted to the water, driving their plump bodies through the surface. Sometimes they bounced

off the rubbery film and spun around on the surface several times before trying again. The trout really keyed in on the insects as they hit the water or twirled about on the surface. If you ever encounter such a flight, a size 12, tan Devil Bug splatted to the surface will be highly effective.

Giant Water Bug

Looking like an overgrown Backswimmer or Waterboatman, the Giant Water Bug belongs in the family Belostomatidae. This flattened, oval-shaped bug is a powerful swimmer and fierce predator. Its long proboscis is used to pierce the prey and draw out the body juices—or give you a good nip if you're careless when handling one. Other insects and small fishes (including trout) are its prey.

The Giant Water Bug is a summer time inhabitant of ponds and lakes. There, it hangs out in the weeds searching for prey. Like the other aquatic bugs, it must submerge with its air bubble. Often living in stillwaters more suited to bass and pike, the Giant Water Bug is really only significant to trout fishers in the fall. At this time of year, they leave the lakes and fly to nearby streams where they overwinter. These flights occur in mid-afternoon and can be heavy enough to get even the big fish feeding alertly on them. The big insects make a distinctive buzzing sound as they divebomb into the river. I've encountered good flights in late September in the Lake States.

One could develop a specific pattern to represent these bugs, but since the opportunity to fish them is so slight, I just use a size 4 or 6 Silver Leech (page 159) with the tail clipped off to suggest the bug's bulk and the flashy diving bubble it carries. The fly is plopped into the water and worked with quick, short pulls. If you're ever fortunate enough to encounter this phenomenon, don't use a light tippet. The fish hit these bugs H A R D.

TERRESTRIALS

Terrestrial insects—those born and bred on land—sometimes fall into or are blown onto the water. Their significance as trout food has been recognized since Dame Juliana's time; she described flies for a wasp and a moth in her book "A Treatise on Fishing with a Hook," published in 1496. For the fly fisher, the most important terrestrials are ants, beetles, grasshoppers, leafhoppers, and inch worms. Ants (which overwinter as adults) and beetles (the most numerous of all insects) can be found in trout stomachs during all the warm months of the year; the others, however, show a definite seasonableness of abundance. Inchworms are prevalent in late spring and early summer whereas grasshoppers and leafhoppers reach the peak of their growth in mid through late summer.

Trout often feed opportunistically on terrestrials. In meadow streams, these insects may comprise over 50 percent of the summer diet of the fish. Sampling of the stomach contents of these trout, however, has shown that no one terrestrial is consumed preferentially. Thus, in such places, the fish are simply watching the surface for any food item that comes along—and most of what comes along are terrestrials. If you enjoy fishing dry flies during opportunistic periods, tie on a terrestrial.

But sometimes one type of terrestrial will fall to the water in such abundance that the fish become selective to them. I've seen selective feeding to all the major terrestrials. In summer, ants will often swarm in numbers beyond imagining. On warm spring evenings, when the big June Bugs (really beetles) are buzzing about,

they often get into the water in heavy numbers; likewise, other smaller beetles—most notably various species of bark beetles and the Japanese Beetle—are frequently numerous enough to bring on selective feeding, and I've encountered the big trout of New Zealand feeding preferentially on the Manuka Beetle so prevalent in the forested regions of that country. When the inchworms are falling to the surface of Michigan's Ausable River (and other streams throughout the Lake States and East), the knowledgeable angler will fish an imitation of these chartreuse or tan-colored insects. From Canada's Bow and Montana's Bighorn rivers to Pennsylvania's Letort Spring Creek, grasshoppers are part of the trout's summer diet and are often abundant in numbers that produce selective feeding. Leafhoppers (or jassids) were one of the insects that stimulated Marinaro's intensive study of terrestrial patterns.

Thus it is, that in the mid- to late-summer period, fishing with terrestrials can be very rewarding. The low, clear waters of late season, however, require a cautious approach on the part of the angler. Wade quietly and watch carefully for feeding fish. Those taking terrestrials are often back under overhanging grasses and bushes, along the edges of undercuts, or out in open water when the winds are blowing strongly. Don't by-pass even the most seemingly insignificant rise. Big trout will take ants and other small terrestrials with surprisingly little disturbance of the surface.

Some thirty years ago, I was wading up a stream near my home in Pennsylvania. It was a hot summer afternoon, and the fly rod hung heavily in my teenage hand. A few small fish dimpled the surface near some overhanging bushes in the tail of a long flat, and I idly pitched a small ant fly to them, thinking that these chubs would at least provide some action. The fly disappeared, and I yanked back, expecting to sail the tiny fish over my shoulder. Instead, the tippet snapped, and a huge brown roared out of the shallows, leaving a very startled boy in its foaming wake.

ANTS

These terrestrials are placed in the insect order Hymenoptera ("membrane wing") along with bees and wasps. Ants occur in every terrestrial ecosystem except *Ant*arctica. They are staggeringly numerous, and because they spend a great deal of time prowling about in vegetation looking for food, they are continually falling or being blown into streams and lakes. Drift samples indicate the presence of ants in trout waters during all the warm months. This continuous presence makes ants a well-known food item to the trout.

While attending graduate school at the University of Wisconsin at Madison in the late 60's and early 70's, I fished the nearby meadow streams extensively. Summer was ant time and afforded me ample refusals from trout feeding on these insects. At first I wrote it off to poor presentations (certainly that was the case much of the time), but then one day as I watched in frustration, I noted that the ants didn't sit up on the surface; rather, they were mired in the film, riding along partially awash. The rear of the body would frequently be deeper in the film than the legs and head, and the ants were usually quite still *(Figure 11-1)*. Because of this motionless, low-rider position, the ant's distinctive outline was clearly visible from underwater, even when the insect was outside the fish's window. My conventionally tied ant fly was riding much too high. To clearly show its ant-shaped outline,

the dry fly imitation of this thin-waisted critter had to be designed to ride with its body awash in the film.

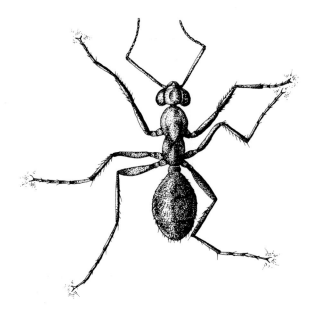

Figure 11-1. *The ant shape is quite distinctive.*

To achieve the correct positioning, I tied an ant pattern with a parachute hackle wound on a post midway along the hook shank. It was the fly I'd been looking for. There was a particular trout that had given me fits; it slurped the Para-Ant on the first drift. While it wasn't a particularly big fish, it was a picky one, and I sorely wanted its approval of the new ant design. The Para-Ant quickly became a standard in my fly box. But while this design was a decided improvement over the standard dry ants of that time, it still had a couple of flaws: (1) the lump of dubbing at the rear of the hook partially occluded the hook gap—a problem on very small hooks, and (2) attaching the hackle post at the center of the hook shank partially obscured the thin-waist profile that is so necessary in a good ant pattern.

But in 1979, Rene Harrop introduced a tying technique that solved these problems. To ape the partially unfurled wings of emerging mayfly duns, he devised a method to affix a ball of dubbing on *top* of the hook shank (page 40). The application of this technique to the Para-Ant was immediately apparent, and I incorporated it into the design. It produced an easy-to-tie pattern with a very strong ant silhouette and with none of the shortcomings of its predecessor. (That's three I owe you, Rene!)

The Para Ant can be fished either wet or dry, and during a hatch can be used as a passable imitation of a floating nymph or emerging midge, especially in sizes 20 and smaller. It's a trick that's saved the day for me many times.

Para-Ant: Dressing

Hook: Sizes 12-28, standard shank length

Thread: 6/0 or 8/0, depending on hook size, color to match body

Abdomen (gaster): Blended fur and sparkle yarn dubbing applied as a ball on top of hook shank

Thorax: Same as abdomen

Head: Optional, I've never found that tying in a separate head makes the fly more effective than one without a head; I believe the eye of the hook sufficiently suggests the head of the natural

Hackle: Dry fly quality of color to match body, tied in at rear of thorax and wound parachute style one or two turns around base of thorax

Para-Ant: Most Used Sizes/Colors (all regions)

Sizes 12-28/Black (BCS 118)

Sizes 16-28/Rusty brown (BCS 66)

Sizes 16-28/Clay tan (BCS 53)

Para-Ant: Tying Instructions

1. Clamp the hook in the vise and wind the hook shank with thread, ending at the standard position.

2. Form a ball of dubbing on top of and at the rear of the hook shank. Use the technique shown for the Floating Nymph (page 40).

3. Wrap the thread forward to the position of the thorax and tie in the hackle; the thorax is placed as far forward on the hook as possible without obscuring the eye—normally this is about three head spaces behind the eye.

4. Form the thorax in the same manner as the abdomen; I normally make it the same size as the abdomen.

5. Wind the hackle one or two turns around the base of the thorax, parachute style, and tie off in front of the thorax.

6. Clip away the excess portion of the hackle feather (there is usually enough left for a second Para-Ant) and tie the finishing knot just ahead of the thorax.

7. Coat all exposed thread with water-thin, flexible head cement; put a drop of cement at the base of each ball of dubbing (*Figure 11-2*).

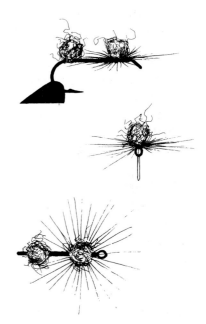

Figure 11-2. *The finished Para-Ant; side view, front view, top view.*

Flying Ant

Once a year an ant colony produces a large number of virgin queens and drones (males). Sometime during the summer, these flying ants leave the nest and form mating swarms. Such flights can be astoundingly vast, and if one should land on the surface of a lake or stream, the fish will feed heavily on the mired, winged insects. Over the years, I've had some fabulous fishing brought on by such falls, and for some unknown reason, I've only seen black or rusty brown flying ants, and I've never seen really small species on the water.

The flying ant rides in the film in the same fashion as the wingless worker ant. The gray wings are held upright over the back, and with only a cursory glance, these insects could be confused with tiny mayflies. From underwater, the wing is as prominent as that of a mayfly, and so it should be represented in the artificial. Although sparkle yarn makes great wings, it has to be well secured or it will pull out. That's one of the reasons I trim the wing butts of the Yarn Wing Dun and Poly Caddis as I do. But on the Flying Ant, leaving the wing butt creates the wrong profile, so I use a winging technique shown to me by George "Chappy" Chapman, a friend from Woodland Hills, California. With Chappy's tactic, the yarn is looped under the hook shank and pulled upright to form a single wing. It's fast and effective; the kind of tying I like.

Like the standard version, the Flying Ant is a good desperation choice when you're out of tiny imitations to suggest mayfly or midge adults. The profile may not be close enough to fool every fish, but it will fool some, and that's certainly better than quitting in frustration.

Flying Ant: Dressing

Hook: Sizes 12-20, standard shank length

Thread: 6/0 or 8/0, depending upon hook size, color to match body

Abdomen: Blended fur and sparkle yarn, applied as a ball on top of hook shank

Wing: Gray sparkle yarn (BCS 108) tied in at thorax

Thorax: Same dubbing as abdomen, wound parachute style around base of wing

Hackle: Cock hackle same color as body, wound parachute style one or two turns around base of thorax

Flying Ant: Most Used Sizes/Colors (all regions)

Sizes 12-20/Black (BCS 118)

Sizes 16-20/Rusty brown (BCS 66)

Flying Ant: Tying Instructions

1. Form the abdomen as for the Para Ant (steps 1 and 2).

2. Wrap the thread forward to the position of the thorax; the thorax is placed as far forward on the hook as possible without obscuring the eye—normally this is about three head spaces behind the eye.

3. Select a strand of sparkle yarn half the desired thickness of the finished wing and fold it up around the hook shank just ahead of the thread.

4. Grasp the ends of the looped yarn in your materials hand and pull the yarn up tight against the shank, then tip it back slightly *(Figure 11-3)*.

5. To secure the yarn, wrap the thread around the shank several times, covering that part of the yarn that's on the underside of the hook

6. Tie in a hackle feather at the base of the yarn wing.

7. Spin dubbing on the thread, leaving an inch or so of bare thread between the hook and the dubbing; use this bare thread to wrap around the base of the yarn wing (just above the hook shank, *Figure 11-4*).

8. Continue wrapping to form a ball of dubbing *around the wing base;* this ball represents the thorax.

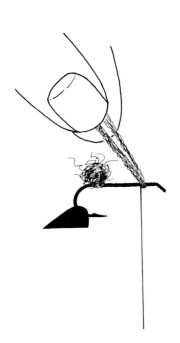

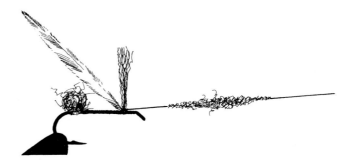

Figure 11-4. *Wrap the thread around the yarn just above the hook shank.*

End with the thread at the front of the thorax.

9. Wind the hackle one or two turns, parachute style, around the base of the thorax; tie down just in front of the thorax. Clip away the excess feather. Tie off the thread, cut it away, and cement as for the Para Ant.

10. Clip the wing to the same length as the hook shank *(Figure 11-5)*.

Figure 11-3. *Tilt the yarn rearward.*

Figure 11-5. *The finished Flying Ant.*

BEETLES

In the mountains, wind is a way of life; but this day, it was being overly zestful. We'd retreated to a small lake where a high bank and stately ponderosa provided us with a tiny crescent of calm water. Expecting only exceptional scenery, we were delighted to find the water covered with the rings of rising trout. Bob Pelzl grabbed a boat and headed out. "The water's covered with beetles," he yelled. And so it was; small black bark beetles, swept in from the surrounding forest lands by the gusting winds. We totally forgot to look at the scenery.

Beetles have two basic shapes: the oval, scarab design, or the more elongate configuration (like a firefly or click beetle). I've taken trout on imitations of the longer beetles, but I've never seen the fish selective to them. The scarab-shaped ones, however, are a different matter *(Figure 11-6)*. Bark beetles, the June Bug, the Japanese Beetle, the Manuka Beetle, and others can fall to the water in huge numbers, and the trout become fixated on them. So, I carry patterns to represent these not-infrequently encountered insects.

They've provided me many memories. There were days when the big, hyperselective fish of Henry's Fork and the Livingston spring creeks threw themselves with abandon on the beetle pattern; nights in the sweet air of New Zealand when my friend Pat Cahill graciously guided me on his favorite waters, pointing out by starlight the dimpling rises of big trout sucking in Brown Beetles; days when Mike Allen and I stalked trout locked on Manuka Beetles; daybreak in the Lake States with June Bugs plopping clumsily to the water; and a host of other experiences that burn bright because of beetles.

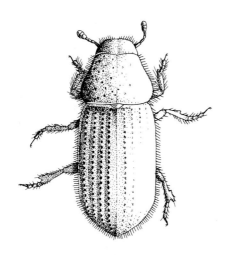

Figure 11-6. *A typical scarab-shaped beetle.*

In the 1940's Vince Marinaro and Charlie Fox spent a great deal of time studying beetle imitations. The Japanese Beetle, which had entered this country in 1916, was enormously abundant in those years, and provided a regular summertime food source for the trout of the Letort and other streams of south central Pennsylvania. In the early days of their studies, they tried all manner of imitations, including half a coffee bean glued on top of the hook. All were somewhat successful. But the super-selective trout of the Letort could not be had on just any old beetle pattern, and that forced Marinaro to search for those qualities that the trout found so attractive in the natural. He discovered that beetles, like ants, basically remain motionless on the surface, and thus the browns of the Letort responded best to a fly designed to show the broad outline and opaque nature of the insect. He developed a very simple fly that provided these two characteristics; it had a palmered hackle body, trimmed top and bottom, and a flat wing of paired jungle cock nails. The trout of the Letort couldn't leave it alone.

Marinaro's Jungle Cock Beetle is still a great fly, but it's difficult to get jungle cock feathers. So, tiers have switched to other designs. However, whether of feathers, hairs, or other materials, all current patterns reflect Marinaro's findings: a broad beetle outline and opaque body. My favorite is Ken Thompson's Foam Beetle—a take off on Marinaro's beetle that substitutes plastic foam for the jungle cock. The cellular foam of Ken's beetle is very tough, easily colored with permanent markers, and provides excellent flotation; it's also very easy to find.

This fly is also a great imitation of land-based, true bugs. They look the same on the water as a beetle, and the trout take them just as readily.

Thompson's Foam Beetle: Dressing

Hook: Sizes 8-22, standard shank length

Thread: 6/0 or 8/0, depending upon hook size, color to match natural

Body: Blended fur and sparkle yarn dubbing on sizes 8-16; thread on smaller sizes

Legs: Cock hackle, one size smaller than normal, palmered over front half of hook shank and trimmed on the bottom.

Shell: Strip of foam plastic dyed with a permanent marker

Thompson's Foam Beetle: Most Used Sizes/Body Color/Hackle Color/ Shell Color (all regions)

Sizes 8-22/Body black (BCS 118)/ Hackle black/Shell black

Sizes 8-22/Hackle brown/Body orange brown (BCS 60)/ Shell dark rusty brown (BCS 65/ 66)

Sizes 12-22/Body black/Hackle black/ Shell bright green (BCS 19/20)

Thompson's Foam Beetle: Tying Instructions

1. Clamp the hook in the vise and wind the shank with thread, ending at the *extended* position.

2. Cut a strip from a sheet of 1/8-inch thick plastic foam. The strip should be as wide as half the length of the hook shank. Color it with a permanent marker. There are many types of foams that will work, just be sure that the material is tough and the air chambers are small.

3. Tie the foam strip in at the rear of the hook with the butt end extending forward to the head of the fly. Wrap the thread forward to the head and then back to the rear in a close spiral pattern. This wrapping compresses the butt end of the foam strip and secures it to the hook.

4. Form the dubbed fur or thread body on the rear half of the hook.

5. Tie in the hackle feather at the middle of the hook.

6. Form the dubbed fur or thread body on the front half of the hook, ending two head spaces behind the eye.

7. Wind the hackle feather forward to the head—5 or 6 turns are sufficient.

8. Push the hackle barbs that are sticking out of the top of the fly down to the sides and fold the foam strip forward over the top of the fly; do not stretch the foam. If the foam is stretched, it will make a narrow body that will curl down around the hook and force all the hackle to stick out of the bottom of the fly, leaving none at the sides for legs. Secure the foam at the head with 5 or 6 turns of thread.

9. Trim away the excess foam, leaving a short clump to form the head.

10. Trim the hackle off the bottom of the fly.

11. Coat the head with cement *(Figure 11-7)*.

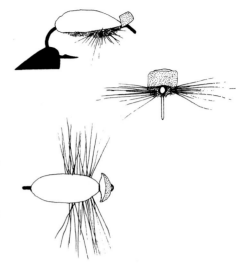

Figure 11-7. *The finished Foam Beetle; side view, front view, top view.*

JASSIDS

These insects are also known as leafhoppers. They're placed in the order Homoptera ("same" wing) along with the closely related treehoppers (leafhoppers that live in the forest rather than in the meadows). These trihedron-shaped insects *(Figure 11-8)* can be hugely abundant in mid through late summer and it's a wise idea to carry imitations of them.

One summer, in the mid 1970's, during our first years of teaching fly fishing classes at Vermejo Park Ranch, we took a day off and went to the lakes to sun bathe and picnic. As we lay there, shutting out all cares and listening to the moan of the wind in the ponderosa pines, I gradually became aware of a soft slurping sound. Suddenly I recognized it as the noise of feeding fish. "Fish," I yelled, leaping to my feet and scaring the wits out of the others. And what a sight it was! The lake was covered with rings. It was also covered with leafhoppers, carried there by the winds. We rigged our gear rapidly, and sun worshipping forgotten, settled into one of the best days of dry fly fishing we'd ever had.

We've been fortunate to experience this same phenomenon a good number of times since.

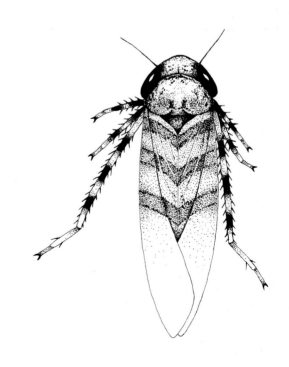

Figure 11-8. *A typical leafhopper.*

Leafhoppers were the critters that nearly drove Marinaro and Fox to distraction. But Vince solved the riddle in the late 1940's, and his justly famous Jungle Cock Jassid fooled trout after selective trout on the difficult waters of the Letort. The fly was a small version of his beetle imitation. And that's just what I use—the size 16 to 22 Foam Beetle in brown and green. They work just great.

GRASSHOPPERS

Late summer is the time of the grasshopper, and they can be exceedingly abundant. In 1986, Jason and I were shooting "The Fabulous Bighorn" video and had completed the early summer segment. As we left Fort Smith, we encountered a huge, dark mass on the highway; it was a migration of immature hoppers. The flightless nymphs formed a column a quarter of a mile wide as they crossed the road from one field to another. We stopped the van and watched in amazement. Five minutes passed and still they came; we were so nonplussed by this phenomenon that we never thought to video it. But, boy! did we tie hopper patterns for our return trip in August. And, boy! was the fishing good. Jason took a 24 1/2-inch brown that refused to go into the net; his antics while trying to land the fish sent us both into a laughing fit. It was such fun that we added the scene to the video.

Grasshoppers develop in the same fashion as the true bugs. A nymph hatches from the egg. It looks like a miniature adult without wings. As it grows and molts, the wings slowly develop. Once mature, the hopper is capable of powerful flight as well as powerful jumping. Its leaping and flying can get the insect into deep water, literally. Bob Ippel, an angling companion and good friend, once encountered the lake trout of Superior feeding heavily on hoppers twelve miles from the nearest land. Needless to say, hoppers can be found in the center of trout streams and ponds of any width.

Hoppers have some distinctive traits that the fly tier needs to carefully consider when building imitations. There's not much fluff on a grasshopper. The body is rather compact, and these insects drop to the water very positively. "Plop" is perhaps the best word to describe the way hoppers fall to the surface. And, they're big, which means that all their parts are readily visible to the trout. Two of the most significant parts, it turns out, are the huge hind legs. Grasshoppers are very active insects, and when they plop to the water, they immediately begin kicking in an attempt to jump off the surface. Those big hind limbs push well away from the body and become a prominent, unique feature. When seen from underwater, the distinctive angle of these big kickers makes the insect look bow-legged *(Figure 11-9)*. And that's just the way I position them on the Bow Legged Hopper. The hopper's body is very similar in size to that of a big stonefly and gives a very similar appearance when seen from below (page 72). So, to achieve a very natural looking hopper body I use the same technique as for the Hair Wing Stonefly (page 73). And like stoneflies, hoppers do not have bushy tails, but the tail of the artificial (which is added to support the rear of the hook) suggests the membranous flight wings of the hopper. It's a perfect marriage of utility and imitation.

Figure 11-9. *A grasshopper seen from underwater.*

Grasshoppers belong to the order Orthoptera ("right angle" wing). Their forewings are leathery and not used for flying; they're held out at right angles to the body during flight. At rest, these tough forewings fold back over the flight wings like a tent. To represent these folded, outer wings, Dave Whitlock came up with the concept of using a segment of lacquered, mottled turkey feather, trimmed to shape and set in on top of the body. It's a great representation that's easily achieved and quite durable. The only problem facing the tier in this day and age is finding good quality mottled turkey. Jack Gartside solved the dilemma by substituting lacquered, mottled body feathers from pheasant, but body feathers from birds such as grouse, and chukkar, also make excellent overwings. In this case, the entire feather is lacquered (page 34) and trimmed to shape. The head can be formed from spun deer hair, as Dave does with his hopper, or from folded deer hair, as in the Henry's Fork Hopper, developed by Mike Lawson. I use the folded hair head because it's easier to apply to my hopper design.

Grasshoppers come in a wide variety of colors, but tan, yellow, and green are by far the most common. Hoppers also come in a broad range of sizes from just plain big to monstrous. And while I usually match the size of the natural in my imitation, there are times when a magnum hopper can outproduce the more conventional sizes. It's always worth a try. A long-time friend, Tom Roney, from Grayling, Michigan, was drift fishing Canada's Bow in late summer and tied some truly huge hoppers so he could see them more easily from the moving boat. The big browns went wild for them! Grasshopper fishing is anything but dull.

In streams, the best hopper fishing is often near shore, since there are usually more insects close to the bank. Trout will move out of deep water and into the near-shore shallows and actively search for the insects. The thin water at the edges of the stream allows the fish to rise to the surface with little expenditure of energy, and near-shore bottom structure frequently offers better feeding lies than the main channel.

On rivers like Montana's Bighorn or Canada's Bow, I've had incredible fishing by wading slowly upstream and prospecting the water ahead with a hopper, especially in riffly areas. Fish of two feet in length or more are often encountered in water that barely covers their backs. It's really exciting to see that huge head poke out and slurp in your fly. It's even more exciting when the hooked fish roars out of the shallows for the cover of deep water, tearing great lengths of line from the reel.

While shallow water is most often found near the bank, there can be areas where midstream shallows are also found: at the heads and tails of islands, where gravel bars cut diagonally across the stream, at the tail out of a pool, in riffles, over a submerged weed bed, and so on. Don't pass up such areas during hopper time. Remember, hoppers can easily get to the center of even huge rivers, and the trout will be watching for them.

Another great way to fish big streams is to float them and cast grasshopper flies in against the bank, often times within inches of dry land. Areas of undercut banks or heavy overhanging vegetation can be especially productive. On the Bow, the water right next to shore is often too shallow to hold fish, but about three feet out, the bottom drops off sharply. The trout hang right at the edge of the deep water and watch for hoppers. When float fishing, don't keep picking up the fly and recasting unless it's necessary. On Montana's Madison, where the fishing is pocket shooting, then the casting is rather rapid fire, but on the long placid glides of the Bow the fly may be repositioned only once ever minute or two.

On small streams, I often don't wade at all. The trout of late summer can be quite spooky, and I have no desire to telegraph my presence to them. Rather, I sneak along and fish likely holds with as much care as possible. A great tactic is to cast the fly delicately into the grass on the opposite bank and then gently pull it off. Be prepared! I've had some really big fish lunge out of the water at the falling fly. I'm usually so startled at such antics that I either break off the fish or simply forget to set the hook. Hopper fishing is anything but dull.

During hopper time, trout ponds can offer some really remarkable fishing. The trout cruise around a foot or two under the surface looking upward for the big insects. When they spot one they often rush it and take it violently, producing sporadic, showy rises. The trick is to remember that the fish are constantly on the move. If you can actually see the fish, cast the hopper fly about eight to ten feet ahead of it and get ready. If you can't see the fish, then toss the fly in the vicinity of the rises and wait it out. Don't try to make the hopper look like it's kicking to shore; a *very occasional* twitch is alright, but it's easy to overdo a good thing. You may have to leave the fly sit for several minutes or a fish may nail it the instant it touches down; you never know. Like I said, hopper fishing is anything but dull.

Bow Legged Hopper: Dressing

Hook: Sizes 6-12, 3XL; for magnum hoppers go as large as size 2, 4XL

Thread: 3/0 or 6/0, depending upon hook size, color to match body

Underbody: Deer body hair

Overbody: Blended fur and sparkle yarn dubbing or a strand of sparkle yarn

Flight Wings: Tips of hair used for underbody and tips of hair used for head

Overwing: Appropriately sized and colored body feather of any bird, or segment of mottled turkey feather; lacquered with flexible head cement and trimmed to shape; tied in on top of body, down-wing style (represents the folded forewings)

Jumping Legs: barbs from pheasant tail or other feathers, knotted to form correct shape, tied in bow-legged style

Forelegs: Tips of hair used for head

Head: Folded deer body hair

Bow Legged Hopper: Most Used Sizes/Body Color/Overwing Color/ Jumping Leg Color/ Head Color (all regions)

Sizes 6-8/Overbody pinkish tan (BCS 58)/Overwing color of mottled turkey (BCS 100 mottled with 103)/Jumping Legs natural pheasant tail color/Head dark natural gray brown deer hair

Sizes 6-12/Overbody yellow (BCS 49)/ Overwing color of dark mottled turkey (BCS 102 mottled with 116)/Jumping Legs natural pheasant tail color or dyed red to imitate Red-Legged Grasshopper/ Head tan deer hair

Sizes 10-12/Overbody bright green (BCS 19)/Overwing dyed olive green (BCS 30) with permanent marker/Jumping Legs dyed olive green (BCS 30) /Head olive green deer hair

Bow Legged Hopper: Tying Instructions

1. Prepare the body as for the Hair Wing Stonefly (steps 1-5, page 73), but cover the rear 2/3 of the body with dubbing or yarn.

2. To prepare the overwing, the entire feather is dipped in head cement, stroked to narrow it, and permitted to dry (page 34). The finished feather should have a width equal to 1/3 the length of the hook shank; if it's too wide, simple cut away the excess. Trim the tip square and then cut off the corners *(Figure 11-10)*. These treated feathers are often longer than a segment from mottled turkey and so can be used easily on the magnum hoppers. I especially like various feathers from pheasant, grouse, and chukkar. If mottled turkey is used, first paint the entire feather with flexible head cement and allow to dry. Then cut out a segment of proper width and trim the tip.

Figure 11-10. *The prepared overwing feather.*

3. Tie in the overwing just ahead of the dubbed portion of the body. The tip end should extend rearward and cover the front half of the tail *(Figure 11-11)*. The ends of the hair tail will suggest the flight wings of the hopper.

Figure 11-11. *The overwing should cover half the hair tail.*

4. The jumping legs may be formed from a wide variety of feathers. Many tiers use pheasant tail barbs because these feathers are the correct color and easily obtainable. However, mottled turkey, dark turkey tail, pheasant rump feathers, grouse tail feathers, and many others are also usable for making hopper

legs. In addition, pre-formed hopper legs are now available from fly shops and catalogs. To make hopper legs from a pheasant tail feather, first remove a clump of 6 to 8 barbs. Wet the clump to keep the barbs together and tie a loose overhand knot in it. A hemostat or hackle pliers is very helpful for getting the end of the clump through the loop of the knot. (Form the loop, reach through it with the tool and grasp the end of the clump, and pull it back through the loop to form the knot. It's easier to get the heavy butt end of the clump through the loop than to get the fine, tip end through.) Hold the loose knot between thumb and forefinger of the materials hand and arrange the ends so that they are at right angles to each other *(Figure 11-12)*. Pull each end to tighten the knot while pinching it firmly with the fingers of the materials hand. Don't pull too hard, just get the knot snug; this will cause the two ends to form a right angle in the finished leg. Tightening the knot too much will cause the finished leg to

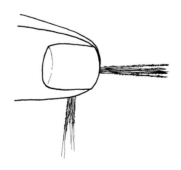

Figure 11-12. *Pinch the untightened knot between thumb and forefinger of your materials hand.*

straighten. Allow the barbs to dry then put a drop of head cement on the knot. Needless to say, it's best to make up a series of legs before beginning to dress the flies. When using feather segments to make hopper legs, I find it best to lacquer the feather and permit it to dry. Small segments are then removed and knotted.

5. Tie in the legs on top of the body so that they angle outward away from the body but at the same time turn them so that the very end of the leg is pointing back in toward the bend of the hook— from the top or bottom the fly will look bow legged (see side and bottom views of the finished fly, Figure 11-15). Wrap the thread forward to just behind the eye of the hook.

6. Select a clump of deer hair for the head. The size of the clump varies with the size of the hook, but remember that the head should be rather robust when it's finished. If the tips are not rather even, then stack the hair.

7. Hold the hair in your materials hand with the tips pointing out over the eye of the fly for a distance equal to the length of the hook shank. Slant the clump downward to that the tips of the hair uniformly surround the eye of the hook while the butts are held above the hook shank *(Figure 11-13)*.

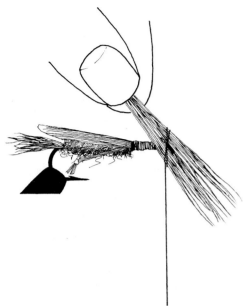

Figure 11-13. *Hold the hair slanting downward and around the eye of the hook.*

8. Keeping a firm grip on the butt end of the clump, make two loose turns of thread around the hair. Pull the turns tight to flair the tips of the hair. Do not let go of the butt end of the clump. Take 4 or 5 more tight turns with the thread to secure the hair.

9. Cut off the butt end of the clump and wrap the thread rearward through the cut end (page 50). Finish with the thread just ahead of the dubbed body.

10. Push the tips of the hair rearward around the fly to form a bullet head and hold them in place with the materials hand. Take two loose turns of thread around the hair and then pull tight, cinching the hair and forming the head *(Figure 11-14)*. Take 3 or 4 more tight turns of thread to form a thread collar and secure the hair.

11. Tie the finishing knot on the thread collar at the rear of the deer hair head and cut away the thread.

12. Trim away the tips of deer hair sticking down under the fly, leaving those sticking to the sides and top.

13. Coat the deer hair head with water-thin flexible head cement; permit to dry and coat again *(Figure 11-15)*.

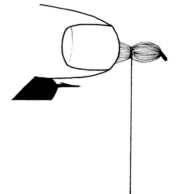

Figure 11-14. *Hold the hair while wrapping the thread at the rear of the head.*

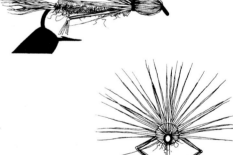

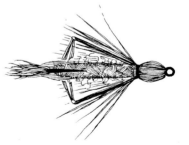

Figure 11-15. *The finished Bow Legged Hopper; side view, front view, bottom view.*

INCHWORMS

In the morning early, the waters slide beneath a veil of mist, whispering as only rivers can about the coming day. Ancient cedars, bowed beneath their years sweep the surface with trailing branches, while high overhead the oaks, basswoods, birches, and maples spread their translucent leaves to the sun. The push of the cool waters is surprisingly strong and the fine gravels of the bottom a delight to wade. Here in 1976, along the banks of Michigan's Ausable River, I learned that inchworms can be more than of passing interest to the trout. I'd gone to teach a fly fishing school at Gates Ausable Lodge, and about mid-morning Cal Gates returned from a fishing excursion, looking a bit shaken. He'd been fishing an oakworm imitation and doing very well on small browns and brookies when a dimpling rise near shore caught his attention. He popped the bright green fly in a couple of feet above it, only to have a huge brown inhale the fly and roar off upstream. Totally unprepared, poor Cal simply stood and watched as the trout disappeared with his fly.

"The oakworms usually come in mid-June right between the Brown Drakes and the Hexes," Cal told me. "And they provide great day-time fishing."

And although, tragically, Cal died a few years later, I can still see the emotionally mixed look of excitement and disappointment on his face as he described his run-in with that big trout.

Every kid has played with inchworms (also called measuring worms) and been fascinated by the peculiar looping way they hitch along *(Figure 11-16)*. These insects are the caterpillars of various species of moths in the family Geometridae (a most apt name). They feed on the leaves of trees, and when ready to pupate, lower themselves to the ground on a silken thread. It is this habit that gets them into trouble with the trout. For, if the insects should drop onto the water, they are sure to become a meal. I've seen hundreds of them hanging in the air, slowly unreeling themselves to certain doom on the waters below.

And I've seen them dragging on the surface, skipping and bouncing on the currents until heartily eaten by a trout. Ah well, their misfortune is my fortune—and yours too if you go alooking for them.

The inchworm lies very still on the surface of the water with its well-segmented body outstretched and simply drifts along totally at the mercy of the currents. And a very simple insect it is to imitate, too. Just an extended deer hair body. No hackle, no wings, no tail; no fuss, no muss, no bother: a paradigm of simplicity that produces a plethora of angling pleasures.

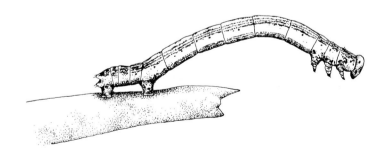

Figure 11-16. *An inchworm.*

Inchworm: Dressing

Hook: Size 12-14, standard shank length

Thread: 3/0

Body: Deer hair, extended body style

Inchworm: Most Used Body Color/Thread Color (all regions)

Chartreuse (BCS 21)/Thread green

Natural dark deer hair (BCS 91)/Thread brown

Inchworm: Tying Instructions

1. Clamp the hook in the vise and wrap the shank with thread back to the standard position and then forward to the head.

2. Select a clump of deer hair for the body; the clump should be 1/2 to 2/3 the diameter of a pencil.

3. Form an extended body as for the Hair Wing Dun (steps 7-12, page 49); however, do not hold the rear, extended portion up at a 45 degree angle, keep it straight as when making the Parachute Spinner (page 60). In addition, make the extended portion of the body as long as that portion on the hook shank.

4. The thread is tied off at the rear of the fly. It's easily done by holding the tips of the deer hair between forefinger and thumb of the materials hand and tying the knot with the middle finger of the materials hand. The loop of the knot is taken *back* around the tips of the deer hair rather than forward over the head of the fly. This procedure produces a body with a single, spiral, thread rib that nicely suggests the well-segmented body of the natural

5. Coat the body with water-thin flexible head cement; permit it to dry and coat it once more *(Figure 11-17)*.

Figure 11-17. *The extended body inchworm*

Sinking inchworm imitations can also produce great fishing. Barry Beck, a friend and superb fisher specializing in low, clear-water fishing, has spent two decades testing such patterns and has found a size 14, 2XL, chenille-bodied fly in fluorescent chartreuse green (BCS 21/24) to be highly effective. If necessary the fly can be ribbed with silver wire to add weight or weighted with lead wire before the chenille is wound on. Barry's success with this fly makes the pattern a very worth while addition to any angler's fly box.

CRUSTACEANS SNAILS AND WORMS

CRUSTACEANS

Too often in fly fishing we become so entranced with the idea of trout eating tiny, delicate insects that we forget that the fish, after all, must survive—and survival means eating whatever the fish can find. Crustaceans are certainly one of those things that fish can find. These organisms occur in lakes and streams world wide, and often in numbers that require a bit of imagination to accept. Regardless of their abundance, however, I have found trout feeding truly selectively to crustaceans only a few times, but very frequently I've found them feeding on crustaceans opportunistically. Thus, it's a good idea to carry imitations of the three principle crustaceans: scuds, cressbugs, and crayfish.

Scuds

If I were to design a trout stream I would want it to be large. Of such magnitude that its fish were not totally accessible to the angler, where there would always be a haven of refuge for them—but with flats, riffles, side channels, and tail-outs where fish would feed freely and the angler could wade in safety. It would be clean; of a clarity that would allow the observant angler to see its feeding fish; to stalk them individually; to test skills one-on-one. And there would be trout, a hundred thousand of them; big browns and rainbows that would take the angler's offering at all hours of the day. It's waters would be as fertile as the earth could make them; laden with nutrients extracted from the shells of long-since-dead creatures that have been fused and hardened to stone. Abundant plant life, both microscopic and macroscopic in scale, would populate its currents to harvest the sun and provide the fodder for the unimaginably abundant scuds I would seed there. Why scuds? Because trout love them and grow fat on these crustaceans. Many, many times on many, many spring creeks, rivers, and lakes, I've taken huge fish after countless huge fish with a scud and strike indicator.

Stream-dwelling scuds, along with some species of mayfly nymphs, caddis and blackfly larvae, and a few other organisms, participate in behavioral drift. They leave the protective cover of the bottom to be carried away by the currents. The normal time for behavioral drift is just before dawn and just after sunset; at these times the fish feed opportunistically because of the wide mix of organisms. But I have, on rare occasions, seen scuds drifting heavily during the daylight hours; the fish were selective to them because they were the only organism in the water column.

Lakes are also super scud habitat, and these crustaceans can be inconceivably abundant in stillwaters. A reading of the data on the many, large, trout silhouettes hanging in Dan Bailey's Fly Shop will convince even the skeptic that the trout of lakes eat these crustaceans. Scuds are creatures of shallow edges and weedy areas; they rarely go deeper than three feet. In such places the imitation is fished with a slow Hand Twist retrieve or Strip/Tease tactic. I normally use a floating line, but under windy conditions, I switch to an intermediate. In addition, a scud pattern is highly effective when casting to visible, near-shore cruisers.

Scuds, also called freshwater shrimp, belong to the order Amphipoda ("both legs," referring to differences in front and hind legs). The body is flattened at the sides, plated, and hinged like that of an armadillo *(Figure 12-1)*. In fact, when placed in the hand they curl up in a defensive posture similar to an armadillo. This has caused a great deal of controversy among fly fishers about the preferred shape of the artificial: straight or hump-backed. Well, I cast my vote with those who tie the pattern straight. Why? Because that's the way a scud swims. It's body is very straight and its little legs are a whir of motion. In his last edition of "Tying and Fishing the Fuzzy Nymphs" Polly Rosborough makes a strong point of tying scuds (and other imitations) on straight shank hooks, and then says, "I've no doubt murdered some pet beliefs and that was intended—I make no apologies. I want to start you thinking, to do more examining of facts." Right on, Polly.

Scuds come in a range of sizes, but 10-14 has served me very well over the years. They also come in a range of colors; but again, tan, gray, and olive will fill the bill most of the time—except when you need an orange one. Female scuds carry their bright orange eggs in a pouch (a marsupium); these highly visible eggs clearly show through the translucent body of the incubating female and make the organism easily seen by foraging trout. Thus it is that fly fishers have begun fishing, with great success, orange, pink, and red imitations of this little crustacean.

In addition, when scuds die, they turn a pinkish orange color (BCS73/74). In tail water fisheries that experience tidal flux due to power generation, scuds can be left high and dry as the water drops rapidly. These dead orangish creatures are then flushed into the currents with the next rise in water level. Because of this, on rivers such as Utah's Green below Flaming Gorge Reservoir or the Colorado below Glen Canyon Dam, an orangish scud imitation is a highly effective fly

For me, the scud was a natural candidate for imitation with the hair leg technique, and I've found this design very effective. It's certainly not the only dressing that will catch trout, but it does embody those characteristics that I believe to be important in a scud pattern: straight, segmented body with shell back and easily seen legs. When I first developed the fly, I used a segment of mallard flank over the back, but in 1979, Jason began tying it with a strip of latex to give the imitation a more translucent look. I like his modification and use it on the earth-tone scuds. On the fluorescent colors, I use a piece of yarn for the back. Otherwise, the tying procedure is exactly the same.

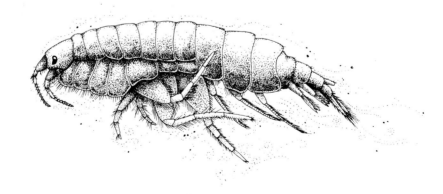

Figure 12-1. *Scuds are flattened at the sides and hinged like an armadillo.*

Hair Leg Scud: Dressing

Hook: Sizes 10-14, standard shank length

Thread: 6/0, color to match body

Body: Blended fur and sparkle yarn applied on dubbing loop; weighted with lead wire

Legs: Guard hairs or other suitable hairs

Shell: Strip of latex dental dam or strand of yarn

Rib: Copper or silver wire

Hair Leg Scud: Most Used Body Colors/Shell Color/Hair Legs/Rib (all regions)

Body smokey gray (BCS 108)/Shell gray/Gray Squirrel guard hairs for legs/Rib silver

Body blend of hare's mask, fox squirrel, and tan sparkle yarn to give overall sandy color (BCS 61)/Shell natural cream/Cottontail rabbit guard hairs for legs/Rib copper

Body olive green (BCS 30)/Shell natural cream colored with permanent marker to match color of body/Guard hairs from olive dyed hare's mask or squirrel skin for legs/Rib silver

Body fluorescent pinkish orange (BCS 73/74), red (BCS 81), or pink (BCS 79)/Shell a strand or two of yarn to match color of body/Legs of dyed calf tail, guard hairs, or filaments of coarse yarn to match color of body/Rib gold or silver

Hair Leg Scud: Tying Instructions

1. Clamp the hook in the vise and wrap the thread to the standard position.

2. Form a dubbing loop and let it hang there for use later on.

3. Tie in a piece of 32 gauge wire for the rib.

4. Weight the middle 1/2 of the shank with lead wire and secure with thread (page 30); end with the thread at the front of the lead.

5. Cut a strip of latex as wide as 1/3 the length of the hook shank. Lay the latex strip on top of the hook shank with the butt end at the *front* of the lead and the free end pointing *forward over the eye*. Secure the latex with the thread by wrapping forward to the head of the fly. Yarn can be used in the same manner (*Figure 12-2*).

6. Spin dubbing on one side of the dubbing loop, insert the hair legs, and spin tight (page 32).

7. Wind the dubbing-leg combination forward and tie off at the head. Once the material is well tied in, wrap the thread a couple of turns in front of the latex.

8. Push the hair legs on the top and sides of the fly down toward the underside and stretch the strip of latex back over the top of the fly. Stretch it fairly tight. This stretching reduces the thickness of the latex (making it more translucent) and reduces its width. When properly stretched, the latex strip will cover the back and top half of each side of the fly.

9. Secure the latex at the rear of the body with one turn of wire. Then wrap the wire forward as a rib. Be careful as you wrap not to trap the hair legs.

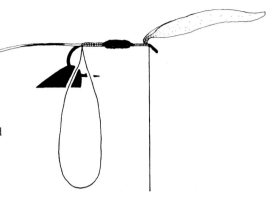

Figure 12-2. *Tie in the latex strip at the head so that it extends forward over the eye.*

Speed Tying Tip: I find it easiest when wrapping the rib not to use a tool (such as a bodkin) to maneuver the legs out of the way. I simply wrap the wire over the top of the fly and then wiggle it back and forth a bit as I wrap through the legs. It's surprising how easy it is to get the wire through the rather stiff hair in this manner.

10. Secure the wire rib just ahead of the latex shell, finish the head, tie off the thread, and cut it away. Cement the head.

11. Clip off the latex so that it forms a short tail extending about 1/2 the way around the hook bend (*Figure 12-3*).

Figure 12-3. *The finished Hair Leg Scud; side view, front view, top view.*

Cressbugs

A close kin to the scud is the cressbug (order Isopoda, "equal legs"). But, whereas scuds are flattened at the sides, cressbugs are flattened top to bottom *(Figure 12-4)*. These creatures are of only local importance, but can be quite abundant where found. I've seen them in the spring creeks of south central Pennsylvania, Michigan's Ausable, Wisconsin's Knapp Creek (where "Way of a Trout" was filmed), and in other streams. Occasionally, I've found them in small lakes. Like scuds, cressbugs are creatures of shallow water. Unlike scuds, they are very poor swimmers and simply dead drift when caught in the currents.

Where the isopods are abundant, the fish definitely eat them. On the Letort, for example, cressbugs are one of the principle winter foods of the trout. The fish will actually root these organisms out of the weeds, wiggling their bodies violently to dislodge the crustaceans and then backing down current to eat those that were shaken loose. And while there's an abundance of insects to select from in the summer, opportunistically feeding trout will certainly take a drifting cressbug. I've had wonderful angling with cressbug imitations, including a stunning morning on Big Springs when I took four fish between 2 1/2 and 5 pounds in a short, two-hour stretch.

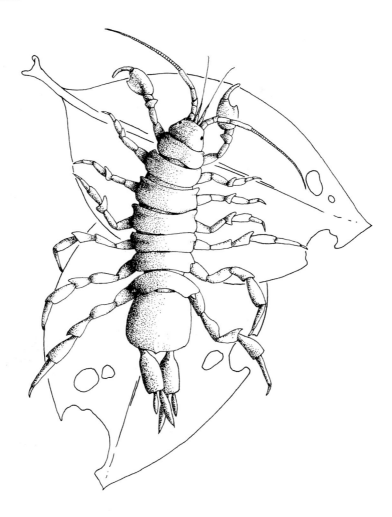

Figure 12-4. *The cressbug is flattened top to bottom.*

For the angler designing trout flies, there are several traits that should be taken into account when considering these critters. As mentioned, cressbugs are not swimmers; they hold the body straight when drifting in the currents; they have many legs sticking out to the sides; and they have a translucent appearance. The fly fishers that frequent the spring creeks of south central Pennsylvania have been well acquainted with cressbugs for many years, and the writers among them, such as Marinaro, Fox, Koch, and Shenk have all described effective isopod patterns and techniques for fishing them. I prefer a Hair Leg Cressbug similar to the fur chenille style used by Ed Shenk. It's fast and easy to tie and certainly effective. It's nothing but a dubbed body with hair legs along its full length. And while the fly can be trimmed top and bottom to more closely approximate the natural, I've found this version of the Hair Leg Wooly Worm to be extremely effective when left untrimmed. The pattern may be ribbed with silver or copper wire or left unribbed. Two other patterns that work very well to suggest either the cressbug or scud are the Muskrat Nymph and a well-brushed-out Fur Caddis Larva. And while cressbugs come in a variety of colors, I've only found two of any significance, gray and olive brown.

Hair Leg Cressbug: Dressing

Hook: Sizes 12-18, standard shank length

Thread: 6/0, color to match body

Body: Blended fur and sparkle yarn; weighted with lead wire

Rib: (Optional) silver wire for the gray version, copper wire for the olive brown version

Legs: Guard hairs spun in dubbing loop

Hair Leg Cressbug: Most Used Body Colors/Hair Legs (all regions)

Olive brown (BCS 100)/Legs of fox squirrel guard hairs

Smokey gray (BCS 108)/Legs of gray squirrel guard hairs

Hair Leg Cressbug: Tying Instructions

1. Clamp the hook in the vise and wrap the shank with thread ending at the standard position.

2. Form a dubbing loop and leave it for a later step; tie in the rib if used.

3. Weight the center 1/2 of the shank with lead wire and secure with thread (page 30); finish with the thread at the head of the fly.

4. Spin dubbing on one side of the loop. Insert guard hairs in the loop—use more than normal—close the loop, and twist tight (page 32).

4. Wind the dubbing-leg combination forward to the head and tie off; wind the rib, if used.

5. Form a smooth head; tie off the thread and cut it away. Apply head cement.

6. Trim the guard hairs off the top and bottom of the fly, leaving those sticking out to the sides to form legs. Lightly roughen the top and bottom of the fly with a dubbing brush *(Figure 12-5)*.

Figure 12-5. *The finished Hair Leg Cressbug; side view, front view, top view.*

Crayfish

If ever there was a creature to excite a big trout, this is it; a juicy, highly caloric mouthful that's abundant in the cold waters that trout prefer. And if ever there was a creature to confound the fly tier, this is it; a big critter with plenty of parts to lead the artisan astray. It is very possible to conceive and produce a pattern with two, widespread pincers, ten walking legs, a long, segmented abdomen and flared telson. It's even possible to catch fish on such flies. But catching a fish on a fly—any fly—is not much of a trick. The trick is consistency and quantity. And for this trick, the perfect, museum-mount flies are not nearly as successful as patterns that look like a fleeing crayfish.

Trout rarely take a crayfish with outspread pincers—the trout have no more desire to get pinched than you do. But let a crayfish dart away, and the trout is after it in a flash. As it turns out, the male crayfish usually has bigger pincers and stays to do battle, while the smaller-pincered female flees. And when this crustacean flees, it no longer looks like the classical pose in which crayfish are shown. Rather, the pincers are shut and held together, the legs are stowed under the body and pointing toward the head,

and the long abdomen is tucked under and furiously chopping away as the crayfish swims backward *(Figure 12-6)*. And that's what we should be imitating: Bulk, linear form, plenty of motion, and correct coloration.

The Muddler Minnow makes a good fleeing crayfish imitation. Fished with a split shot on the leader just ahead of the clinch knot, this pattern has done remarkable things for me in seasons past. However, since I developed the Strip Leech series, I've fished them exclusively to imitate minnows, leeches, and crayfish (page 152). The pattern is bulky, has plenty of motion, and the fish eat it with wild abandon. The brown, olive, or gold Strip Leech do extremely well where crayfish are abundant, but I also carry a specific crayfish imitation that's a variation on the Upside Down Leech (page 164). This Fleeing Crayfish has performed wonders. It can be fished right on the bottom without worry of getting snagged. I vary the retrieve from quite rapid strips to rather slow pulses. Because most crayfish are various shades of rusty brown with hints of olives and creams, I've found that one color scheme is effective nearly everywhere I fish. Vary the colors if necessary to more closely simulate the crayfish in your home waters.

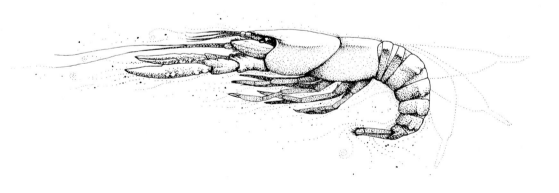

Figure 12-6. *The swimming crayfish looks very different than the stationary one.*

*Fleeing Crayfish:
Dressing*

Hook: Sizes 4-10; 2XL shank

Thread: 3/0, rusty brown

Tail: Pale olive green (BCS 27) marabou; as long as hook shank

Body: Rusty brown (BCS 63) fur spun in a pale tan (BCS 91) yarn loop

Weight: Chrome-plated lead eyes tied on top of hook shank (this causes fly to ride upside down)

Hackle: Iridescent bronze body feather from pheasant with marabou fluff left on

Fur Strip: Rusty brown (BCS 63) hung on hook as for Upside Down Leech

*Fleeing Crayfish:
Tying Notes*

Tie in the tail of marabou and then dress the body as for the Fur Chinelle Dragon (page 114), adding lead eyes and a fur strip tail as for the Upside Down Leech (page 164).

SNAILS

Behold the lowly snail. A one-footed slug in spiral, armor plate. A great delicacy to the gourmet, and a highly important trout food. Fish feed both opportunistically and selectively on these mullosks. Selective to snails? You bet, and when they are, the fishing can be incredible.

As often happens in fly fishing, a particular incident proves to be the catalyst for exploration of patterns and techniques to imitate a specific food organism. For Bob Pelzl and me, an in-depth study of snails began in the late 1970's. We were fishing Munn Lake on the Vermejo Park Ranch in New Mexico and having only moderate success. Rummaging through his fly box for a different pattern to try, Bob came across a Peacock Nymph. As he waited for the fly to sink a few feet, a fish struck. Hard. It jerked Bob's rod tip down sharply, and the 3X tippet broke instantly.

Bob could only stare in amazement. He called to me, and as I watched his second cast, another fish took the fly with the same vigor as the first. This time the rod tip stayed up, and the fish was brought to net. It's belly was distended out of proportion, and its anal vent was swollen and hemorrhoidal. When Bob lifted the fish, it's stomach contents shifted like a fist full of gravel.

"Snails," we chorused.

"Uh, Bob, I'll trade you six damsel nymphs for one of those peacock nymphs."

Since that first moment when we realized the true significance of snails as trout food, we have had many pleasurable hours feeding artificial escargot to the fish.

Snails are mullosks placed in the order Gastropoda. There are both terrestrial and aquatic forms. Of the 283 families of snails, only 14 occupy the freshwaters of the United States, but they are nearly ubiquitous, being absent from only the highest alpine lakes and heavily polluted waters. They reach their greatest abundance in slow waters; they are lacking from swift waters and wave-swept beaches. Snails almost never occur in areas where the pH falls below 6.2 and are most abundant in alkaline waters (pH above 7). Dissolved oxygen also limits the distribution of snails, and so most species are found in water less than 10 feet deep (where oxygen content is high). They prefer waters that remain above 32 degrees and below 80 degrees F. Some lake snails will migrate to find the zone of most favorable temperature. Snails may inhabit all types of substrates from sand to dense beds of vegetation, but in trout waters they are most significant where there are abundant aquatic plants. They feed on algae and decaying materials.

The snail's shell varies in shape from a flat spiral *(Figure 12-7)* to a steep, cone-shaped spiral *(Figure 12-8)*. The most common form is a short cone *(Figure 12-9)*. The majority of the snail's body is inside its shell; it does extend its muscular foot (which it uses as a means of locomotion)

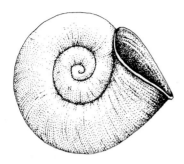

Figure 12-7. *A flat, spiral-shaped snail shell.*

the sunken plants, then the Peacock Snail is fished deep just over the beds of vegetation. The fly is retrieved at different speeds. First a slow hand twist retrieve, then a Strip/Tease retrieve (strip slowly and at the same time twitch the rod tip). Or the fly is retrieved in sharp, foot-long pulls. Often the fish will prefer one or the other of these retrieve tactics. If one does indeed seem to be favored, then use that method exclusively.

and its tentacles (used for a sense of touch). Snails are drab hues of olives and grays and browns. However, minute ridges on the shell act as a diffraction grating and give the animal an iridescent luster.

Snail imitations have been tied to closely mimic the coiled shell or even several snails together. Bob Pelzl once tied a fly to imitate several small snails on a stick. It was very life-like, with perfectly shaped polypropylene shells on a green and brown chenille background. It was fun to play with, but not an effective fly. In actuality, highly effective snail imitations are surprisingly simple to tie. The fore and aft Peacock Nymph that Bob first used to take snail-eating trout is the basis of our Peacock Snail pattern.

The peacock herl suggests the color and iridescent quality of the snail's shell. Brown, dry-fly-quality hackle wound fore and aft serves to suggest the animal's foot and adds a bit of movement to the retrieved fly. To add the coppery tones often seen in snails, I added a copper wrapping in the herl body. Bob and I also discovered that trout very rarely eat large snails—the fish can't digest the snail's shell, and big ones would be too difficult to pass. Thus we found it necessary to tie the fly on only size 10-14 hooks.

There are several ways to fish snail flies in lakes. The best tactic depends upon the behavior of the snail and the water conditions. When the lake is relatively calm, and the snails are in

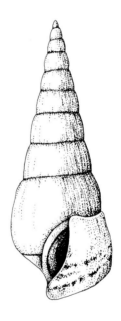

Figure 12-8. *Some snails have elongate, cone-shaped shells.*

The Peacock Snail can also be fished in pockets of emergent weed beds. Use a floating line and plop the fly into the pocket. Let it sink for several seconds, but watch your leader or line tip very carefully; fish often grab the fly as it descends. Don't neglect the edges of the weed beds; fish often cruise along them searching for food. Which line you use to fish the edges of the weeds depends upon the depth at which you are fishing. Normally, I use a sinking line of appropriate density when fishing the lake side of the weed bed. When fishing the shore side, where the water is usually only a few feet deep, I generally use a floating line.

Another extremely effective time to fish the Peacock Snail is during or after heavy winds. Wind causes waves which are actually wheels of water rolling across the lake. Only one-eighth of this wheel protrudes above the surface to form the "wave". As these wheels of water head shoreward, they sweep through the sunken and emergent weeds, whisking the snails off the plants and rolling them up toward the surface.

Under such conditions, trout cruise over sunken weeds and in the shallows, watching selectively for the hapless mullosks. One great way to fish the snail under such conditions is with a floating line. The up and down bobbing motion imparted to the line by the waves is

transmitted to the snail. Trout find this jigging action irresistible. When Jason and I were video taping "Fishing Crustaceans and Snails" we encountered a windy day just made for this tactic. Trouble was, I lost the first three fish I hooked. I stopped in disgust and began talking with Jason. To keep the line from getting tangled, I idly pitched it into the shallows next to shore and tucked the rod under my arm. As we lamented my poor luck (skill?), the rod tip jerked down and the reel sang. I snatched the rod from under my arm, and Jason hit "record." It was a very nice brown that proved most photogenic. Thank goodness for the jigging snail.

If you have trouble casting a floating line into the wind, use an intermediate line. Its narrow diameter allows it to knife into the breeze, and treated with flotant it will ride on the surface. Untreated, it sinks very slowly allowing the fly to be fished just over the sunken weeds. Retrieve the fly with sharp, foot-long pulls punctuated with pauses of several seconds each.

While snails are more likely to be important as trout food in lakes, they can be significant in slow-water areas of streams, especially where there are weed beds. In backwaters and ponded areas, the Peacock Snail has proved to be an excellent pattern to fool cruising fish. This fly has also proved successful in slowly flowing water when fished over the tops of sunken weed beds or at their margins.

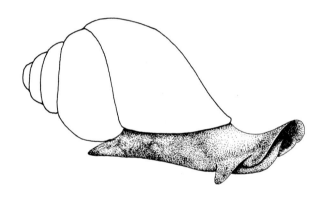

Figure 12-9. *Most snails have a short cone-shaped shell.*

Peacock Snail: Dressing

Hook: Sizes 10-14, regular shank length

Thread: 6/0, olive, brown, or black

Body: Peacock herl; robust, cigar shape; weighted with lead wire

Rib: 32 gauge copper wire twisted with herl

Hackle: Brown dry fly hackle applied fore-and-aft style: three turns at rear of body and three or four turns at front of body

Peacock Snail: Tying Instructions

1. Clamp the hook in the vise and wrap the shank with thread, ending at the standard position.

2. Tie in a hackle feather; wind the hackle three turns and tie off; cut away the excess (save for use at the front).

3. Weight the center of the shank with lead wire and secure with thread (page 30), ending with the thread at the rear of the lead.

4. Lay a length of 32 gauge copper wire on top the hook shank and secure in place by wrapping the thread rearward over the wire. End with thread just in front of the hackle.

5. Select a clump of 3 or 4 strands of select grade peacock herl. Cut the butt end of the clump square. Hold the clump on top of the hook with the butt end at the rear of the lead and tie down by wrapping the thread forward over the herl. Wrap the thread forward to about two head spaces behind the eye.

6. Twist the wire and peacock herl together into an open spiral *(Figure 12-10)*. The idea is to strengthen the herl with the wire and at the same time add a bit of copper coloration.

7. Wind the twisted wire-herl combination forward to the head and tie off. Cut away the excess.

8. Tie in the brown hackle and wind it four turns at the front of the body; tie off, cut away the excess.

9. Form a smooth head, tie off, cut away the thread. Apply head cement *(Figure 12-11)*.

Figure 12-10. *The wire and herl are twisted together.*

Figure 12-11. *The finished Peacock Snail; side view, front view.*

Floating Snail

Floating snails can also be significant. Bob and I use the floating pattern about twenty-five percent of the time when we're fishing with snails. After a heavy wind, look for these buoyant gastropods in near-shore waters. Snails may also float intermittently to the surface to breathe. And, at times, usually midsummer, vast numbers of snails will often appear at the surface. This phenomenon may be related to high water temperatures and attendant lowered oxygen levels. The snail floats with its foot in the surface film and its shell hanging down.

The English have noted this phenomenon on their reservoirs, and they fish floating snail patterns with great success. In fact, my Floating Snail is a modification of a cork-bodied fly developed by the master English angler John Goddard. The foam underbody of the Floating

Snail makes it easier to tie than Goddard's cork-bodied version. In addition, the foam underbody allows the fly to ride lower in the water and in a vertical orientation: hackle at the film and hook point down. This posture is identical to that of the natural and has made the Floating Snail highly effective.

One would think that trout take the non-mobile, floating snail in an unhurried manner, but in fact the rise is usually quite strong. Certainly such energy expenditure is not necessary to pursue the snail. Perhaps the bold rise is necessary to facilitate the swallowing of such a crusty morsel. Regardless of the reason, the point is that the strong, sometimes splashy, rise can be misleading. On the Vermejo lakes there is a large caddisfly that emerges at about the same time that there are large numbers of floating snails. Since fish take the caddis adults vigorously, it's easy to be fooled if you automatically assign such rises to a caddis emergence.

The floating snail is fished on a floating line. If fish are actively rising, simply cast the fly into a feeding area and let it sit. The fish will find it. If the rises are intermittent, give the fly an occasional strip. Such movement is attractive to foraging fish.

In all cases you have to be ready for the take. As noted earlier, trout take snails hard. I always use the strongest tippet I can get away with and try to strike by gently lifting the line, but in the excitement of snail fishing, that's not always possible.

Floating Snail: Dressing

Hook: Sizes 10-14, standard shank length

Thread: 6/0, olive, brown, or black

Underbody: Any cellular foam material that does not absorb water, cut into 1/8" to 1/4" wide strips and wound onto the hook to form a cone-shaped body with apex at rear of hook; color the underbody with olive, brown, or black permanent marker

Overbody: Peacock herl

Rib: Copper Crystal Hair, Flashabou, or Krystal Flash twisted with herl

Hackle: Four turns of brown cock hackle at head of fly

Floating Snail: Tying Instructions

1. Clamp the hook in the vise and wrap the shank with thread ending at the standard position.

2. Lay a single strand of copper Flashabou or similar material on top of the hook, and wrap the thread forward to secure it.

3. Select a clump of 3 or 4 strands of select grade peacock herl. Cut the butt end of the clump square. Hold the clump on top of the hook with the butt end near the middle of the shank and tie down by wrapping the thread rearward over the herl. End with thread at the standard position.

4. Tie in a piece of cellular foam and secure by wrapping the thread forward. End with the thread about two head spaces behind the eye.

5. Form the underbody by stretching the foam and wrapping it tightly at the rear of the hook; relax the tension on the foam as it's wound forward until there's no tension at all on the last wrap. This technique produces a cone-shaped body with the apex at the rear *(Figure 12-12)*. Also, the flotation qualities of the foam at the rear of the hook are eliminated by compressing it. This causes the rear of the hook to sink and the front to float, achieving a vertical orientation of the fly in the water.

6. Twist the Flashabou and the peacock herl into an open spiral as was done with the wire in the Peacock Snail *(Figure 12-10)*. The idea is to strengthen the herl with the Flashabou and at the same time add a bit of copper coloration.

7. Wind the twisted Flashabou-herl combination forward to the head and tie off. Cut away the excess.

8. Tie in a brown hackle feather and wind it four turns at the front of the body; tie off, cut away the excess.

9. Form a smooth head, tie off, cut away the thread. Apply head cement *(Figure 12-13)*.

Figure 12-13. *The finished floating snail.*

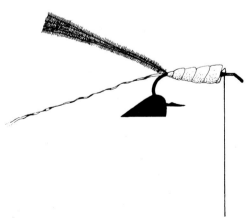

Figure 12-12. *Form the cellular foam into a cone-shaped underbody.*

Worms

"We'll fish worms;" Bob Pelzl had told me, "the big trout of the San Juan can't resist them." I was silent in disbelief, surely Bob knew that I preferred to fly fish. And, I thought, he too had long since given up fishing with bait. Bob held out a closed hand. "Here's your bait." As I opened my mouth to decline, he opened his hand to reveal a cluster of orange and red flies of unique design tied on 3XL hooks *(Figure 12-14)*. "We call them the San Juan Worm," he laughed. "Had you going didn't I"? I vaguely remember mumbling something about Bob's ancestry.

It was early morning in August of 1976, and we were nearly to the pools that Bob had described. Mist rose from the water into the cold air of the high desert dawn, and the down vest and chamois shirt felt good. As we waded into the stream at the "log run," I was startled by its chill. The thermometer registered 44 degrees F. While I rigged my rod and threaded a strike indicator onto the leader, Bob explained, "The discovery was accidental. Jim Aubrey and I were fishing here a couple of years ago, and this fly, which was designed as a shrimp pattern for alpine lakes, really knocked 'em dead. Our subsequent investigations revealed an abundant population of aquatic worms living in the silt of the river's bottom, and this fly turned out to be a rather good imitation of these annelids. You'll have to give Jim a hard time about it, though, he still refuses to call his fly a 'worm.'"

Worm fly or not, the solid, silver-bright rainbows of the river loved it. The take was never gentle; the indicator would leap upstream as the fish grabbed the fly and dashed away over the stony bottom or cartwheeled into the rapidly warming air. And they came to the fly with stunning regularity; often we'd be simultaneously hooked up.

It was fishing of such quality that only when the feeding slowed did we realize how hot the August day had become. As we drove back to the temperature-controlled environment of our motel room at "Abes," I sat quietly, thinking of the stark beauty of the arid landscape and the magnificent fishery where for the first time since childhood I'd caught trout on worms.

Bob and I keyed the worms and discovered that they are truly aquatic, not earthworms that have simply fallen or been washed into the river. These aquatic annelids belong to the family Lumbriculidae. They live in the sand and silts of the river bottom, and are especially abundant in tailwater fisheries and spring creeks.

Since that first, wild fling of worm fishing with Bob, I've given myself to this annelid with utter abandon. And what a ride it has been: I've fished it everywhere, and in rivers like the Bighorn, Green, Bow, South Platte, San Juan, Henry's Fork, Silver Creek, Armstrong's Spring Creek, Yellow Breeches, Little Lehigh, and many others, it's been so good that it's almost embarrassing—almost.

Figure 12-14. *Jim Aubrey's original San Juan Worm.*

The design of the San Juan Worm has changed over the years. When Bob and Jim's secret finally got out, anglers on the San Juan began playing with an incredible array of materials and designs: marabou, Larval Lace, yarn, Ultra-Chenille, floss, and just about anything else that can be imagined. And they all work. The biggest improvement, however, was not in the materials used in the body, it was in the hook.

I don't know who first thought of using a English bait hook for the worm design, but the concept is brilliant. This hump-backed hook twists and turns when fished dead drift, giving the worm fly a very natural motion. I tie the pattern in three colors, using yarn for the body and ribbing it with wire. Extremely simple and extremely effective.

San Juan Worm: Dressing

Hook: Sizes 2-10, English bait hook

Thread: 3/0, color to match body

Body: Yarn

Rib: 26-32 gauge wire, depending upon hook size

San Juan Worm: Most used colors/Rib (all regions)

Fluorescent orange (BCS 73/74)/Silver wire rib

Fluorescent red (BCS 81)/Copper wire rib

Fluorescent pink (BCS 79)/Silver wire rib

San Juan Worm: Tying Instructions

1. Clamp the hook in the vise and wrap the shank with thread, ending well down on the rear curve.

2. Tie in a length of wire for the rib, wrapping the thread forward and then rearward to secure the wire tightly.

3. Tie in a length of yarn, wrapping the thread forward to the eye.

4. Wrap the shank with yarn and secure at the head. Cut away the excess.

5. Rib the fly with the wire, keeping the turns relatively close; tie off at the head and cut away the excess.

6. Form a smooth head; tie off the thread and cut it away. Cement the head *(Figure 12-15)*.

Figure 12-15. *The San Juan Worm on an English bait hook.*

LEECHES, MINNOWS, MICE AND MORE

In my early years of fishing, I knew only the worm; it sufficed for all manner of fish, from chubs to scrappy little bluegills, to perch and bullheads. But as my angling skills evolved, and I began to focus more and more on the most highly prized of fishes, the trout, I branched out to other baits. Hellgrammites and softshells became regular additions to red worms and night crawlers, but the one that held the greatest mystery and attraction for me was the minnow. Stories in the outdoor magazines reported of huge, hook-jawed trout that shunned all baits and lures but fell easy prey to a properly fished minnow.

I would lie awake at night in my room under the eves and visualize the pools and riffles of the streams I fished. I'd see myself casting a minnow into a dark and secret hold under the roots of a hemlock and feel the big trout take it with a gentle pull that only a gifted few ever come to know. Oh, if only it had been so. But alas, my minnows caught, what were to me, only other minnows.

A couple of years thereafter, I put aside bait for the fly. But the longings of those early years would not go away so easily, and rather quickly I found myself devoted to streamers. They became my bread-and-butter flies. While I struggled to learn the necessary skills for nymph and dry fly, the streamers caught trout: little brookies in headwater streams buried deep in the forested hills where my pony carried me, freshly stocked rainbows in the washouts under the highway bridges, and an increasing number of, shy, holdover browns. And then I learned that in the twilight of morning and evening, streamers would take those big browns that had possessed my dreams for all the years of my youth. But even now, even after those dreams of boyhood have become reality, I still dream of secret places where hook-jawed trout steal from cover to cautiously mouth my streamer fly in a way that only a few ever come to know.

In the three and a half decades that have passed since I first took up the fly, I have only grown more attached to the streamer. Though I first used these long flies to imitate minnows, I have learned that they can do so much more. They are excellent representations of leeches, eels, tadpoles, and crayfish as well. On the other hand, they can be tied in a range of exotic colors that no fish has ever seen and provoke savage strike after savage strike. They take all gamefishes: the coldwater trout and salmon; warmwater species like bass, pike, and muskies; and saltwater fishes like tarpon, bones, and redfish. Streamers deserve the serious attention of every fly fisher.

In the early days of fishing the long flies, I came to realize that color and movement were very important traits in the design. Slowly, the stiff-haired bucktail patterns disappeared from my box, replaced with streamers of marabou and other soft feathers. As a freshman at Penn State's Mont Alto Campus in 1962, I took a fly tying course from the late Bill Pfiffer and heard of the night fishing exploits of his close friend George Harvey. From those discussions I learned that bulk and size were also desirable traits in streamer designs. My favorite pattern quickly became the Marabou Muddler. It could be tied in any color and size and had a bulky head and pulsing, undulating wing. It worked miracles on the trout of the Falling Spring Creek that next trout season.

I transferred to the main campus in the fall of 1963 and began frequenting the Fisherman's Paradise stretch of Spring Creek. It was Big Brown City! There were days, when using two marabou muddlers hooked in tandem, I'd take over twenty trout each over twenty inches in length. It really was paradise.

A little over a decade later, Royce Dam showed me his Strip Fly, and streamer design took a new direction for me. For, in addition to using Royce's concept on the Strip Nymph (page 36), I used it to make a leech imitation. I'd been using marabou to tie leeches, but the undulations of the fur strip looked ever so much better in the water. The Matuka (a New Zealand pattern) had gained great popularity in this country at about that time, and I saw a way to marry Royce's fly and the Matuka concept to make a leech. I wanted a fly that was bulky and on which every part moved, so I used a tail of marabou, a body of brushed-out mohair yarn, a fur-strip wing attached Matuka style, and a big soft hackle. The body was weighted so the fly could be fished like a jig, teasing it up and down to create a strong fluid movement. The Strip Leech was more than I had hoped for. It not only looked like a leech, it caught fish. Big fish. In one season I caught more big fish on the Strip Leech than I'd ever caught on any other pattern. And during that season, I also realized that this same basic design would be ideal for minnows, crayfish, tadpoles, salamanders, and diving mice. All that was required were slight modifications to the materials used. Since then, I've essentially abandoned every other streamer design. For me the Strip Leech has worked wonders, and I shall not be without it.

I'm not saying that you should toss all your streamers into the garbage. I'm not saying that the Strip Leech is the long-hoped-for magic fly that no fish can resist. What I am saying is that the essence of a number of widely different organisms can be distilled into this one design. When minnows, leeches, eels, salamanders, tadpoles, and diving mice are examined in the element where they interact with fish, they have two outstanding characteristics: (1) they all display a great deal of movement and (2) they all have significant bulk. And that's just what the leech series was designed to provide.

LEECHES

These members of the phylum Annelida are separated into the class Hirudidae and are widely known for the blood-sucking habits of some species. Leeches are widely distributed in lakes and streams around the world and in some lakes can reach densities of several hundred per square yard. Most species are black or shades of browns or olives, often with purple, green, or red markings on the underside. Many species are quite small, but the blood-sucking species can reach lengths of half a foot or more in the extended swimming position. Leeches are rather secretive, remaining hidden in beds of aquatic weeds, bottom trash, or in the interstices among stones. In morning and evening, however, they do venture out. They are strong swimmers, moving with fluid, sinusoidal movements (*Figure 13-1*). Trout grab them at every available opportunity.

I fish the Strip Leech in a number of ways. In streams, I often use the Broadside Float, perfected by the late Joe Brooks. The fly is cast across stream or across and up and the line mended as necessary to keep the fly drifting sideways to the current. This tactic is especially effective when used with a floating or sink tip line in riffle waters that are knee to waist deep. The drifting leech fly actually swims as the line tugs on it and the currents shift it around. The

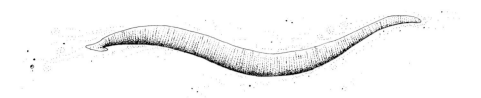

Figure 13-1. *The swimming stroke of the leech is very smooth.*

lead wire causes the fly to bob up and down, the marabou tail waves and pulses open and shut, the mohair of the body adds bulk while the teased out hairs wiggle, the soft hackle adds bulk and plenty of action, and the fur strip performs a whole series of exotic movements. It not only looks great in the water, it is great.

When Jason was ten, we went to fish Wyoming's Green River with Ralph and Betty McConahy, friends from my childhood. Nancy and the McConahy's headed off upstream; Jason and I would fish down. We waded into position at the head of a long pool, just where the waist-deep riffle dumped in. I demonstrated the Broadside Drift, showing Jason where to cast and how to mend. A very nice, 18-inch brown took the fly exactly where it was supposed to and I played it to net. On the next cast, I took a 17-inch brown. "OK, Jason" I said, "I've got them all warmed up; now it's your turn."

I helped him get the presentation right, then turned to wade down stream. There was a deep, rolling splash behind me, and I thought Jason had fallen in. Turning quickly I saw it wasn't Jason, it was a fish, a big fish, and Jason was rooted to the spot by the feel of it against the line.

The fish fought deep in the dark waters of the pool and slowly drew Jason toward the rapids below. Though we had earlier admired the shining mountains towering over us, the sweet smell of the grasses, the squabbling of jays, and the pastel splash of wild flowers, all that was lost to senses that concentrated solely on the big brown.

As the fish dropped back into the heavy flow of the rapids, I grabbed the back of Jason's vest to steady him, and we ran for shore. Running and holding the rod to the side, he pumped against the fish, finally drawing it into the near-shore water. When I scooped up the 25-inch brown, Jason hollered so loud that Nancy heard him from half a mile upstream.

In slower stream areas, I use an active retrieve, moving the fly at various speeds and with various amounts of twitching and pumping. In stillwaters, I fall back on the Strip/Tease retrieve, either using a floating line in the shallows or probing deep with a sink tip or full sinking line. When drift fishing from a boat, I use the Strip Leech as a searching fly, casting as close to the bank as possible and fishing the fly with either a Broadside Float or an active retrieve. On the Bow, Bighorn, Madison, and other rivers, this strategy has usually produced the biggest fish of the trip.

Another technique that has worked for me, especially in deep, fast, pocket water, is fishing a Strip Leech dead drift near the bottom. Use a compound tippet and strike indicator (page 77) and present the pattern upstream with a Tuck Cast. Aim the line high as for a false cast; the weight of the shot and fly will cause the end of the leader to flip over and tuck under the line. As the cast drops, the tucked leader piles up, allowing the fly to sink rapidly. Presenting the Strip Leech with the Leisenring Lift (page 37) or Brooks Method (page 118), so that the artificial swings across just in front of a suspected lie, can be astoundingly productive as well.

Strip Leech: Dressing

Hook: Sizes 8-2/0 (or larger), 3XL shank

Thread: 3/0, color to match body

Tail: Clump of 20-30 chartreuse marabou barbs, same length as hook

Body: Mohair or other fuzzy yarns or coarse dubbing, well brushed out

Rib: 24-30 gauge wire depending upon hook size

Wing: Fur strip (cut from tanned hide with fur intact, page 177); any soft fur will work; strip should be 1/8 to 3/8 inch wide depending upon hook size

Hackle: Pheasant rump feather with iridescent metallic green or blue coloration; or other feather of similar color

Strip Leech: Most Used Color of Body and Wing/Rib (all regions)

Black body and wing (BCS 118)/Rib silver

Brown body and wing(BCS 87)/Rib copper

Olive body and wing(BCS 43)/Rib silver

Strip Leech: Tying Instructions

1. Clamp the hook in the vise and wrap the shank with thread, ending at the standard position.

2. Tie in a clump of chartreuse marabou for the tail, wrapping the thread forward over the rear 1/3 of the hook. I use chartreuse because it's easily seen by the fish, and I like the contrast it gives in the fly. Other colors that work well are purple, black, olive, pink, orange, green, and brown—take your choice.

3. Tie in a piece of wire for the rib, wrapping the thread rearward to the standard position.

4. Tie in the yarn for the body, again wrapping forward over the rear 1/3 of the shank.

5. Weight the front 2/3 of the shank with lead wire, beginning just ahead of the materials and ending about 3 head spaces behind the eye; secure with the thread, ending with the thread about two head spaces behind the eye.

6. Wrap the yarn forward to form a robust body; secure with the thread and cut away the excess.

7. The width of the fur strip for the wing will depend upon the size of the hook; normally I make it the same width as the body of the fly. Prepare the front end of the fur strip as for the Strip Nymph (Figure 4-25, page 37) and tie in just ahead of the body.

8. Separate the fur of the strip just above the rear end of the body and wrap the wire through the separation, pulling it tight to secure the strip to the rear of the hook *(Figure 13-2)*.

9. Wrap the wire forward in a riblike fashion, securing the fur strip to the top of the body, Matuka style.

Speed Tying Tip: If the wire is simply wrapped forward like a rib, the fur of the wing will get trapped as the wire is wound over the top of the fly. To prevent this and still allow rapid tying, I use the following tactic. First, stroke the fur of the wing upright. Next, wrap the wire under the body and about half way across the top of the fly. The fur will be partially trapped by the wire. At this point, stop wrapping and brush the trapped hair out of the way with your fingers. This forms a slot in the fur through which the wire can then pass.

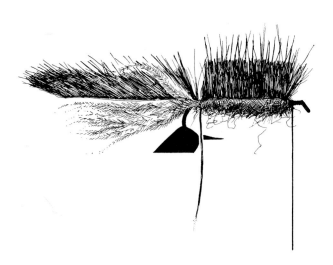

Figure 13-2. *Part the hair and secure the strip with a wrap of the wire.*

10. Secure the wire at the head of the fly.

11. Prepare, tie in, and wind on the rump feather hackle and finish the fly in the same manner described for the Fur Chenille Dragon (page 114).

12. Cut the wing so that it's as long as the tail *(Figure 13-3)*.

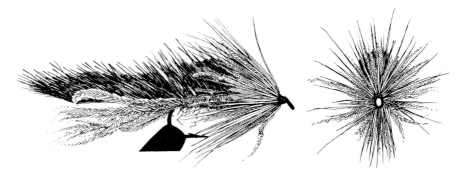

Figure 13-3. *The finished Strip Leech; side view, front view.*

Minnows

More properly, this category should be "food-fishes" because it's not just members of the minnow family that are eaten by the trout. In fact, trout will eat any fish smaller than themselves—including other trout. In Alaskan waters, the char feed heavily on the salmon smolts that are migrating out to sea, and a smolt fly will catch fish until you get physically exhausted. Certainly salmon smolts are not minnows. But "angler speak" is not changed easily, and food fishes will probably always be "minnows." In most trout waters, there are two principle food fishes: the true minnows and sculpins. Many species of minnows *(Figure 13-4)* inhabit our waters, living out their tenuous existence in the shallows at stream or lake edge. Kingfishers, herons, and bitterns prey upon them from the world above, and trout, mink, and otter seek them in the world below. And while these members of the family Cyprinidae are normally only a few inches in length at maturity, some species of minnows such as the squawfish and carp can attain lengths of several feet and weights in excess of fifty pounds.

Big trout, reclusive and secretive by day, move into the shallows to feed on minnows during the twilight and dark hours. These large fish often wallow and thrash about in water too

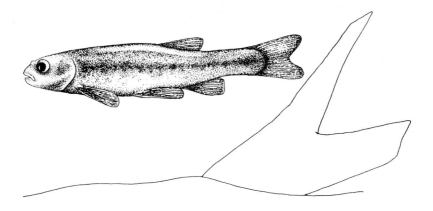

Figure 13-4. *A typical minnow.*

shallow to cover their backs as they pursue the fleeing minnows. Daylight hours will find big trout feeding on minnows—sometimes in the shallows, but more often when the minnows stray out into the deeper water.

Sculpins are another matter. These toady-looking, mottled members of the Cottidae family *(Figure 13-5)* are bottom dwelling fishes that live not only in the shallows but in the deeper waters as well. They poke about in the cupboards of the bottom, never straying more than a few inches above the protective crevices and gaps in the stony reaches they prefer. They can attain lengths of six inches or more—should they live so long. Their range neatly overlaps that of the trout, and they are a readily available item on the menu of all stream trout, day or night. Sculpins also occur in some cold-water lakes, and trout there know them well.

The first time I fished a brown Strip Leech, it reminded me of a sculpin. I immediately began playing with body materials to tailor the design to represent food fishes. Very soon, the Gold Leech and the Silver Leech took form. The tail can be omitted or tied of marabou, Flashabou, or Crystal Flash. I decided upon tinsel chenille for the body because it not only sparkles, but it moves in the water. The fur strip and hackle were changed in colors only. Since a frightened minnow flares its gill plates and shows it gills, I added a bright red throat of craft fur. These leeches-turned-minnows have done exceedingly fine things for me over the years; they are the fly fisher's version of the Rapala, and every bit as deadly on big trout.

Shortly after I dressed the first Silver Leech flies, we took a trip to Pennsylvania to visit our families. On the way home, we detoured through the Carlisle area to fish the spring creeks. One afternoon found us on the Boiling Springs. I was casting to some small, highly selective fish dimpling in the currents when Jason came running up to tell me of a very large fish he had spotted. Sure enough, it was large. And holding right in the middle on a barren bottom in crystalline water. In its exposed position, it could see us as well as we could see it and no manner of fly would persuade it to feed. Until I tried the Silver Leech. That big rainbow—all 23 inches of it—came off the bottom in a flash and grabbed the fly before it had sunk six inches. I was so startled I only stared. The fish set the hook itself.

Since then, we've fished the Gold and Silver Leeches with smashing success on many, many rivers and lakes. And it's been as effective for salmon as for trout. For Jason's sixteenth birthday we journeyed to Alaska to fish the Kanektok with John Gary. The "Tok" comes from the hills strong and swift and pushes its way through the lowland tundra to the Bering Sea. In August, the silver salmon come, as bright as freshly polished metal, and as hard.

On a day that spoke more of duck marshes than trout waters, our guide took us down to tide water to cast for fresh silvers. They were holding in the flats at river mouth, resting and waiting to ride the next tidal surge upstream. I'd used the leech series with great success several times

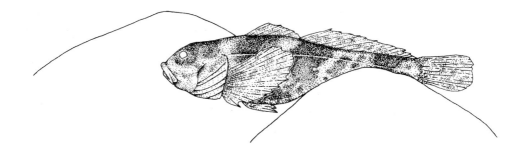

Figure 13-5. *Sculpins are creatures of rocky bottoms.*

before in Alaska, and this day the Silver Leech possessed the salmon. They came one after the other to the undulating, steel and fur sham. Fighting with an almost tireless strength they twisted the water about themselves, forcing us to struggle as much as they. And so it went for the week, whether we fished at the tide or high up in the braided channels of the river. The leeches took salmon, the uniquely spotted leopard rainbow, arctic char, and even grayling. Paradise is probably warmer than Alaska, but the fishing certainly can't be any better.

And some day, we've promised ourselves, we'll go back. After a shore lunch of salmon, we'll lie on a bar of river-sorted pebbles and look up at the clouds as they march in from their birthing place over the icy sea. We'll wait to feel the touch of the weak arctic sun on our cheeks and to smell of the land—the pure, sweet air scented with the fragrance of willows and the musk of tundra. We'll dwell on the raucous noise of quarrelsome gulls, the rasp of wind over the stones, the haunting pipe of the curlew. And we'll fish again those magnificent pools and runs where the big salmon and trout came so readily to the Gold and Silver Leeches.

These flies can be fished in variety of ways. All those described for the Strip Leech work very well for the Gold and Silver Leeches, too. Another favorite way of fishing these flies in streams is to cast down and across a riffle area into the slow water along the far bank. The fast water of the riffle will immediately cause the line to belly, dragging the fly out into midstream at right angles to the flow of the current. Like the Broadside Float, the dragging fly is presented to the fish in full side view; however, the fly is moving as if frightened. This presentation has produced many good fish.

Some anglers have evidenced concern that long tails on a fly produce short strikes. Striking a real minnow short would mean that the trout nibbles on its tail; a surefire way to lose lunch. When a big fish wants to eat a big minnow, it does not strike short. The trout seizes and crushes the minnow sideways across the midsection before swallowing it. They do the same to the leech flies. Once, when fishing a lake, I spotted some trout rushing into shallow water and slashing into the schools of minnows that tried to take refuge there. Quickly knotting on a big Silver Leech, and using some dense trees for cover, I ran to the spot where the trout were feeding. A four-pound brown came racing in from deep water; using the Bow-and-Arrow Cast, I plopped the fly about five feet ahead of it. The response was as dramatic as it was instantaneous. The trout grabbed the pattern across the middle and shook it like a terrier would shake a rat. I jerked, hard. The brown tore itself from the water in a magnificent leap, landing in a dead bush on shore. In a flash, the fish made another wrenching leap, landing back in the lake and departing hencewith. It held my fly. The bush held my leader. Where's the camera when you need one?

Gold or Silver Leech: Dressing

Hook: Sizes 8-2/0 (or larger), 3XL

Thread: 3/0, tan or white

Tail: None or pearlescent, gold, silver, or other similarly tinted Flashabou or Crystal Flash, same length as hook shank

Body: Gold or silver tinsel chenille

Rib: Gold or silver wire

Wing: Fur strip (page 156) of golden tan mink (BCS 55) or silver mink (BCS 92) or other similarly colored fur; strip should be 1/8 to 3/8 inch wide depending upon hook size

Throat: Bright red (BCS 85) craft fur

Hackle: Bronzy pheasant rump feather for Gold Leech, silver pheasant body feather for the Silver Leech

Gold or Silver Leech: Tying Instructions

These flies are dressed the same way as the Strip Leech (page 156), except a red throat is added before the hackle is applied.

MICE

Alaska's Talachulitna is a lovely stream. One whose very appearance gladdens the heart of the fly fisher. Not overpowering in its midcurrents, it is, none-the-less, a fair-sized stream with long, deep pools, and plenty of holding water for trout and salmon. The bottom is a marvel of small to medium-sized gravels, a gift from the gods for the wading angler who is sometimes made careless by the urgency of reaching a good holding lie. Its cold waters strengthen the fish, and they fight as if possessed.

It was my first Alaskan river. And the first night in camp, as the moon crowded over the spruce trees to the east, I heard the hunting call of wolves. The flesh on my arms tingled and my scalp grew tight at the primal sound—this was their world that I had come to share in, and they had called to me. To that part which is still wild. To that part that knows the way of the hunter and the hunted. To that part that had come to learn of the things that only wilderness rivers can teach.

The silver salmon were late in that year of low water, but the big resident rainbows were abundant and very cooperative. They held tight against the outside corners of the deep pools and took the Gold Leech within seconds of its noisy entry into the water.

"They're probably taking it as a mouse," our guide, Dave McDivitt, explained. "There are plenty of mice and voles in the grass, and they're always getting into the water." "These big 'bows also take a floating mouse with gusto."

I'd used mice many times at night for big browns, but not in the day for rainbows. That night, back at the Gray Bow Lodge, I tied some floating mice. We fished them as Dave had told us, casting down and across, tight against the far bank, and allowing the currents to drag the fly back toward the river's center. The results were smashing! The big rainbows would crash onto the fly like largemouth bass. Since then the floating mouse has been a standard Alaskan

pattern for me. And it's served many others equally as well.

Mice and voles are common in all areas of the world where trout are found, and if these mammals get into the water, they're fair game for big trout. When fishing for big browns at night, I plop the fly down hard and move it almost as if it were a bass popper, chugging and gurgling it and then resting it for a bit. I usually fish this big, air resistant fly on a floating line with a five-foot leader ending in a 15-pound tippet. The floating line stays out of underwater snags, and the heavy tippet allows me to horse a big fish out of the dense cover where they're often found. It also allows the fly to be ripped out of the trees where it frequently lands when casting in total darkness.

A real mouse does not sit on top of the water anymore than a dog or cat sits on top of the water when swimming. The critter is mostly subsurface, it's little legs pumping furiously and its tail streaming out behind (Figure 13-6). It no longer looks like a cute little bundle of fur with button eyes, delicate whiskers, and wiggly nose. It looks like lunch—a big "chunk-a-lunch." Thus, my Down and Dirty Mouse is not nearly as realistic in outward appearance as those of many other tiers. It is realistic in its appearance in the water, however. To get the necessary bulk, the fly is tied of deer hair, but the hair is not packed, as is the standard procedure with most floating, spun-deer-hair flies. The unpacked hair picks up water and causes the fly to ride low. The bulk and low riding habit allow the Down and Dirty Mouse to push a lot of water like the real mouse. Certainly it catches fish, and it's fast to tie.

On a recent trip to the Sutton River in northern Ontario, Jason, John Pinto, Jim Martin, and I found the Down and Dirty Mouse to be just what the big brookies had ordered. We'd cast across and allow line drag to plow the half-sunken artificial back across the currents. The explosive takes by those big, wild brook trout were stunning.

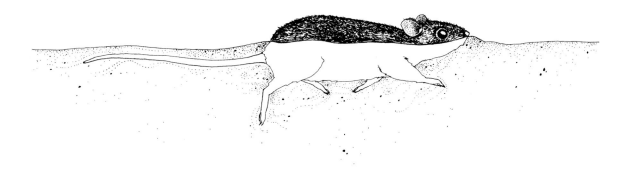

Figure 13-6. *The swimming mouse.*

Down and Dirty Mouse: Dressing

Hook: Sizes 4-4/0 (or bigger), 2XL

Thread: 3/0 brown

Tail: Four grizzly hackle feathers (other colors work just as well) tied two on either side of the shank with concave sides facing out

Body: Natural deer hair or other similar hair

Down and Dirty Mouse: Tying Instructions

1. Clamp the hook in the vise and wrap the shank with thread, ending at the standard position.

2. Select four hackle feathers and pair them, placing one feather on top of the other and aligning their tips. Tie one pair on the far side of the shank (wrapping the thread forward) and one on the near side (wrapping the thread rearward); face the concave sides outward *(Figure 13-7)*.

3. Select a clump of deer hair about twice the diameter of a pencil and cut it from the hide. With the materials hand, hold the hair by the tip end; cut off the butt

end so the clump is the same length as the hook shank.

Figure 13-7. *The tails of the Down and Dirty Mouse are tied in with the concave sides facing outward.*

4. Hold the clump on top of the hook shank and wrap the thread loosely two times around the clump and the hook. Hold the clump so that these wraps are placed 3/8 to 1/2 inch from the butt end.

5. Maintaining a tight grip on the tip of the clump with the materials hand, pull the thread tight to flare the butt end of the clump.

6. Wrap the thread forward through the butt end of the clump, placing one turn immediately ahead of the last; it should take about 10 turns. This process spins the butt ends of the hair

around the hook while the tips remain unspun *(Figure 13-8)*.

7. Do not compress the spun portion of the hair.

8. Repeat steps 3-7 as many times as necessary to completely cover the top of the hook, placing each clump of hair immediately ahead of the previous one.

9. When you reach the eye, form a smooth head, tie off the thread, and cut it away.

10. Trim the mouse flat on the bottom if you so desire *(Figure 13-9)*.

Figure 13-8. *The tips or the hair remain unspun.*

Figure 13-9. *The finished Down and Dirty Mouse; side view, front view.*

Cone Head Mouse

This is a product of Jason's imagination, modelled on the principle of Larry Dahlberg's Diver. And a good product it is, too. It's a diving mouse that can be pulled under and then allowed to float back to the surface. Such action can produce savage takes. It's especially good in lakes and slow-water areas of streams.

The diving, ascending action can be achieved with any floating popper or mouse by using a sink tip line and a strip/pause retrieve. Once the tip sinks, a fast, strong strip on the line causes the fly to dive; during the pause the fly floats back to the surface. With Jason's Cone Head Mouse, however, the same action is attained with a floating line—a boon where underwater weeds and sticks could hang up the sink tip line.

The trick of the Cone Head Mouse is in the trimming. Tie the fly as described for the Down And Dirty Mouse, but pack the hair and then trim the front half of the fly into a long pointed cone *(Figure 13-10)*. This can be done at streamside or lakeside.

Wet Mouse

The Northern Water Shrew is a commonly found streamside inhabitant of the northern conterminous US, Canada, and Alaska. This 3 1/2-inch long, dark grayish brown, mouse-like critter actually dives underwater and feeds on aquatic insects. It has webbed feet and can swim quite rapidly. No, trout do not get selective to diving shrews, but yes, they do eat them. A brown Strip Leech is a good representation of the these organisms. So is a Fur Chenille Dragon, with or without a fur strip tail *(Figure 13-11)*.

Figure 13-10. *The finished Cone Head Mouse; side view, front view.*

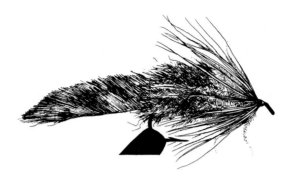

Figure 13-11. *The Fur Chenille Dragon with fur strip tail.*

MORE

Another opportunistic food item that can be nicely emulated with the Strip Leech is the tadpole *(Figure 13-12)*. These immature frogs are especially prevalent in some lakes, and in the spring of the year, tadpoles are often part of the trout's daily fare. In addition, some lakes have especially abundant populations of "water-dogs," really aquatic salamanders. Both of these organisms are easily imitated with a black or brown Strip Leech.

Crayfish are another important food stuff that can be nicely matched with the leech flies (page 152). I normally tie on the Fleeing Crayfish (page 145) to suggest these crustaceans, but if you don't have one in the box, let me suggest the Gold Leech or brown or olive Strip Leech.

Work the fly with plenty of action; in places where crayfish are abundant, these leech patterns have performed exceptionally well, especially on very large trout.

Of course, the leech flies are not restricted to five colors, and they're not restricted to the salmonids. I've tied them with every shade of fur that I can get my hands on. In purple and with doll eyes, they are Di-No-Mite on largemouth bass; in red and white they are super pike flies, they've caught walleyes, salt water fishes, and so on. The leech flies can be tied with a monofilament weed guard. They can also be tied to ride hook point up so they can be fished right on the bottom, exactly like a jig. The design borrows from Dan Blanton's Crazy Charlie bone fish fly and the old Johnson Silver Minnow and pork rind combination for bass and pike.

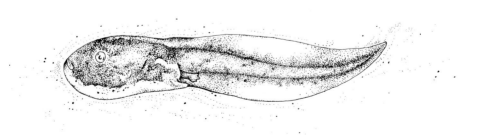

Figure 13-12. *A typical tadpole.*

Upside Down Leech: Dressing

Hook: Size 6-2/0 (or larger), 2XL or standard shank length

Thread: 3/0, color to match body

Tail: Fur strip; 1/4 to 3/8 inch wide

Body: As for regular leech designs

Weight: Lead eyes tied on top of hook shank

Throat (weed guard): Bucktail, calftail, or other stiff hairs

Hackle: Pheasant rump feather or other appropriate feather

Upside Down Leech: Tying Instructions

1. Clamp the hook in the vise and wrap the shank with thread, ending at the standard position.

2. Tie in the body material and wrap the thread forward to about three head spaces behind the eye.

3. Tie in a pair of lead eyes (either plated or unplated depending upon color of fly). These should be set in on top of the shank. Use figure-8 wraps, and secure them well *(Figure 13-13)*.

Figure 13-13. *Figure-8 the lead eyes to hold them securely.*

4. Wind the body material forward and make one figure-8 turn around the stem of the eyes; tie off in front of the eyes and cut away the excess.

5. Tie in a clump of hair for the throat. The hair should cover the point of the hook and extend slightly beyond it. Some tiers find it easier to turn the hook over in the vise for this step.

6. Apply the hackle as for the other leech patterns. Finish the head of the fly, tie off the thread, and cut it away. Cement the head.

7. Cut a strip of fur to the desired length; this can be any length, depending upon the organism you intend to imitate. Because of the placement of the lead eyes, the fly will ride hook point up, so stab the hook through one end of the strip from the leather side *(Figure 13-14)*.

The interesting feature of this fly is that the tail can be added at any time. In fact, I carry several colors of long fur strips and add them to the body when fishing. This way, I can add a purple tail to a silver body, or a yellow tail to a gold body, or a red tail to black body, etc. The strip can then be cut to any length desired—didn't I say pork rind and silver minnow?

Figure 13-14. *The finished Upside Down Leech.*

EGGS

When salmon spawn in rivers holding trout, the trout often get selective to salmon eggs—either to single eggs or to egg clusters. As with any other food item, the trout can be very picky about what they want. The imitation should be the correct color, size, shape, and have the same behavior (dead-drifting on the bottom). I fish egg imitations with a compound tippet (page 77) and split shot to keep the unweighted fly hovering near the gravel.

I use the standard egg pattern tied with Bug Yarn in fluorescent orange (BCS 77), pink (BCS 79), and red (BCS 85); fluorescent chartreuse (BCS 21) has also worked at times. In addition to single egg flies, I use a design that Maggie Merriman showed me. It's tied like a single egg fly but on size 2-8 hooks. Called the "Gob-O-Eggs," it has worked wonders for me. There was a trip to Alaska with Jason and Bob Ippel when the three of us landed and released nearly 2,000 fish during our one week stay. It was an easy trick. The silver salmon were spawning and the river was thick with arctic char and rainbows feeding heavily on loose eggs. We decided to go for numbers as well as size and a quality experience, so for several hours we'd fish for big rainbows with the Strip Leech, Down and Dirty Mouse, and the Gob-O-Eggs; shift over to 1- to 4-pound arctic char and rip out 50 to 70 apiece on the Gob-O-Eggs; and then hunt salmon with the Strip Leech, Gob-O-Eggs, and skated, dry muddlers. It was easy for each of us to take over a hundred fish a day! The Gob-O-Eggs has also worked very well for salmon and steelhead here in the Lake States, and single egg flies can be deadly on trout anywhere.

FEATHERS, FUR, AND STEEL

Feathers, fur, and steel. The three, principle raw ingredients from which the fly designer constructs deception. Obviously, the more a tier knows about these elements the better will be that deception. And there's enough to be known that it can be the subject of books such as Eric Leiser's excellent "Fly Tying Materials." It is not my intention to repeat what Eric and other writers have done. Rather, I want to add some further thoughts and information about the qualities of feathers, fur, and steel, about substitution, about experimentation, about fly design.

FEATHERS

Although feathers are used as an ingredient in a great number of patterns, tiers know less about them, in general, than about other materials. True, dry fly hackles are well understood and have been thoroughly discussed in journal articles and texts such as "The Book of the Hackle" by Frank Elder. In addition, tiers are quite familiar with the properties of feathers such as pheasant tail, turkey tail, mottled turkey, peacock herl, mallard primaries, wood duck flank, and a few others. But what about other feathers?

Soft Hackles

In the 1850's soft hackles were the darling of the fly tying community, and much was written about them. But somehow, over the past century, soft hackles have become second-class

citizens in the fly designer's world. Gradually, tiers have lost intimacy with soft hackles and have experienced a concomitant loss in associated tying skills. Currently, there's little information available on soft hackles beyond Syl Nemes' books and few notes in texts such as Darrell Martin's "Fly Tying Methods" and Jim Leisenring's "The Art of Tying the Wet Fly." So, when a soft hackle of moor hen is specified in a pattern, the tier dutifully follows the recipe or, if moor hen feathers are not available, simply doesn't tie the fly. But perhaps the fly would be tied if the angler knew that golden plover, starling, and coot all have feathers that could be substituted for the specified moor hen. Perhaps, too, this loss in proficiency with soft hackles has occurred because many feathers once used for this purpose (dotterel, sea swallow, lapwing, and landrail, for example) are no longer readily available, and patterns using these feathers have been dropped from the fly tier's repertoire. But soft-hackles don't deserve this second-class status. They are still the first-class choice in many fly designing situations.

Body Feathers

Body feathers have received almost no attention other than their use for tailing or legging materials, but there's a wide range of possibilities offered by these feathers. Jack Gartside has developed a whole series of delightfully successful patterns based on feathers from every body area of the ringneck pheasant, but Jack is one of only a few that have ventured outside the ordinary; not many tiers understand body feathers the way Jack does. And yet, as fly designers, we should, for, in the development of new tying concepts and applications, feathers offer many avenues to be explored. When designing with feathers, it's necessary to not only consider the color of the feather but its texture and other characteristics as well.

When I first began experimenting extensively with soft hackles nearly two decades ago, I was struck by the dearth of information about them. So, I began to collect first-hand information on readily available feathers and to read what scanty angling information I could find on uses of various feathers for soft hackles. During the process, I also accumulated information about body feathers in general. I was struck by the vast range of feather colors and types available on the market.

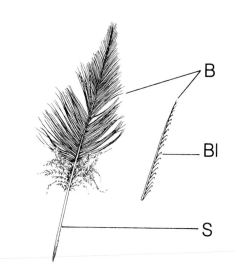

Figure 14-1. *Anatomy of a feather: S = shaft; B = Barbs; Bl = Barbule.*

Anatomy

Even though feathers vary from the superbly pigmented, stiff, genetic hackles to nondescript marabou fluff, they all have the same basic anatomy. The center rib of the feather is called the "shaft". The fibers that arise from the shaft are "barbs"; the barbs of most feathers bear small hooks or "barbules" that allow adjacent barbs to stick together *(Figure 14-1)*; the barbs of some feathers (such as stiff cock hackle) lack barbules.

Feather Types

Feathers on different parts of the bird perform different functions, and thus have different forms in terms of both overall shape and texture. Based on such variations, feathers of the body can be separated into neck (or hackle cape), throat, back, breast, rump (or saddle), flank (region covered by the folded wing), tail coverts, belly, and tail *(Figure 14-2)*. The feathers of the wing can be separated into dorsal marginal coverts, lesser coverts, greater coverts, bastard wing, ventral marginal coverts, undercoverts, primaries, and secondaries *(Figure 14-3)*.

Figure 14-2. *Typical feather regions of the bird body: N = neck (or hackle cape), Th = throat, Bk = back, Br = breast, R = rump (or saddle), Fl = flank (region covered by the folded wing), Tc = tail coverts, Bl = belly, and Tl = tail.*

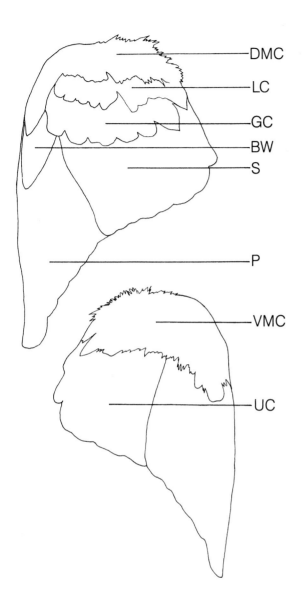

DMC

LC

GC

BW

S

P

VMC

UC

wing cases. Feathers from the back of the bird usually have rounded tips and heavy stems and barbs. That's because these feathers are exposed to the harshest of environmental factors and must also provide some protection against the teeth or talons of predators. Such feathers are useful to make the outer wings of grasshoppers or the shells of beetles. Breast feathers are often short and have squared tips and long, very soft barbs. They're also heavily endowed with long, basal, marabou fluff. Such feathers are useful as marabou soft hackles. Belly feathers are softer than breast feathers, but are sometimes longer and more rounded at the tips. These longer ones are useful where a very webby, marabou-type hackle is needed. Flank feathers tend to have less basal fluff than breast feathers and may vary from an elongate form to one with a squared end and long thin barbs. The barbs of flank feathers are often used for tails and wings of dry flies and legs of nymphs. Feathers of the rump patch are fairly long with a relatively thin stem and medium-length to long barbs. Often as much as half of the barbs are of the marabou type. These feathers make very nice hackles on larger flies—such as the Strip Leech—where the marabou fluff is an important component of the design. In addition rump feathers make excellent outer wings for grasshoppers. The stems of the tail coverts and tail feathers are usually too heavy to make these feathers useful for hackling purposes, but the barbs may be used for wings, tails, throats, legs and other structures.

Figure 14-3.   Typical feather regions of the bird wing: DMC = dorsal marginal coverts, LC = lesser coverts, GC = greater coverts, BW = bastard wing, VMC = ventral marginal coverts, UC = undercoverts, P = primaries, and S = secondaries

Feathers from the nape (hackle cape) may be elongate with relatively short barbs. Depending upon their stiffness, such feathers are very good for dry fly hackles or for heavily dressed soft hackle flies. Or the nape feathers may be short and square tipped like those usually found on the throat. Such feathers make good nymph

Dorsal and ventral marginal covert feathers of the wing are often of different colors (the ventral ones are usually of a lighter shade) but are shaped the same. They are relatively short feathers with medium-length barbs and medium-weight stems. They are also small. For example, it is not unusual to find the marginal coverts of grouse in sizes as small as size 20 or 22. It is these feathers that have traditionally been specified for soft hackle flies. Undercoverts and the greater and lesser coverts are elongate feathers with medium length barbs and medium weight stems. These feathers are great for making "half" feathers for palmering Soft Hackle Wooly Worms.

The stems of the flight feathers (primary and secondary feathers) and those of the bastard wing feathers are too stiff and heavy to make these feathers useful for soft hackles, but the barbs are used for wings, tails, and legs.

Selecting Feathers

When selecting feathers, I first consider the characteristics I'm trying to build into the fly. Then I consider colors, textures, barb lengths, and shaft diameters and how these features could contribute to the design. For example, when designing the Strip Leech, I wanted a feather that would add bulk and movement to the fly, and, because it would be basically an opportunistic pattern, I wanted the feather to provide a bit of attractive, iridescent flash. Pheasant rump feathers had soft barbs of sufficient length for use on the big flies while simultaneously offering iridescence. Furthermore, the large amount of marabou fluff at the base of the feather could add significant motion. The shaft diameter at the base of the feather was a bit large, but once I developed a method for handling it (page 115), this feather proved to be just what was needed.

To help you select feathers for your particular needs, I've listed the most commonly available ones in the tables below. Use Table 14-1 to select the birds having the general color(s) that you need, then go to Table 14-2 to narrow the color selection and choose the feather type you need.

Table 14-1. Selecting plumage according to general color requirements. Borger Color System (BCS) numbers are given in parentheses; "i" means iridescent.

COLOR	PLUMAGE	COLOR	PLUMAGE
White (107)	English grouse, sage grouse, mallard, Amherst pheasant	White mottled with grays or browns	moorhen, golden plover, blue grouse, Amherst pheasant, ringneck pheasant, Bob White quail, snipe
Pale gray (105)	mourning dove, coot, Mearns quail		
Grays (109, 110)	scaled quail, jackdaw, Gambles quail, Mearns quail, California quail	Gold (50, 67)	golden pheasant
Dark Grays (113/114, 117)	American woodcock, coot, crow, jackdaw, magpie, spruce grouse	Buff (58)	Courtnix quail, chukkar, hen ringneck pheasant
Olive grays (108, 108/112)	mallard, scaled quail, spruce grouse, ruffed grouse, blue grouse, Gambles quail, California quail, scaled quail, Bob White quail, English grouse, golden pheasant	Dark tan (94)	California quail, Gambles quail, scaled quail
		Oranges (76, 73)	red pheasant
Dark olive gray (116)	golden plover, moorhen, starling, coot, spruce grouse, Amherst pheasant	Orange browns (60-63)	American and English woodcock, Courtnix quail, English grouse, jay, kingfisher, red pheasant
Charcoal (114)	coot, Gambles quail, mourning dove	Red browns (65, 66)	Bob White quail, ruffed grouse, kingfisher, golden pheasant
Mottled grays	blue grouse, sage grouse, Mearns quail	Dark browns (64, 87, 98, 99)	snipe, jay, chukkar partridge, Courtnix quail, cock ringneck pheasant
Black (118)	crow, jackdaw, kingfisher, red pheasant	Mottled browns & browns mottled with blacks	ringneck pheasant (cock and hen), chukkar partridge, snipe, bobwhite quail, English grouse, ruffed grouse, English woodcock
White & black barred	silver pheasant, Amherst pheasant		

IRIDESCENT COLOR	PLUMAGE	IRIDESCENT COLOR	PLUMAGE
Blue (i136)	kingfisher	**Green (i22, i23)**	Amherst pheasant, starling
Purple blue (i128)	magpie, silver pheasant	**Dark green (i10)**	ringneck pheasant
Deep purple blue (i144/145)	Amherst pheasant	**Gray green (i6)**	golden pheasant
		Dark gray green (i9)	Amherst pheasant
Purple (i130)	starling	**Medium olive (i28)**	ringneck pheasant
Deep purple (i132)	golden pheasant, silver pheasant	**Dark olive green (i33)**	Amherst pheasant
Light blue gray (i105)	ringneck pheasant	**Bronze (i86)**	ringneck pheasant
Dark blue gray (i141)	kingfisher	**Scarlet (i81)**	golden pheasant

Table 14-2. Specific colors of various feathers from commercially available bird plumages; some are available as wings only, others as entire capes. This table is not meant to be a complete listing of all available or useful plumage. N = nape; Th = throat, Bk = back, Br = breast, R = rump, F = flank, Bl = belly, Tc = tail covert, DMC = dorsal marginal covert, VMC = ventral marginal covert, GC = greater covert, LC = lesser covert, UC = under covert. Numbers refer to the Borger Color System. Those numbers separated by a slash (/) indicate a color between the two given color numbers. The given colors indicate the most prominent shades of the feathers; natural variations may occur.

Colors of Readily Available Wing Plumage

Crow

DMC, GC, & LC	black (118) with indigo (132) iridescence
VMC & UC	dark blue gray (117)

English Grouse

DMC	orange brown (63) barred with black (118)
GC & LC	black (118) with orange brown (63) bars
VMC	medium olive gray (112) mottled with orange brown (63) and white (107)
UC	white (107)

English Woodcock

DMC	orange brown (63) mottled with black (118)
GC & LC	orange brown (63) to medium orange brown (60) mottled with olive gray (108)
VMC & UC	buff (58) mottled with medium olive gray (112)

Golden Plover

DMC, GC & LC	dark olive gray (116) marked with light orange (67)
VMC	mottled dark olive gray (116) and white (107)
UC	white (107) mottled with light dun brown (95)

Jackdaw

DMC, GC & LC	black (118) with indigo (132) iridescence
VMC & UC	dark blue gray (117)

Jay

DMC, GC, & LC	dark dun brown (99)
VMC & UC	dark tan (61)

Magpie

DMC	almost black (118) with hint of iridescent green (i10)
GC & LC	dark iridescent purplish blue (i128)
VMC & UC	dark blackish gray (117/118)

Mallard

DMC, GC, & LC	dun gray (108/112)
VMC & UC	white (107)

Moor Hen

DMC, GC & LC	dark olive gray (116) with dark olive drab tint (103)
VMC	white (107) spotted with charcoal (114)
UC	charcoal (114) spotted with white (107)

Mourning Dove

DMC, GC, & LC	charcoal (114) washed with medium olive drab (100)
VMC & UC	light blue gray (105)

Colors of Readily Available Bird Skins

Chukkar

Bk, DMC, GC, LC	dark dun brown (99)
F	barred with black (118), medium brown (87) and buff (58)bars
R	medium olive gray (112)
VMC & UC	buff (58)

Coot

N, Th, VMC, & UC	charcoal (114)
Bk	dark blue gray (113/114)
Br, F, & Bl	light blue gray (105)
R & TC	dark olive gray (116)
DMC, GC, & LC	dark gray (114/117)

Grouse, Blue

Th & Br	white (107) with dark blue gray (117) tip
Bk	olive gray (108) with dark tan (61) mottled tips
R & TC	dark olive gray (116) with medium gray (110) mottles
Bl	charcoal (114) with white (107) tips
DMC, GC, LC & VMC	olive gray (108) with charcoal (114) bars and buff (58) mottles
UC	white (107)

Grouse, Ruffed

N	mottled orange brown (63) and black (118)
Th	light orange brown (60) with ecru (91) and black (118) bars

Grouse, Ruffed (cont.)

Bk, R, & TC	red brown (87) speckled with dark olive gray (116), ecru (91) eye on feather
DMC	dark brown (64) with buff (58) edges and center
GC & LC	red brown (66) with buff (58) along stem
VMC & UC	medium olive gray (112) with white (107) tips

Grouse, Sage

VMC	white (107) with dark olive gray (116) bars
UC	white (107)
All other feathers	dark olive gray (116) with buff (58) and ecru (91) bars and spots

Grouse, Spruce

N	charcoal (114)
Th	white (107) with charcoal and buff (58) mottles
Bk	dark olive gray (116) with dark tan (61) bars
R & TC	dark olive gray (116) with dark tan (61) and medium gray (110) mottles
Bl	medium gray (110) with white (107) tips
DMC	olive gray (108) with dark tan (61) edges
GC & LC	olive gray (108) with dark tan (61) mottles
VMC	same as DMC or white (107)
UC	white (107)

Kingfisher

N & Br	dark red brown (65)
Th	dark gray green (9)
Bk & LC	iridescent dark blue gray (i141)

Kingfisher (cont.)

R	iridescent blue (i136)
F	white (107) base with sandy (61) tip
Bl, VMC, & UC	sand (61)
DMC	dark red brown (65/66)
GC	black (118)

Pheasant, Amherst

Crest	small feathers iridescent dark olive green (i33), elongate feathers scarlet (81)
N	white (107) edged with iridescent purple-black (i129)
Th, Bk, & Br	iridescent green (i23) edged with black (118)
R	iridescent dark gray green (i9) tipped with orangish yellow (50)
F & Bl	white (107)
Tc	black (118) tipped with a bar of white (107) followed by a bar of scarlet (81)
DMC	dark olive gray (116)
GC & LC	iridescent purplish blue (i144/145)
VMC & UC	brown (87) mottled with white (107)

Pheasant, Golden

Crest	short feathers red orange (76), long feathers gold (50)
Nape	top portion deep orange (73/76) with black (118) bars, lower portion iridescent gray green (i6) edged with black (118)
Th, Br, & Bl	iridescent scarlet (i81)
Bk, R, & Tc	gold (67)
F	red brown (66) tipped with iridescent scarlet (i81)
DMC	red brown (66) barred with black (118)
GC	deep orange brown (66/76)

Pheasant, Golden (cont.)

LC	iridescent deep purple (i132)
VMC	red brown (66)
UC	olive gray (108)

Pheasant, Red

Crest	black (118)
N & Th	rusty orange (76)
Bk, R, Tc, BMC, GC, & LC	dark olive gray (116) barred with pale tan (91) and dark tan (71) with black (118) center and ecru (92) eye
Br, F, & Bl	rusty orange (76) with pale blue gray (134) eye
VMC	orange (73)
UC	pale rusty orange (60)

Pheasant, Ringneck, Cock

Crest	dark olive tan (29)
N	iridescent dark green (i10) with white (107) collar
Th	same as N and iridescent bronze (i86)
Bk	light rosy orange (68) with white (107) and dark olive gray (116) center, dark green (10) tips; also red brown (83) with ecru (91) and black (118) mottled center
Br	iridescent bronze (i86)
R	iridescent medium olive (i28) to iridescent light blue gray (i105) barred with ginger (54) and dark olive gray (116)
DMC	dark brown (64) with light blue gray (108) bars and tips
GC	dark ecru (104)
LC	iridescent bronze (i86) with ecru (91) center
VMC	white (107)
UC	light gray (106) washed with medium ginger (51)

Pheasant, Ringneck, Hen

N & Th	light dun brown (95) variously barred with black (118) and dark orange brown (66)
Bk:	light dun brown (95) with black (118) and buff (58) barred tips
F	pale ginger (48) to buff (58) with dark brown (64) bars
R	black (118) with pinkish (69) edges
Bl	ecru (91) with medium olive gray (112) bars
DMC, GC, & LC	buff (58) with dark brown (64) bars
VMC & UC	mottled pale tan (91) and buff (58)

Pheasant, Silver

Crest	iridescent deep purple (i132)
N & Br	black (118) with indigo (i132) iridescence
Bl	dark olive gray (116)
All other feathers	white (107) with black (118) bars

Quail, Bob White

N	medium brown (87) mottled with black (118)
Th	light rosy orange (68)
Bk	medium brown (87) with black (118) bars and mottles
Br	dark pinkish tan (71) with black (118) bars
R	yellow brown (62) barred with charcoal (114) and ecru (91)
DMC	olive gray (108) with dark orange brown (66) blotches
GC & LC	red brown (66) with pale tan (91) and dark brown (64) bars
VMC	olive gray (108) with white (107) bars
UC	medium gray (110) with white (107) bars

Quail, California

N & Th	mottled grays (105, 109) with charcoal (117) edges and center
Bk	smokey gray (108) to medium olive gray (112)
Br	blue gray (109)
R & TC	medium olive gray (112)
F	rusty brown (66) tipped in black (118), to creamy orange (48) with brown (102) edges and center, to dark olive gray (116) with white (107) center
Bl	creamy orange (48) with brown (102) center
DMC, GC, & LC	smokey gray (108) tinted with rosy tan (121)
VMC	buff (94) with rosy brown (99) overtones
UC	medium gray (110/114)

Quail, Courtnix

N	orangish tan (62/63) with charcoal (117) and pinkish tan (58) centers
Th & Br	fleshy tan (61) with red brown (66) mottling
Bk, R, & Tc	brown (87) with black (118) mottles and creamy orange (48) center
F	fleshy tan (61) with black (118) mottles and pale tan (91) center
Bl	pinkish tan (58) with red brown (66) and black (118) mottles
DMC, GC, & LC	brown (87) tinted with smokey gray (108)
VMC	pinkish tan (58)
UC	white (107)

Quail, Gambles

N, Th, Bk, R, & Tc	smokey gray (108) with rosy tan (121) overtones
Br	medium gray (110) tipped in creamy tan (91)

Quail, Gambles (cont.)

F	dark rusty brown (83) with white (117) center
Bl	creamy tan (91) with dark rusty brown (83) center
Wings	same as California Quail

Quail, Harlequin or Mearns

N	mottled white (107) dark tan (61) and olive gray (108)
Th, Br, & Bl	charcoal (114) mottled with white (107)
Bk	black (118) with dark tan (61) bars and white (107) along stem
R	mottled light blue gray (105), dark tan (61), and black (118)
Tc	same as **R** and with white (107) along stem
DMC & VMC	medium blue gray (109) with white (107) spots
GC	medium blue gray (109) with black (118) spots and white (107) along stem
LC & UC	light blue gray (105)

Quail, Scaled

N	blue gray (105/109) tipped in charcoal (117)
Th	pale blue gray (105) tipped with charcoal (117)
Bk, R, & Tc	smokey gray (108) tinted with rosy tan (121)
Bl & Br	creamy tan (91) tipped with charcoal (117)
F	same as **Bk**, but with white (107) center
Wings	same as California Quail

Snipe

N	mottled tan (58) and dark brown (64)

Snipe (cont.)

Bk   black (118) with buff (58) tips

F, VMC, & UC   white (107) barred with dark brown (64)

Tc   dark orange brown (66) barred with black (118)

DMC   dark chocolate brown (98) with white (107) tips

GC & LC   dark brown (64) tipped with ecru (91)

Starling

N & Th   iridescent purple (130) tipped in tan (94)

Other body feathers   iridescent green (22) tipped in tan (94)

DMC, GC, & LC   dark olive gray (116) with dark blue green (22) iridescence, edged in medium ginger (51)

Starling (cont.)

VMC & UC   dark olive gray (116) edged with medium ginger (51)

Woodcock, American

N, Bk, R, and TC   dark olive gray (116) with pinkish ginger (54) bars

Th   medium gray (110) washed with pinkish ginger (54)

Br, F, & Bl   light orange brown (60) to buff (58)

DMC   dark olive gray (116) with light orange brown (60) edges

GC & LC   light orange brown (60) with dark olive gray (116) bars

VMC & UC   dark tan (61)

FUR

As you've noticed, I like dubbed bodies. Which means that furs are very important in my tying. Both natural and artificial furs. And, as you might guess, I have a rather wide ranging collection of them.

Selecting Furs

When selecting natural furs I look for three things: texture, length, and color. By texture, I'm referring to the diameter of the dubbing fur fibers as well as the number and diameter of the guard hairs. If I want to tie smooth-bodied flies (and therefore need only the dubbing fur) then the fewer guard hairs the better. If, on the other hand, I want coarse dubbing then the more guard hairs the better. The length of the fur is also important. Long dubbing fur is easier to

spin than very short fur, and long furs can act as binders when blending. Because of dyes, and because furs can be blended, the natural color of the fur is less significant than the diameter (denier) and length of the fur. However, I still like to have as wide a range of natural colors as possible.

In addition to selecting furs for dubbing, I also look at the length and color pattern on the guard hairs. Partially because I like to blend them with fine furs to get coarse dubbing for nymphs, but more importantly to evaluate their use for hair legs. Most guard hairs have a mottled pattern that makes them a good match for the mottled legs of many insects. And, guard hairs have a unique shape that makes them especially useful for hair legs. The hair is thin in diameter on its basal half and thick in diameter on the apical half *(Figure 14-4)*. When guard hairs are plucked from the skin (page 32), they tend to break at the point where the thin, basal half meets the thick apical half. Thus, if the hairs are plucked rather than cut, the tier can be assured of getting hairs of known length. This length will vary from animal to animal and from area to area on a pelt. For example, the guard hairs from the back of the cottontail rabbit are suitable for hook sizes 8-12; the guard hairs from the mask of the rabbit are best for hook sizes 14-16; the back of a squirrel has hairs that make good legs on hook sizes 12-16; and so on.

The natural furs I use most often are white domestic rabbit (dyed any color needed), cottontail rabbit, gray squirrel, fox squirrel, muskrat, mink, hare's mask, mohair, and Australian possum. For a good technical discussion of fur and hair diameters, shapes, and other traits, see Darrell Martin's book "Fly Tying Methods."

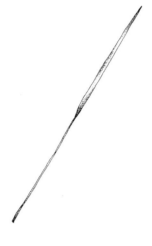

Figure 14-4. *The normal shape of a guard hair.*

Synthetic furs are also very useful in fly tying. For large flies of one color, I find yarns very helpful. But often, I prefer to use synthetics in the form of dubbing; either used alone or blended. The material is cut into 1/2- to 1-inch long chunks and mixed in a food blender. The artificial furs add highlights, texture, or unique properties to the blend. For instance, sparkle yarns contribute their unique, sparkling translucency; polypropylene yarns can add coarse texture and translucency, and acrylics can add a splash of color. Some of the fine-diameter, synthetic dubbings such as Fly Rite can be used directly as dubbing or used as a binder when blended with coarser materials. Steve Fernandez, an extraordinarily gifted fly tier from southern California, uses blended flosses in many of his patterns. It produces a beautiful, translucent look that is very reminiscent of seal fur.

Blending Furs

Blended furs are often better than a single fur alone. Mixtures can be created to produce both specific colors and specific textures not available from any one natural or synthetic material. Furthermore, the heather hue produced by blending is a good match for the usually mottled appearance of most of the trout's food organisms. But, furs cannot be blended like paints. A mix of green, red, and yellow furs may look olive from five feet away. However, from five inches away a trout closely inspecting a fly made from the mix will not see olive; it will see bits of green, red, and yellow furs. So, when blending furs, I start with a color and/or texture that's close to the final product I want, or at least contains the major component I'm looking for. I than add other colors/textures to provide highlights and achieve the final product. For example, suppose I want to blend a sandy tan (BCS 61) dubbing with a coarse texture for nymph bodies. I start with the light-colored fur from a hare's mask, add some dark tan sparkle yarn, and round it out with the fur from the back of a fox squirrel. And, I keep notes on what I've done so I can easily repeat it.

The small, gourmet-style coffee blenders are good for a quick fix, but for serious blending, you need a big food blender. The cost is often no more than that of the smaller ones, but the capacity is significantly greater. The big blending chamber allows materials to mix faster and more thoroughly, and of course, allows more materials to be blended at one time. Some tiers blend the material wet, some dry. Actually both methods have merit. The wet method allows the tier to match colors of subaquatic insects. The dry method is great for dry fly blends.

Fur Strips

What would I do without fur strips? I honestly don't know. At this writing, Jason and I have just returned from the far north of Ontario where we were fishing for big brook trout. Knowing the aggressive, piscivorous nature of these char, we took plenty of Strip Leeches. We were not disappointed. Those 2-5 pound squaretails took the fur-strip flies extremely well. In the first two hours of fishing, we landed and released 71 big brookies on the Gold and Silver Leeches. What a trip!

I cut the strips from a wide range of furs, selecting them for the required color and fiber length. The trick to cutting the strips is to use a very sharp razor blade or number 11 scalpel and keep the hide up off the table top while slicing it (this keeps the blade from cutting the fur fibers). For this you need three hands, so I grip one edge of the hide with the clamp of a clip board. This way I can lift the opposite edge in my materials hand and use my bobbin hand to hold the scalpel. I cut the strips with the "grain" of the fur—from head to tail.

STEEL

The hook serves two critical purposes: (1) it is the foundation upon which the fly is built, and (2) it is the means by which the fish is secured and held until brought to net. The ideal hook would be eyeless, so thin as to be nearly invisible, super strong, come in an infinite variety of lengths, have a point that never gets dull, and be barbless but with the retention power of a barbed hook. Obviously such a hook does not exist. That leaves us with a less than perfect world in which to operate and a number of decisions to make.

Eye Styles

First, eyed or eyeless? An eyeless hook does allow the tier to dress a slightly more realistic pattern (what food organism has a loop of wire sticking out of its nose?). However, the inconvenience of attaching an eyeless hook to the leader far outweighs any benefit gained. So our hooks are eyed. But tiers have not considered the eye to be part of the representation of the food organism; rather, the eye (like the hook bend and point) is regarded as a necessary evil.

Thus, when selecting hooks most tiers consider only the length of the shank (from the rear of the eye to the bend). But in fact, the eye should be considered in the overall length of the imitation, especially when tying flies sizes 16 and smaller. In these smaller sizes, variations in length are much more evident than in larger sizes (page 46). Time and time again I've had highly selective fish refuse my fly only to readily take the same imitation tied one size smaller. In these situations, the length of the hook shank of the first fly I chose was the same length as the natural's body. For the fly one size smaller, the length of the shank plus the length of the eye matched the body length of the natural, and that's the fly they wanted. Thus for flies size 16 and smaller, the eye must be considered an integral part of the overall length of the design.

Some designs lend themselves very nicely to hiding the eye. For instance, in the Braided Butt Damsel, Yarn-Wing Dun, Devil Bug, and Poly-Caddis, the eye is overarched with the trimmed, butt end of the wing. In other designs, the eye sticks out beyond the fly proper like a proverbial sore thumb. In these instances, I consider the eye of the hook to represent the head of the insect.

When I first began tying flies thirty years ago, I was confused about the various eye configurations. Drawings or photos of salmon flies all showed them on up-eye hooks, trout flies were shown on down-eye hooks, and bait fishermen found ring-eye configuration best. If there were advantages offered by any one style, they weren't readily apparent by usage.

Some anglers suggested that the angle of the eye determined the direction that the tippet pulled on the hook. That is, a down-eye hook was best because it caused the leader to pull the hook down into the fish's mouth (even though the angler was pulling up on the line) whereas an up-eye hook was inferior because it caused the leader to pull the hook up and out of the fish's mouth. A little experimentation showed this to be a myth. Whether a hook is knotted on the tippet with a turl, clinch, or any other knot, the direction of pull against a hook is the same, regardless of eye angle. The leader does not pull up on up eye hooks or down on down eye hooks.

Nor does eye angle influence the way the hook behaves when it's set, because regardless of eye position, when the hook point catches, torque develops and rotates the eye end of the shank downward *(Figure 14-5)*. This in turn angles the point downward. On a hard surface such as a block of wood, the point can't dig in very far, and the shank rotates downward until the line of pull is straight from the hook point to the eye *(Figure 14-5)*. But, in the flesh of the fish's mouth, the hook point is buried almost immediately, and the line of pull shifts rearward up onto the bend of the hook *(Figures 14-6, 14-7, 14-8)*.

Bend Shapes

A hook buries itself to the rear-most position on the bend. On a flat surface, a hook with a square bend penetrates only to the lower angle on the hook *(Figure 14-6)*; such hooks therefore need long points to allow a secure grip. In addition, all the stresses are concentrated on the upper and lower angles of the bend, and such hooks must be made of very strong material to prevent bending or breakage. The same holds true for the Limerick bend which is curved at the top but then angled at the bottom *(Figure 14-7)*; this lessens the stresses on the upper part of the bend only to concentrate it at the lower angle. A model perfect hook has a uniformly curving bend. Given points of the same length, it will

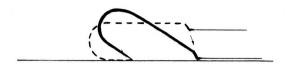

Figure 14-5. Torque rotates the eye downward until the line of pull is straight from point to eye.

dig in deeper than a square or Limerick bend *(Figure 14-8)*. In addition, the stresses are uniformly distributed around the bend of the model perfect hook. For these reasons, I prefer hooks of the model perfect design.

Gap

Eye design does influence initial effective gap, and so can be important on hooks size 18 and smaller. A down-eye hook has a smaller, initial effective gap than hooks with a ring eye or up eye *(Figure 14-9)*. For this reason you might wish to consider an up-eye or ring-eye configuration in small hooks.

Anglers most frequently miss fish on small hooks, regardless of eye position, because the gap is so tiny that the hook doesn't catch well in the trout's toothy mouth. To help the hook point catch, I slightly offset the point to the side *(Figure 14-10)*. In addition, it's very necessary to wait a second or two after the take to give the fish time to close its mouth and turn its head downward. When the tiny hook is set at this time, the leader draws the fly back into the corner of the fish's mouth where it will almost always dig in.

Figure 14-6. A square bend hook fully set on a flat surface.

Figure 14-7. A Limerick bend hook fully set on a flat surface.

Figure 14-8. A model perfect bend hook fully set on a flat surface.

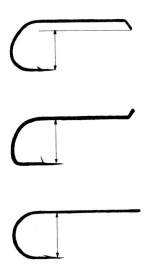

Figure 14-9. *Initial effective gap for down-eye, up-eye, and ring eye hooks.*

Shank Length

Some anglers have contented that a long-shank produces better hooking capability than a short-shank, and therefore, since the angle of the eye effects overall hooking length, ring-eye hooks are best. Certainly, on a flat surface, there's a *tiny* bit more hooking length on a ring-eye hook than on either an up-eye or down-eye hook *(Figure 14-11)*. Certainly, the shorter the shank, the less the distance from the point to the end of the eye. And certainly, on a flat, perfectly smooth, hard surface, this can effect the angle that the point assumes when the hook is set *(Figure 14-12)*. From these observations it would *seem* that a very short-shanked, up-eye hook would have no bite at all; the angle of penetration would be so steep that the point would simply slide along and not dig in, even when the hook has been "beaked" to change the point's initial angle of penetration *(Figure 14-12)*. Thus the angler foolish enough to use such diabolically manufactured, short-shanked hooks would lead a life of missed strikes and needlessly lost fish. This must certainly be news to the thousands of successful anglers who regularly use such hooks and to the hundreds of thousands of trout and salmon such anglers have caught on these hooks.

Figure 14-10. *Offsetting the points on tiny hooks helps them dig in.*

The fact is, a trout's mouth is anything but hard, perfectly smooth, and flat. It's soft and fleshy and filled with a variety of angled and rolling landscapes, edges, corners, cavities, and other obstructions. Thus, the hook point has many protuberances to catch on before it's whisked away by the anxious strike of the angler. In addition, the hook is not merely sliding loosely over the interior of the fish's mouth. The fish is biting the fly; trying to kill it; eating it. This masticating grip is of great assistance in getting the hook point in. Here's an experiment that clearly shows how much the fish helps the angler set the hook. Tie a short-shank, up-eye hook onto a piece of tippet. Lay the

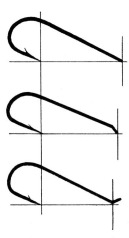

Figure 14--11. *On a flat surface, a ring-eye hook has a slightly longer hooking length than a down-eye or up-eye hook.*

Figure 14-12. *The shorter the shank length the steeper the initial hooking angle on a flat surface.*

hook in your open palm and pull on the leader. The hook slides easily off your hand. Now repeat the experiment, except close your hand tightly over the hook before you pull.

In fact, fish often hook themselves when they chew on the fly. I've seen it happen many times. For instance, when Jason and I were video taping "Fishing Damsels and Dragons," Bob Pelzl was fishing nearby. Unknown to us, I called for "quiet on the set" just as Bob cast a damsel nymph into an area where some trout were cruising. As Jason and I worked, a rainbow moved in and picked up Bob's fly as it lay motionless on the sandy bottom. Bob dropped the rod tip to take all tension off the line and waited, hoping the fish would spit out the fly and move on. The fish chewed on the fly, shook its head a few times and then slowly swam off. It had hooked itself. Bob quickly paid out line to keep all tension off the fish. Nearly a minute passed before Jason and I were finished video taping, and all the while the fish cruised back and forth in front of Bob as if nothing was wrong. When we finished, Bob asked, "Can I fish now?" At the affirmative answer, he let out a whoop and tightened the line. The fish was still on, and we rushed over to watch in amazement as Bob recounted the story and landed the fish.

Sharp Points

Experiences such as Bob's have only reenforced my belief in using the sharpest hook I can get—and keeping them sharp. Vince Marinaro gave the best criterion for a sharp hook that I've ever read: When scraped across the top of a thumbnail, the hook should be sharp enough to dig in and not slide. The new chemi-

cally sharpened hooks are that sharp right out of the box. What a boon they've been to my tying; they've saved me all the time I used to spend sharpening hooks before I tied. And, they've been a boon to my fishing because many more fish (like Bob's) now hook themselves.

Hook Selection

Like the eye, the extra material in the bend and point are often ignored by the tier. They shouldn't be. They are part of the fly, and unless they are de-emphasized and balanced with the design of the fly, they can call unnecessary attention to themselves, in which case, the fish may notice them and reject the offering. For most nymphs and drys, I use standard length hooks with high carbon, 1X fine wire. This length balances very well with most of my designs, and I've found the strength of the wire quite satisfactory for even very large fish.

However, there are designs for which such hooks are not the best choice. For example, a thinly dressed nymph tied on a standard, size 10 hook emphasizes the bend and point rather than blending with them. I'm convinced that the fish's attention is often called to the overly noticeable bend and point. So convinced, that for thinly dressed patterns size 14 and *larger* I use 2XL hooks. These provide a smaller (less evident) gap for the same shank length (for example, a size 12, 2XL has the same shank length as a standard size 10). I've had trout in lakes refuse thinly dressed flies only to take the same dressing on a 2XL shank. It's happened too often to be a fluke.

At the other end of the spectrum are the very tiny flies dressed on hooks with almost impossibly small gaps. For these I may dress double flies (page 64) or use 2X short shank hooks. For designs such as the Strip Leech or Bow Legged Hopper, which are imitations of elongate, large organisms, I normally use 3XL hooks with standard wire diameter. The curved, English bait hook (or others of similar design) are excellent for worms and some larvae, and the 5X-short-shank hook works great for egg flies.

Barbed or Barbless

Barbless hooks have received a great deal of press in recent years as conservation tools. Certainly on heavily fished waters, barbless hooks have prevented unnecessary damage to many fish, and I fully agree with the rationale of their usage. In addition, barbless hooks, or those with very small barbs, penetrate faster and easier than hooks with large barbs. But barbless hooks are not available in the wide range of styles produced in barbed hooks, so I often find myself pinching the barb down. If the barb is large, it has usually been cut so deeply into the wire that the metal of the point often fractures when the barb is crimped. Therefore on hooks with large barbs, it's best to pinch them down before the fly is tied. Filing them off is an alternative. I prefer to buy hooks with very tiny barbs. These can be pinched down without injury to the hook wire.

When fishing in areas that are *not* mandated as "barbless only," I normally do not pinch the barb completely shut on hooks size 10, 3XL and larger. I pinch the barb almost shut. This allows the hook to penetrate quickly, but still maintains the retention capability of the barb. This is necessary because the weight of a big fly makes it easy for a jumping fish to literally shake the artificial out of its mouth. Small, light-weight flies are nearly impossible to dislodge in this manner.

Due to normal variations occurring in the printing process, the colors of the imitations shown in the photos in this book may not exactly match the specified BCS colors.

Chapter Fifteen

THE FLIES

MAYFLY NYMPHS

Hair Leg Nymph
Feather Leg Nymph
Strip Nymph

Mayfly emergers

Parachute Floating Nymph
Wet/Dry Fly

Mayfly duns

Yarn Wing Dun
Loop Wing Dun
Hair Wing Dun

MAYFLY SPINNERS

Parachute Spinner
X-Wing Spinner

STONEFLIES

Mono Stonefly Nymph
Hair Wing Stonefly

Caddisfly Larva and Pupa

Peeking Caddis
Fur Caddis Larva
Sparkle Caddis Pupa

CADDISFLY ADULTS

Devil Bug
Poly Caddis
Diving Caddis

MIDGES

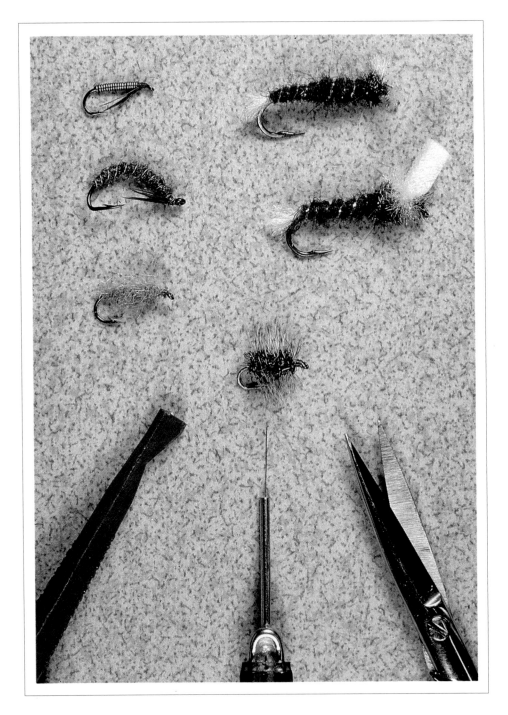

Brassie   Jumbo Lake Pupa-Sinking
Fur Midge Larva   Jumbo Lake Pupa-Suspender
Sparkle Midge Pupa

Griffith's Gnat

CRANEFLIES

Fur Cranefly Larva
Troth Skater

DAMSELS AND DRAGONS

Marabou Damsel Nymph
Braided Butt Damsel-Adult
Braided Butt Damsel-Teneral
Fur Chenille Dragon

WOOLY WORMS AND AQUATIC BUGS

Hair Leg Wooly Worm
Sparkle Boatman

TERRESTRIALS

Inchworm-Floating
Para Ant
Flying Ant
Thompson's Foam Beetle
Bow Legged Hopper

CRUSTACEANS

Hair Leg Scud
Fluorescent Scud
Hair Leg Cressbug
Fleeing Crayfish

Snails and worms

Floating Snail
Peacock Snail
San Juan Worm

Leeches and minnows

Strip Leech
Silver Leech
Upside Down Leech

Mice and eggs

Down and Dirty Mouse
Cone Head Mouse
Gob-O-Eggs

ANNOTATED BIBLIOGRAPHY

In putting together this collection of reference materials cited in the text, I've listed the most recent (and therefore most readily available) editions of the books. Annotations are mine.

Anonymous. 1954. Family Circle's Guide to Trout Flies and How to Tie Them. Family Circle, Inc., USA. My first book on fly tying; still a good reference.

Arbona, Fred L., Jr. 1989. Mayflies, the Angler & the Trout. Lyons & Burford, NY. An authoritative look at the biology of the major mayfly groups of the U.S.

Atherton, John. 1971. The Fly and the Fish. Freshet Press, Rockville Centre NY. A reprint of the 1951 edition; the book that firmly established impressionism as a methodology in fly tying.

Beck, Barry. 1990. "The Sinking Inchworm." Fly Fisherman Magazine, vol. 21 (5): 40ff. Barry's description of how to tie and fish his sinking inchworm.

Bergara, Juan de. 1984. El Manuscrito de Astorga. Flyleaves, Denmark. A reprint of the 1624 edition; a very interesting study in early hackled fly development.

Berners, Dame Juliana. 1979. A Treatise On Fishing With a Hook. Van Resse Press, NY. A copy of the 1496 edition; the first book on fly fishing.

Borger, Gary. 1979. Nymphing: A Basic Book. Stackpole, Harrisburg, PA. A discussion of all the major nymph fishing tactics for streams and lakes.

Borger, Gary. 1980. Naturals: A Guide to Food Organisms of the Trout. Stackpole, Harrisburg,

PA. Natural history of the fish's food organisms as related to imitations and fly fishing tactics.

Borger, Gary. 1986. Borger Color System. Gary Borger Enterprises, Inc., Wausau, WI. A standardized system for recording colors of the trout's food organisms and their imitations.

Borger, Gary. 1986. South Island Sampler (video tape). Gary Borger Enterprises, Inc., Wausau, WI. How to spot, stalk, and catch the big trout of New Zealand's South Island.

Borger, Gary. 1987. The Fabulous Bighorn (video tape). Gary Borger Enterprises, Inc., Wausau, WI. Advanced nymph fishing on the Bighorn River in Montana.

Borger, Gary. 1991. Fishing Crustaceans and Snails (video tape). Gary Borger Enterprises, Inc., Wausau, WI. The biology of crustaceans and snails as related to fly design and presentation tactics.

Borger, Gary. 1991. Fishing Damsels and Dragons (video tape). Gary Borger Enterprises, Inc., Wausau, WI. The natural history of these important lake insects, flies to match them, and tactics that take fish.

Brooks, Charles E.. 1970. Larger Trout For the Western Fly Fisherman. A.S. Barnes and Company, Cranburry, NJ. A most interesting look at the tactics of a big fish addict.

Brooks, Charles E.. 1974. The Trout and the Stream. Crown Publishers Inc., NY. An excellent treatise on what makes good trout waters and how to locate fish in them.

Brooks, Charles E.. 1976. Nymph Fishing For Larger Trout. Crown Publishers Inc., NY. Where to find them and how to catch them on nymphs; no BS here.

Brooks, Joe. 1972. Trout Fishing. Harper & Row, NY. A fine introductory book by one of America's most-loved masters of the sport.

Brynes, Gordon. 1990. "How Trout See." Fly Fisherman Magazine, vol. 21 (5): 56ff. A good discussion of the current scientific information on vision of the trout.

Caucci, Al and Nastasi, Bob. 1986. Hatches II. Winchester Press, Piscataway, NJ. An excellent book on mayfly hatches with tying instructions and presentation tactics.

Dunne, J. W. 1924. Sunshine and the Dry Fly. A. & C. Black, Ltd., London. A unique study on light quality as it influences feeding behavior of trout during the hatch.

Elder, Frank. 1979. The Book of the Hackle. Scottish Academic Press, Edinburgh. An excellent discussion of the properties of dry fly quality hackles.

Flick, Art. 1972. Art Flick's Master Fly-Tying Guide. Crown Publishers, NY. A great source of information on a wide ranging series of patterns.

Fox, Charles K.. 1967. Rising Trout. Foxcrest, Carlysle, PA. A fun book of stories that illustrate some masterful angling tactics; good information on Fox's and Marinaro's early work on terrestrials.

Fox, Charles K.. 1971. The Wonderful World of Trout. Freshet Press, Rockville Centre, NY. More stories that illuminate the thoughtful mind of one of America's great fly fishers.

Goddard, John. 1975. Trout Flies of Stillwater, 3rd Edition. Adam and Charles Black, London. A thorough examination of English stillwater patterns with presentation tactics.

Goddard, John. 1977. The Super Flies of Still Water. Ernest Benn Limited, London. A pattern dictionary of the best stillwater flies for England's stillwaters.

Goddard, John. 1982. Stillwater Flies How and When to Fish Them. Ernest Benn, London. A by-the-month guide to stillwater fishing in England.

Goddard, John and Clarke, Brian. 1980. The Trout and the Fly: a New Approach. Ernest Benn Limited, London. A remarkable book filled with astute observations; a must for all fly fishers.

Grant, George F. 1971. The Art of Weaving Hair Hackles for Trout Flies. George Grant, Butte, MT. An excellent description of the weaving process.

Grant, George F.. 1980. The Master Fly Weaver. Champoeg Press, Portland, OR. An excellent history of the weaving process with much insight into George's design tactics.

Hafele, Rick and Hughes, Dave. 1981. The Complete Book of Western Hatches. Frank Amato Publications, Portland OR. A good source of information on hatches west of the Rockies.

Halford, F. M. 1973. Dry Fly Fishing. Barry Shurlock & Co. Reading, England. A reprint of the 1889 edition; a classic study by the great dry fly apologist.

Harrop, Rene and Harrop, Bonnie. 1978. "Floating Nymphs." Fly Tyer Magazine, vol. 1 (3): 8-9. Describes the technique of using a ball of dubbing for emerging mayfly wings.

Hewitt, Edward R. 1972. A Trout and Salmon Fisherman for 75 Years. Van Cortland Press, NY.

A reprint of the 1948 edition; provides much insight into the life and times of one of America's most brilliant fly fishers.

Koch, Ed. 1988. Fishing the Midge: A New and Revised Edition. Stackpole Books, Harrisburg, PA. As it says, a new version of the 1972 edition; great info!

LaFontaine, Gary. 1981. Caddisflies. Nick Lyons Books, NY. The most extensive angling text available on caddis biology, fly design, and angling tactics; extremely well researched.

LaFontaine, Gary. 1990. The Dry Fly. Greycliff Press, Helena, MT. Another extremely well researched book that examines the trout's response to the dry fly; a must for the fly designer.

Lawrie, William H. 1967. All-Fur Flies and How to Dress Them. Pelham Books, London. A thorough look at a unique tying methodology.

Leisenring, James E. and Hidy, Vernon S. 1972. The Art of Tying the Wet Fly and Fishing the Flymph. Crown Publishers, Inc, NY. A reprint of Leisenring's 1941 book with added notes by Hidy; much good information in a slim volume; required reading for all soft hackle enthusiasts.

Leiser, Eric. 1973. Fly Tying Materials Their Procurement, Use, and Protection. Crown Publishers, NY. THE book on this subject.

Marinaro, Vincent C. 1970. A Modern Dry-Fly Code. Crown Publishers, Inc, NY. A reprint of the 1950 edition; this is the work that set off modern interest in terrestrials and thorax style mayfly designs; a host of careful observations.

Marinaro, Vincent C. 1976. In the Ring of the Rise. Crown Publishers, Inc, NY. A great study in trout feeding behavior on the spring creeks.

Marsh, Ed. 1971. "A Fly for All Seasons." Field and Stream Magazine, vol. 75 (12): 38ff. Describe the original South Platte Brassy.

Martin, Darrell. 1987. Fly-Tying Methods. Nick Lyons Books, NY. Great information on tools, hooks, hairs, and furs and some very interesting thoughts on tying procedures.

Matthews, Craig and Juracek, John. 1987. Fly Patterns of Yellowstone. Blue Ribbon Press, West Yellowstone, MT. A good look at the most used fly patterns for America's fly fishing Mecca.

McClane, A. J. 1975. The Practical Fly Fisherman. Prentice-Hall Inc, Englewood Cliffs, NJ. A precocious text by a superb master fly fisher.

Merwin, John (Ed.) 1980. Stillwater Trout. Nick Lyons Books, Garden City, NY. A fine study of stillwaters and the flies and tactics to fish them.

Nemes, Sylvester. 1975. The Soft-Hackled Fly. The Chatham Press, Old Greenwich, CT. A love story; Syl restores soft hackles to their rightful place in our boxes.

Nemes, Sylvester. 1981. The Soft-Hackled Fly Addict. Sylvester Nemes, Chicago, IL. Love turns to addiction; Syl finally admits to his cravings.

Nemes, Sylvester. (forthcoming). Soft Hackle Fly Imitations. Syl Nemes, Bozeman, MT. A reformed (?) addict turns to exacting imitation; Syl's forthcoming book on soft hackle flies as specific imitations of both floating and subaquatic organisms; a modern examination of this tying style.

Odier, Georges. 1984. A Revolutionary Approach to Successful Fly Fishing. Stone Wall Press Inc, Washington, DC. How to fish diving caddis imitations—tactics that work.

Ovington, Ray. 1974. How to Take Trout on Wet Flies and Nymphs. Freshet Press, Inc, Rockville Centre, NY. Some good solid information from a good solid fly fisher.

Pritt, T. E. 1886. North-Country Flies, 2nd ed. Sampson, Low, Marston, Searle, & Rivington; London. Pritt was the first to truly comprehend the value of soft-hackle flies as imitations of hatching insects.

Pulman, G. P. R. 1851. The Vade-Mecum of Fly Fishing, 3rd ed. Longman, Brown, Green, and Longmans; London. An early and well-informed, provocative discussion of impressionism.

Richards, Carl; Swisher, Doug; and Arbona, Fred Jr. 1980. Stoneflies. Nick Lyons Books, New York. A solid description of the insects, the patterns to mimic them, and the tactics to fish them.

Roberts, Donald V. 1978. Flyfishing Still Waters. Frank Amato Publications, Portland, OR. One of only a few American books to examine this subject; some good reading here.

Rosborough, E. H., "Polly". 1988. Tying and Fishing the Fuzzy Nymphs, 4th ed. Stackpole Books, Harrisburg, PA. You must read at least one edition of this book; many invaluable lessons for the fly designer.

Sawyer, Frank. 1973. Nymphs and the Trout. Crown Publishers Inc, NY. A reprint of the 1958 edition; anyone who has fished the pheasant tail nymph or used a tuck cast is a kindred spirit with Sawyer; much good information in this volume.

Schwiebert, Ernest. 1973. Nymphs: A Complete Guide to Naturals and Imitations. Winchester Press, NY. A richly informative, detailed look at subaquatic food organisms of the trout by one of America's most knowledgeable and experienced fly fishers.

Shenk, Ed. 1989. Ed Shenk's Fly Rod Trouting. Stackpole Books, Harrisburg, PA. A glimpse of the man behind the rod and the flies he fishes so successfully.

Skues, G.E.M. 1949. The Way of the Trout, 4th ed. Adam and Charles Black, London. More information than can be assimilated in one reading; Skues had a brilliant mind and it shows in this volume.

Skues, G.E.M. 1974. Nymph Fishing for Chalk Stream Trout and Minor Tactics of the Chalk Stream. Adam and Charles Black, London. A reprint of the 1939 and 1910 editions; the genesis of nymphing by one of the most original thinkers in fly fishing.

Solomon, Larry and Leiser, Eric. 1977. The Caddis and the Angler. Stackpole Books, Harrisburg, PA. The first really good examination of these insects; some good patterns and tactics.

Stewart, W. C. 1905. The Practical Angler or the Art of Trout Fishing More Particularly Applied to Clear Water (revision of the 1857 edition). Adam and Charles Black, London. So important in its time that fly fishers carried it on stream; introduced the upstream presentation as a valid fly fishing tactic and established soft hackle designs as a separate tying methodology.

Swisher, Doug and Richards, Carl. 1971. Selective Trout. Crown Publishers Inc, NY. The catalyst for much modern thinking about fly designs; introduced the No-Hackle patterns.

Thompson, Ken. 1980. Thompson Foam Beetle. Fly Tyer Magazine, vol. 3 (2): 54. Describes Ken's tying technique for this effective fly.

Troth, Al. 1978. "Daddy Long Legs." Fly Tyer, vol. 1 (3): 24-25. Describes the tying and fishing of the Troth Skater.

Walton, Izaak and Cotton, Charles. 1915. The Compleat Angler. Humphrey Milford Oxford University Press, London. There have been many editions of Walton and Cotton's 1676 work; Walton fished bait, Cotton the fly; the origins of many of our modern concepts of fly fishing.

Whitlock, Dave. 1982. Guide to Aquatic Trout Foods. Nick Lyons Books, NY. A discussion of trout foods and fly designs by one of our most innovative tiers and fly fishers.

INDEX

NOTES

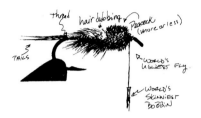

Foxy Fur Wings, NICE '88

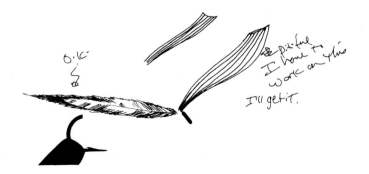